Pursuing Justice

RALPH WEISHEIT
Illinois State University

FRANK MORN
Illinois State University

THOMSON

WADSWORTH

Australia • Canada • Mexico • Singapore • Spain
United Kingdom • United States

THOMSON

━━━━✳━━━━ ™

WADSWORTH

Executive Editor, Criminal Justice: Sabra Horne
Assistant Editor: Brian Gentes
Editorial Assistant: Elise Smith
Technology Project Manager: Susan DeVanna
Marketing Manager: Dory Schaffer
Marketing Assistant: Andrew Keay
Advertising Project Manager: Stacey Purviance
Project Manager, Editorial Production:
    Matt Ballantyne
Art Director: Vernon Boes
Art Editors: Yvo/Carolyn Deacy

Print Buyer: Karen Hunt
Permissions Editor: Sommy Ko
Production Service: Forbes Mill Press
Copy Editor: Robin Gold
Proofreader: Sue Boshers
Cover Designer: Yvo
Cover Image: Copyright © Corbis
Text and Cover Printer: Webcom, Limited
Compositor: Linda Weidemann,
    Wolf Creek Press

For more information about our products,
contact us at:
Thomson Learning
Academic Resource Center
1-800-423-0563

For permission to use material from this
text, contact us by:
Phone: 1-800-730-2214
Fax: 1-800-730-2215
Web: http://www.thomsonrights.com

Wadsworth/Thomson Learning
10 Davis Drive
Belmont, CA 94002-3098
USA

Asia
Thomson Learning
5 Shenton Way #01-01
UIC Building
Singapore 068808

Australia/New Zealand
Thomson Learning
102 Dodds Street
Southbank, Victoria 3006
Australia

Canada
Nelson
1120 Birchmount Road
Toronto, Ontario M1K 5G4
Canada

Europe/Middle East/Africa
Thomson Learning
High Holborn House
50/51 Bedford Row
London WC1R 4LR
United Kingdom

Library of Congress Control Number:
2003112652

ISBN 0-534-62391-3

We dedicate this book to

Ryan "The Jazzman" and Carol — RW

Carlos and Maura — FM

and to those who pursue justice in search of a better world.

Contents

Chapter 3

Social Justice   30

Part Two

FORMAL SYSTEMS OF JUSTICE   43

Chapter 4

Common Law Systems   45

Chapter 5

Civil Law Systems   61

Chapter 6

Islamic Law Systems   77

Postscript
Justice as an Evolving Concept   237

Appendix
The United Nations'
Universal Declaration of Human Rights   241

Preface

This book was designed to introduce the reader to the many dimensions of the concept of justice, to provide several examples of the range of issues relating to justice, and to highlight some of the strategies that have been used to achieve justice. This book is designed to fill a gap in the literature on justice by combining a discussion of the concept of justice with efforts to pursue it. Some academic fields, such as philosophy, deal extensively with the concept of justice, but stop short of applying the concept to real-world efforts to pursue justice. Reading about philosophical views of justice provides little insight into the concrete steps that individuals, organizations, communities, or nations might take to achieve justice. In contrast, more applied academic programs, such as criminal justice, political science, and peace studies, often examine strategies for pursuing justice without defining justice or providing a sense of the variety of ways the term might be used.

That a gap in the literature exists may seem surprising given that for each of the chapters in this book there are dozens, sometimes hundreds, of books and thousands of articles. That so much has been written about issues of justice has complicated the task of writing an introductory overview. For us, the chapters represent broad overviews of each topic rather than comprehensive coverage. Space restrictions also made it necessary to limit the number of topics included in the book. This has meant leaving out such important issues as poverty, domestic violence, police brutality, and privacy. The topics selected for inclusion were chosen to encourage the reader to think about the issue of justice more broadly. We hope that the information in these chapters will serve as a springboard for further study, and the reader who wants to pursue the topics in this book further is encouraged to begin with the many references provided with each chapter.

Not a day goes by without news about some injustice in the world. Whether it is rape and torture committed by paramilitary groups in a developing country or more local concerns about the sentence given a drunk driver, we are continuously faced with issues of justice. Our awareness of these issues is heightened by improved communications systems that show us real-time images of injustices around the globe—including hunger, child prostitution, and the civilian casualties of war. Deciding what constitutes injustice and what is the best way to right a wrong is not always easy. One purpose of this book is to stimulate the reader to think about the meaning of justice and strategies for achieving it.

Part One considers key sources of thought about the concept of justice. Talking about justice is, at the same time, simple and maddeningly complex. On the one hand, justice is an idea that we hear every day. We use the terms *justice* and *injustice* on a regular basis and routinely apply them to everyday situations, often without thinking about what we mean by the terms. Although most people know what they mean when they use the term *justice,* few of us are able to give a concise definition that fully captures its meaning. Justice is something that is difficult to precisely define but, "We know it when we see it."

Justice may be a short simple word, but the concept it describes is quite complex. Religion, philosophy, and political science each provide a perspective on the concept of justice, and the chapters in Part One illustrate how the concept of justice has evolved in each of these areas. These chapters are important in helping the reader to recognize the many dimensions of justice and to appreciate that justice is a constantly evolving concept, one that both shapes and is shaped by world events.

Simply talking about justice does not always convey a sense of how the concept might apply to real world situations. Two sections of the book specifically address this issue. In Part Two, formal systems for achieving justice are described. Often, people living under a particular justice system are unaware of alternative ways of structuring formal justice systems. Someone who understands alternative systems of justice will find it is easier to recognize the strengths and weaknesses of their own system. These chapters also reinforce the idea that justice is not a fixed concept, but is shaped by the culture and time in which it operates.

Part Three provides concrete examples of issues related to justice. These issues were selected to represent both domestic and global concerns, with the focus on issues that have far-reaching implications. Domestic terrorism, slavery, genocide, and the environment each illustrate issues in justice. These selected issues also make clear that questions of justice pervade our everyday lives, whether we are aware of it or not. When we buy clothes made by slave labor, we are supporting injustice. Becoming aware of how justice issues are woven through our everyday decisions is an important first step in righting wrongs.

Finally, Part Four addresses the issue of responding to injustice. The discussion ranges from what individuals can do, to the role of organizations, to global approaches to justice. Most people are aware that individuals can make a difference and that organizations have a role to play in pursuing justice. Individuals and organizations will continue to be important agents in the pursuit of justice, but global approaches are increasingly necessary as the world moves toward a global economy. Global approaches are relatively new, and have yet to be fully developed, but as the globe continues to shrink, these approaches will become crucial.

Ultimately, there will always be injustice, but ignoring injustice only breeds further injustice. Governments, agencies, and people who are perceived as unjust quickly lose their legitimacy and ultimately their authority. Injustice is also an underlying cause of war. "No justice no peace" is more than a slogan, it is a reflection of reality. The battle for justice may be never ending, but it is a battle that must be fought. Recognizing injustice and taking steps to correct it is one of the things that distinguishes us from animals.

Acknowledgments

We wish to thank Shelley Murphy at Wadsworth who first encouraged us to write this book. We also wish to thank Robin Gold whose editing skills did much to improve the flow of the manuscript and Linda Weidemann of Wolf Creek Press who went above and beyond the call of duty to keep the project on schedule. Finally, we wish to thank Sabra Horne who oversaw the project, made suggestions that substantially improved the book, and kept it (and us) moving on schedule.

WHAT IS JUSTICE?

W hat is justice? What constitutes a just society? What are the responsibilities of citizens to their neighbors, their government, other humans? Should everyone be treated equally? Or should people be treated based on some special status? Is there anything called a just war? Why do we punish people? What is our responsibility to the environment? These questions have been raised by every civilized society. Answers to such questions are embedded in ancient traditions, mythology, philosophy, theology, history, law, and political theory.

In the final analysis, the notion of justice is a human construct used to describe the actions of humans. We do not describe earthquakes as "unjust," although we might use that term to describe inequities in the way assistance is provided to the victims of an earthquake. As Aristotle has observed, if we lived in a perfect society we would not need to define and dispute this notion of justice. Generally speaking, justice may be divided into two main spheres. One is concerned with the justice of the individual in relation to other human beings and to the organized community itself, the state. The other is concerned with the justice of the state—its form of government and its laws, its political institutions, its military postures, and economic arrangements—in relation to the human beings that make up its population.

In the language of justice, five words act as justice markers:

- **Equality:** Everyone being given the same treatment and access to goods.
- **Merit:** Getting what one deserves.
- **Need:** Some sort of "safety net" for those who cannot function in society.
- **Rank:** Many institutions—military, universities, churches—think of rank structures as a means to think about justice.

- **Fairness:** Justice is treating people fairly if not equitably. Law is often the last interpreter of what is just, even if a law is considered unjust.

Although justice is a short, simple word, it is a complicated idea with many dimensions. Presenting a broad overview of these dimensions is the task of the next three chapters. In these chapters, our discussion will focus on religious and philosophical perspectives, justice and the state, and social justice.

RELIGIOUS AND PHILOSOPHICAL PERSPECTIVES

Humans have considered questions of justice from the very beginning. Perhaps the first formal efforts to delineate the meaning and implications of justice can be found in religion and philosophy. Both religion and philosophy seek to give meaning to the world, to account for injustice, and to outline proper responses to injustice. In addition, religion and philosophy form the foundation for other perspectives of justice.

The notion of justice has been central to both religion and philosophy, and for this reason, there is an extensive body of literature on justice from each perspective.[1] The purpose of this chapter is to provide a broad overview and to highlight key aspects of these perspectives, and in doing so, to set the tone for the chapters that follow.

RELIGION AND JUSTICE

Initially, justice was harsh and vengeful and closely connected to religion. In the ancient Babylonian culture, which arose on the banks of the Tigris and Euphrates rivers, an area today known as Iraq, issues of justice were being addressed around 1750 B.C. The *Hammurabi Code*, an ancient text of laws, reflected a rigid static society where obligations and responsibilities were well known and fixed. Consequently, justice was rigid, uncompromising, and absolute. For example, if a building collapsed because of faulty design, the architect could be put to death. If a person under medical care died, the physician likely would face death. However, there was some proportionality. For example, if the daughter of a gentleman was struck and suffered a miscarriage, the fine was 10 shekels; the same thing happening to the daughter of an ordinary man resulted in a fine of 5 shekels. In like fashion, if the ordinary citizen's daughter died, the perpetrator was liable for a heavy fine; if it was a gentleman's daughter, the wrongdoer could face execution. This code established the concept of an eye for an eye and a tooth for a tooth, an idea that found its way into the law outlined by Moses in the Bible.[2]

Judaism and Christianity

The earliest stages of Old Testament justice were theocratic, with God's reactions being swift and uncompromising. Probably written around 1000 B.C., the Pentateuch, or Torah, struck themes that continue in Western culture. When Adam and Eve were tricked into sin by a serpent, the creature and its progeny were cursed to crawl the earth forever. Adam and Eve were exiled from the Garden of Eden. Eve, and all women thereafter, was to suffer in childbirth; the man was to struggle to earn a living by the sweat of his brow. When Cain murdered his brother, Abel, God did not sentence the killer to death, but to life as a fugitive and vagabond. The story of Cain and Abel has been used by generations of reformers to defend alleged murderers against the death penalty. Later, the wickedness of the world compelled God, with the exception of a small party of elect in an ark, to destroy all the inhabitants of the earth. Young and old alike were drowned in the deluge. Sodom and Gomorrah met a similar fate with the Divine promise that only the innocent would be saved. Even Lot's wife, whose only sin was to look back on her home with longing, was condemned and turned into a pillar of salt. Moses brought plague and death to thousands of Egyptians, even innocent children, because of the actions of the Pharaoh.

When Moses was crafting a new set of nation-state laws, to be found in the first five books of the Bible (Genesis, Exodus, Leviticus, Numbers, and Deuteronomy), he set forth a justice system that affected much of Western culture for thousands of years.

As the roaming Israelites settled and began to build a distinct culture in a new homeland, issues of justice emerged again. In an attempt to bring some softness, proportionality, and reason to justice, they introduced *lex talionis,* or an eye for an eye. For example, Leviticus 24: 17–22 states,

> If anyone takes the life of a human being, he must be put to death. Anyone who takes the life of someone's animal must make retribution—life for life. If anyone injures his neighbor, whatever he has done must be done to him: fracture for fracture, eye for eye, tooth for tooth. As he has injured the other, so he is to be injured. Whoever kills an animal must make restitution, but whoever kills a man must be put to death. You are to have the same law for the alien and the native-born. I am the Lord your God.

Numerous offenses warranted capital punishment. For example, profaning the Sabbath could result in death (Exodus 35: 2; Exodus 31: 14–15; Numbers 15: 32–36). Blasphemy and sacrifice to other gods resulted in death (Leviticus 24: 11–14; Exodus 22: 20). The twentieth chapter of Leviticus commanded death for a variety of familial and sexual violations, including adultery, incest, homosexuality, and bestiality (Leviticus 20: 9–16).

The appearance of Jesus Christ in the New Testament seemed to remove some of the harshness of older scriptures. Jesus preached in Matthew 5:

> You have heard that it was said, "Eye for an eye, and tooth for tooth." But I tell you, Do not resist an evil person. If someone strikes you on the right cheek, turn him the other also. And if someone wants to sue you and take your tunic, let him have your cloak as well. If someone forces you to go one mile, go with him two miles. Give to the one who asks you, and do not turn away from the one who wants to borrow from you.

Though taking off some of the sting of previous years, this still relegated those who did not follow Christianity to eternal punishment. However, Christ's followers were not so eager to leave behind hundreds of years of tradition. For example, Paul acknowledged justice flowing from secular power and of death as an appropriate punishment:

> Let every soul be subject to the governing authorities. For there is no authority except from God, and the authorities that exist are appointed by God. Therefore, whoever resists the authority resists the ordinance of God, and those who resist will bring judgement on themselves. (Romans 13: 1–4)

Justice was a vital concern of the ancient civilizations forming some four thousand years ago. These early peoples found the answers to their perplexing questions about justice along religious lines. Judaism and Christianity, based on their holy books and interpretations, provide a cultural bedrock on justice for Western civilization. Harshness was tempered somewhat with mercy, especially as time went by and these cultures became more sophisticated economically and politically. Another important religious tradition that would profoundly affect considerable parts of the world also grew out of Judaism; we can see some differences in the religion of Mohammed based on the desert cultures from which its originators came.

Islam

Islam's *Qur'an,* (also spelled *Koran*) revealed to Muhammad in the seventh century is filled with references to justice as well (see also Chapter 6). Central to Islam is submission to and fear of Allah who is both "terrible in his retribution," and "all-forgiving and compassionate." The goal of the *Qur'an* is to establish ethical and egalitarian society:

> O ye who believe! Be ye staunch in justice, witness for Allah, even though it be against yourselves or parents or kindred. (*Qur'an* 4: 135)

And again:

> Let not hatred of any people reduce you that ye deal not justly. Deal justly, that is nearer to your duty. (*Qur'an*, 5:8)

Economic and social inequalities were to be avoided. Those who did receive riches were not to be condemned, however, if they used this wealth to help others. The decay of any society is caused by neglect and self-absorption of the prosperous. The *Qur'an's* main goal is to prevent people from corrupting the earth by falling into decadent ways. When a civilization becomes decadent and decrepit, it needs to be swept away and start again. Therefore, vengeance and retribution are central, but they are to be tempered by mercy. In Islam, the poorest and most incapacitated person still has a claim on equal rights; all are the servants of God in this world and the next. Therefore, almsgiving is not a charity, a sign of one's goodness but, rather, it is a duty. Considerable justice and mercy is extended to the fellow believers with warnings against being an aggressor[3]:

> And fight in the way of God with those who fight with you, but aggress not: God loves not the aggressors. And slay them wherever you come upon them, and expel them from where they expelled you; persecution is more grievous than slaying. (*Qur'an* 2: 185–190)

And again later:

> O believers, be you securers of justice, witness for God. Let not detestation for a people move you not to be equitable; be equitable—that is nearer to godfearing. (*Qur'an* 5: 11)

Islam can be quite forgiving of the killer of a nonbeliever:

> Whom God leads astray, thou wilt not find for him a way. They wish that you should disbelieve as they disbelieve, and then you would be equal; therefore take not to yourselves friends of them, until they emigrate in the way of God; then, if they turn their backs, take them, and slay them wherever you find them. (*Qur'an* 4: 91–94)

Unlike the Jewish/Christian tradition, killing a believer of Islam called forth much different consideration:

> It belongs not to a believer to slay a believer, except it be by error. If any slays a believer by error, then let him set free a believing slave, and bloodwit is to be paid to his family unless they forgo it as a freewill offering. If he belong to a people at enmity with you and is a believer, let the slayer set free a believing slave. If he belong to a people joined with you by a compact, then bloodwit is to be paid to his family and the slayer shall set free a believing slave. But if he finds not the means, let him fast two successive months—God's turning; God is All-knowing, All-wise. And whoso slays a believer wilfully, his recompense is Gehenma [hell], therein dwelling forever, and God will be wroth with him and will curse him, and prepare for him a mighty chastisement. (*Qur'an* 4: 94–95)

Islam takes many forms. One is the Shiite (representing 10 to 15 percent of the Muslim population). Muhammad's successor was his son-in-law Ali.

Shiites believe that the ruling of the nation is not a public matter; it is a theocratic one. The ruler is infallible and never makes mistakes. Shiites believe the rulers reflect the will of Allah. The people have no right to select or challenge the rulers. The Sunnis represent 85 to 90 percent of the Muslim world. According to Sunni beliefs, the successors to Muhammad were the four caliphs or religious leaders. Government is a secular matter without any religious authority. Rulers come and go from power based on the will of the people.

Over time, many Muslim countries modernized and deviated from the pure teachings of the *Qur'an.* In response, some fundamentalists arose. Most notable is that of Muhammad ibn Abd al-Wahhab. Today Wahhabism represents an austere conservative brand of Islam. Followers of Wahhabism believe the *Qur'an* is the ultimate blueprint for life. All questions can be answered by a careful reading and application of that holy book. Some countries—Saudi Arabia, Iran, and Afghanistan, for example—construct their entire political and social structure around this sect. Punishments come right out of the *Qur'an* (see Chapter 6 on Islamic law). Theft results in the right hand being amputated. Adulterers are stoned to death. Murder and sexual deviation warrant beheading. Women should be covered and largely secluded. In more modern interpretations of the *Qur'an,* many fundamentalists would not allow females to drive an automobile or attend school. There are no theaters in Saudi Arabia because the Saudis detest the mixing of the sexes and the corrupting influences of Western culture. These Muslims see any deviation from the *Qur'an,* or their interpretation of it, as sacrilege. Any government contrary to The Book is the Great Satan.

Buddhism

Buddhism stands in contrast to both Christianity and Islam. Ancient Buddhist texts are called the *Tripitaka* or three baskets and consist of the Sutra (thread), Vinaya (regulations), and Abhidharma (commentaries). Buddhists believe all things are impermanent. Human suffering is natural and caused by one's own actions in this life and previous ones. In this sense, justice is a cosmic phenomenon and society has little to do with it. In this justice system, what a person is now is the result of the accumulation of what they had been before. However deterministic this seems, there is a desire to live a just life now to ensure a better life later. For the individual, the good or just life is the middle path. One needs to avoid extremes. Do not pursue worldly things nor be an ascetic. A just person and society walks the middle way along the Noble Eightfold Path. This means the person, rulers, and society should have correct

1. views
2. thoughts
3. speech
4. conduct

5. livelihood
6. effort
7. mindfulness
8. concentration

"It is the neglect of the rulers to perform their duties fairly and equitably that theft, violence, sexual immorality, lack of piety and moral decline come."[4]

MODERN RELIGIOUS VIEWS OF JUSTICE

Modern religious views of justice can be presented in several categories, which have emerged over time. Although there are many, here we will concentrate on only two of these views: Protestantism and Catholicism.

Protestantism and Justice

The religious revolt against the entrenched elitism of the medieval Catholic Church in the sixteenth century was caused by a desire for reformation. Unfortunately, most of the protestant denominations did not stray too far from the Catholic Church when it came to justice. When issues of justice are raised, the New England Puritans quickly come to mind. However, some theologians did address the problem of inequality and injustice. Perhaps the greatest twentieth-century theologian to address issues of justice was Reinhold Niebuhr, who saw justice as the balance of power between classes. Absolute justice was likely unattainable, but the ideal would be a harmony in which the weak were protected from the strong. Unlike many theologians, Niebuhr emphasized sin. Sin or conflict is a persistent aspect of human life and sin is injustice. To refuse to value the claims of others or to think your claims are superior is to be unjust. Two principles must be addressed before there can be justice. These principles are freedom and equality. Even though freedom is a cherished notion, if left alone it would harm the poor. Therefore, freedom cannot stand alone unregulated. Equality is Niebuhr's highest standard of justice. Neibuhr believed that equal justice is the greatest goal for society. As he says in *Moral Man,* "the oppressed have a higher moral right to challenge their oppressors than these have to maintain their rule by force."[5]

Catholicism and Social Justice

The history of the Catholic Church is replete with authoritarianism and dogma. Pronouncements of clergy became the source of justice. The Papacy throughout the Middle Ages was dogmatic and dictatorial as were the secular leaders of the church. In fact, because they held the "keys to heaven," many popes were stronger than most Christian monarchs. Such positions led to the Reformation in the sixteenth century. Many today argue that the Papacy remains very conservative and uncompromising on a variety of issues.[6] However, in the twentieth century, many church leaders developed a social justice–oriented tradition. This outlook was framed by the basic affirmation that all humans had dignity and that God gave the abundance of nature to all people. Institutions existed for the sake of the people and not the other way around, these Catholics believed. People have rights that the state or any other institution cannot take away. Any economic system that denies the rights of workers or treats them in an undignified way is an unjust system. Workers should receive a living wage and be able to participate in the production of goods. Earlier Catholics were advised to share their goods as a matter of charity, but for the modern church, it became a matter of justice. If they did not do so, the Church and the state had the right to take away from the rich to give to the poor. The justness of a community was to be determined by how it treated the powerless in society. It may be summed up as all belongs to God and whatever belongs to God belongs to all.[7]

Some Catholic theologians, particularly from the Third World, felt their Church did not address the issue of justice strongly enough. This point of view has been called Liberation Theology. José Porfirio Miranda (*Marx and the Bible*) and Gustavo Gutierrez (*The Power of the Poor in History* and *A Theology of Liberation*)[8] are two significant thinkers of justice from the liberationist point of view. Although not limited to Latin America, the liberationist view has found its greatest expression in these Spanish-speaking regions. The basis of the liberation theology is a rereading of the Bible. Liberation theologists believe God chose to be born poor and to live and teach to the poor. To the liberationist, justice is recognizing the realities of poverty and oppression and the importance of struggling to liberate the oppressed. Leaning on Marxist theory, liberation theology thinks capitalism is unjust. Multinational corporations in the Third World have made the poor into nonpersons and robbed them of their human dignity. Injustice is structured, institutionalized, and systemic. Private ownership of property has come about by injustice. The only way to know God is to do justice. The poor become the litmus test because "To deal with a poor man or woman as Yahweh dealt with his people—this is what it is to be just." Just as God liberated His people, as written in Exodus, nothing short of liberating the poor from all forms of oppression can be done to achieve a just society. Miranda and other liberationists believe the Bible should be read from a Marxist perspective with the goal of liberating the oppressed.[9] Clearly, the liberation theologians look to the Bible and to Karl Marx more than do other types of theologians

JUSTICE AND PHILOSOPHY

Much like religion, philosophy provided some of the earliest systematic think-ing about the issue of justice. During the classical period of Western civilization and Confucian epoch of Eastern civilization, literature and philosophy emerged to give some of the earliest and most compelling themes and definitions of jus-tice. Frequently, these definitions reflected the nature of the society at the time they were promulgated.

Perhaps one of the earliest references to justice in literature occurred in Classical Greece. As early as 800 B.C., Homer's *Iliad,* that grand telling of the battles at Troy, set forth a view of ancient justice as that of revenge. Strikingly familiar to those who understood Judaic traditions, justice meant vengeance, a central theme throughout this epic. The attack on Troy was a result of the desire for retribution. Gods and warrior/princes felt slighted and needed re-venge. When one warrior/prince was captured in battle and begged for his life, Agamemnon argued that in the name of justice all should perish and quickly killed the fallen soldier. Soon the entire culture was obliterated. To the Gods or those defining justice in their name, law offered little compro-mise or mitigation.[10]

The question of justice first reached philosophical importance in Plato's *Republic,* or *Concerning Justice,* written around 380 B.C. Plato's mentor, Socrates, chose to die by execution rather than to give up his principles. Per-haps Plato used his mentor's example when he equated justness with both per-sonal and civic virtue. Arguing against those who thought a person or society does good only under threat of being caught, Plato suggests that people and states should do justice because it was the right thing to do. Plato believed that justice should be "corrective," not just punitive. This is consistent with the So-cratic belief that no one sins on purpose.[11] Justice becomes a quest for har-mony in the soul and in the state. However, that can lead to some confusion. One Greek word used for *justice* was *isotes,* which means equality. When Plato speaks of justice, he uses *dikaiosune* or righteousness. So when Plato speaks of justice as performing the functions for which one's nature is best fitted, he really speaks of righteousness. The just ruler is unselfish; his one aim is the welfare of the citizens. The just citizen is a wiser, a stronger, and a happier per-son than the unjust one.[12]

Plato's student, Aristotle, modernized the definition of justice. Aristotle be-lieved that if all humans were friends there would be no need to be concerned about justice. But human nature demands some moral compass, something to guide people to do the right thing. In his *Nicomachean Ethics* (ca. 322 B.C.), Aristotle divided justice into two categories: distributive and rectificatory.

Distributive justice is what people deserve. Here, the notion of equality becomes important. To Aristotle, equality means proportionality. Equals deserve equal treatment and unequals deserve unequal treatment. But how is equality determined? "For if the people involved are not equal, they will not [justly] receive equal shares; indeed, [there is injustice] whenever equals receive unequal shares, or unequals equal shares. In a distribution, that is the source of quarrels and accusations." Justice becomes one of proportionate equality. Good judgment and a sense of fairness became important.

Rectificatory justice has to do with exchange relationships: Two men before the court for the same crime are to be considered equal before the law even if they are different socially. Aristotle believed, "what is just will be both what is lawful and what is fair, and what is unjust will be both what is lawless and what is unfair." Like Plato, Aristotle favored harmony. Whether in commercial transactions or the settling of a dispute in a courtroom, justice means to restore equilibrium. Equality is equilibrium. In an almost-modern profit/loss analysis, Aristotle asks what the difference is in a theft. One party, the victim, has suffered a loss, while another, the thief, has gained. The judge's job is to restore [take away from the crook and restore to the victim] equality or equilibrium. Justice becomes an intermediate condition between extremes, a golden mean or average.[13]

Thomas Aquinas synthesized Christian theology and Aristotelian philosophy. His thought, written in *Summa Theologica* in 1274 A.D., became the basis of Catholic thinking for centuries. Echoing Aristotle's two categories of justice, Aquinas reaffirmed to medieval Christians that justice was the perpetual and constant desire to render to each person his right. Aquinas believed that all human law was the application of natural law; therefore, human justice must be a reflection of Divine justice. Justice is a virtue to be done knowingly, voluntarily, and resolutely. Justice, which connotes equality, has to do with relations to others. It is meant to rectify human acts. But in addition, justice was a virtue directed at relations with other people. "Now, this may happen in two ways: first, as regards his relation with individuals; secondly, as regards his relations with others in general, insofar as a man serves a community serves all those who are included in that community."[14]

When confronting the discrepancies of offenses, Aquinas dealt with the issue of objective justice. For if one strikes a prince, his opponents argue, he does not receive the same punishment as if he had struck a peasant. Aquinas recognized that "the injury inflicted bears a different proportion to a ruler from that which it bears to a private person; wherefore each injury needs to be equalized by punishment in a different way, and this implies an objective and not merely a rational diversity."[15]

The list of more contemporary philosophers who have addressed the issue of justice is a long one. Thomas Hobbes, John Locke, Jean-Jacques Rousseau and G. W. F. Hegel, to name a few, expounded and elaborated on themes first put forth by Aristotle and Aquinas.[16] Our attention now shifts to two of these thinkers, John Stuart Mill and John Rawls.

John Stuart Mill spoke of **utilitarianism.** Briefly, the ends justify the means. The right thing to do is what produces the most good. For utilitarians, the goal of life is happiness, or the absence of pain. The rightness of acts can be evaluated by their contribution to happiness. Individual rights and claims can be overridden by considerations for the happiness of the greatest number. Mill had a specific idea of what was unjust. There were six common examples of injustice: (1) Depriving people of things they had a legal right to have, (2) depriving them of things they had a moral right to have, (3) not giving people what they deserve— good to those who do right and evil to those who do wrong, (4) breaking faith with people, (5) being partial, and (6) treating people unequally. On the other hand, "justice implies something which it is not only right to do, and wrong not to do, but which some individual person can claim from us as his moral right."[17]

Much of modern philosophical discussion about justice has revolved around the work of John Rawls. First in 1971 with his *Theory of Justice* and then in 2001 with his *Justice as Fairness,* Rawls has reshaped the contemporary philosophical debate about justice. For Rawls, the concept of **fairness** is closely connected to any understanding of justice.

According to Rawls, only principles that everyone can publicly accept can serve the purpose of giving us a fair distribution of goods and privileges, and this leads to justice. We won't accept slavery or the forced importation of religious beliefs. As citizens, we think of ourselves free to have our own way of life and our religion. We no longer believe that anyone is politically superior to another. No more kings and aristocracies by inheritance; as citizens, we are all equal. Though we think of ourselves free and equal, we also agree that some limits need to be placed on freedom. Without such restraints, our freedom and liberty would interfere with the freedom and liberty of others. For example, speed limits restrict our freedom to zoom along public thoroughfares, but this is done to protect the rest of us. We also accept limited inequalities in wealth and status to encourage people to take on difficult and essential jobs.

But where did this societal agreement come from? Rawls asks us to imagine that we are at a meeting at the beginning of time and that we represent all the generations of our family. At that meeting, we are to bargain and hammer out principles that would shape the fundamental institutions of our society: government, economic systems, social arrangements, and such. Everyone at the meeting has to believe that the outcome would be fair. In daily life, some would be richer than others, or stronger than others, or prettier than others, or more talented than others, or better educated than others. But we all agree that those differences do not make a difference in the bargaining process. It would not be fair for the poor to be forced to accept a set of principles forced on them by the rich, and minorities should not be forced to accept whatever proposal the majority favored.

An environment for such a bargaining session can only be ensured if those who are bargaining do so under a veil of ignorance in which the bargainers would not know their sex, race, religion, wealth, intelligence, or special gifts. In other words, all unfair advantages are excluded from the bargaining table. Rawls thinks that stripped of these advantages, with everyone operating on a level moral plane, two principles of justice would emerge, principles agreed to by everyone:

1. Each person has an equal right to a fully adequate scheme of equal basic rights and liberties.
2. Social and economic inequalities are to satisfy two conditions: first they must be attached to offices and positions open to all under conditions of fair equality of opportunity; and second, they must be to the greatest benefit to the least of the least advantaged members of society.

The first safeguards our freedoms to think and speak, to choose careers and lifestyles, and to differ in political and religious beliefs. These liberties are so precious to us that we cannot afford to put them at risk, not even to increase overall happiness. Under the second principle, we recognize that some inequalities exist, and that they improve the overall condition of society. But we must ensure ourselves and our families a share of the benefits. For example, if it turns out you are a day laborer, you get no benefit from the fact that your boss gets a thousand times more income and you may see this as an example of injustice. The insistence that the inequalities also help those worst off protects against this kind of unfairness. When people accept Rawls' principles, they reach an "overlapping consensus." That is the best that can be expected in a democratic society.

Justice as fairness is not just academic speculation; Rawls has a political agenda. For example, he rejects free market capitalism, welfare-state capitalism, and state socialism. Rawls demands an activist government to ensure justice. His approach endorses a system in which economic power is shared by companies and workers. This system uses taxation to keep the differences between rich and poor close to maintain everyone's basic rights and it supports women's rights and gay rights. Thus, according to Rawls, whatever social arrangements we agree to will be fair because none of us can try to skew the distributions of benefits and burdens in our own favor.[18]

CONCLUSION

Neither religion nor philosophy provides a single view of justice and wide variations exist even with particular religious and philosophical perspectives. For example, some Christians use the Bible to justify the death penalty whereas others use the Bible to argue against it. Although neither offers one simple view of justice, both religion and philosophy have played a large role in reflecting and shaping society's view of justice. Each has also provided a valuable framework for organizing thinking about justice. In both religion and philosophy, the earliest notions of justice focused on retribution and punishment. Although these themes have not disappeared, modern views place a greater emphasis on fairness and equality.

For religious prophets and philosophical pundits to talk of justice is one thing, but it must be translated into everyday life. Clearly, the state—government and its political leaders—is in the forefront of any such process. For much of history, the state was an appendage of religion. But as nation-states developed, governmental and religious leaders fought over power. Soon the secular won out over the religious, and a new brand of definers of justice emerged. Religious and philosophical perspectives on justice persisted, but were now filtered through a very different lens, that of politics. Our attention now turns to the role of politics and the state in determining justice.

Discussion Questions

1. Can you think of examples in which religion and religious values shape problems between two countries?
2. Using the example of Moses in the Old Testament and Jesus in the New Testament can you think of why Judaism and Christianity might view capital punishment differently?
3. How does an individual's religious and philosophical definition of the "nature of man" shape the way that person views justice?

Endnotes

1. For an excellent book of readings, see Robert C. Solomon and Mark C. Murphy (eds.), *What Is Justice?: Classic and Contemporary Readings* (New York: Oxford University Press, 2000).
2. G. R. Driver and John C. Miles (eds.), *The Babylonian Laws*, Vol. 2 (Oxford, England: Clarendon, [1956–1960]), pp. 58–108, 406, 494, 501.
3. Fazlur Rahman, *Major Themes of the* Qur'an (Chicago: Bibliotheca Islamica, 1980), pp. 37–64.
4. Trevor Ling (ed.), *The Buddha's Philosophy of Man* (Rutland, Vt.: Everyman's Library, 1981), pp. 119–121.
5. Karen Labacqz, *Six Theories of Justice* (Minneapolis: Augsburg, 1986), pp. 83–90.
6. Philip Jenkins, "The Next Christianity," *Atlantic Monthly* (October 2002), pp. 53–68.
7. Ibid., pp. 66–82.
8. José Miranda Porfirio, *Marx and the Bible: A Critique of the Philosophy of Oppression*, John Eagleson (trans.) (Maryknoll, N.Y.: Orbis, 1974); Gustavo Gutierrez, *A Theology of Liberation: History, Politics, and Salvation*, Caridad Inda and John Eagleson (trans.) (Maryknoll, N.Y.: Orbis, 1973).
9. Jenkins, pp. 100–115.
10. See Solomon and Murphy, pp. 13–14.

11. G. M. A. Grube, *Plato's Thought* (Boston: Beacon, 1958), p. 288.
12. Ernest Barker, *The Political Thought of Plato and Aristotle* (New York: Dover, 1959), pp. 81–119.
13. D. S. Hutchinson, "Ethics" in *The Cambridge Companion to Aristotle,* Jonathan Barnes (ed.) (Cambridge: Cambridge University Press, 1995), pp. 222–224.
14. See Solomon and Murphy, p. 52.
15. Hutchinson, p. 125.
16. For readings on these philosophers, the reader is directed to Solomon and Murphy, pp. 63, 74, 81, 95.
17. See John Stuart Mill, *Utilitarianism,* Oskar Piest (ed.) (Indianapolis: Liberal Arts, 1957), p. 62; and *On Liberty* (Chicago: Henry Regnery, 1955), pp. 109–137.
18. John Rawls, *A Theory of Justice* (Cambridge, Mass.: Belknap Press of Harvard University Press, 1999), pp. 3–22; *Justice as Fairness: A Restatement* (Cambridge, Mass.: Belknap Press of Harvard University Press, 2001), pp. 39–52; and *Political Liberalism* (New York: Columbia University Press, 1993), pp. 4, 47–48.

JUSTICE AND THE STATE

As the national state emerged in the late Middle Ages, more profound questions arose about justice. At first, remnants of the old world remained in such concepts as the Divine Right of Kings. From this perspective, the king was thought to act under the guidance of God, and as a representative of God, the monarch had considerable leeway to draw the lines of justice. This approach also made it difficult to challenge the king's interpretation of justice, for to challenge the king was to challenge God.

In his book, *The Prince* (1513), Niccolo Machiavelli outlined perhaps one of the earliest treatises on the concept of governance and of justice to drift away from the view that government was a divine creation. Machiavelli was born and raised in politically chaotic Italy. After a frustrating career in the politics of Renaissance Florence, Machiavelli wrote *The Prince.* He longed for a ruler who would bring order, stability, and unity to Italy. Questions of a moral or immoral state were wrongheaded, he thought. The state is amoral. The prince must be honest and just but deal with the world as it is and not as it should be. People are devious, gullible, corrupt, and greedy and must be treated accordingly. Being feared by the citizenry was better than being loved. Obtaining and retaining power was the first priority. Every ruler in Europe achieved power by force. The state and its ruler are more important than the people who make up the state. Therefore, the ruler may do unjust things in the name of preserving the state. Hence, politicians must break promises, conceal their deals, distort the facts, ignore the masses, and pose as righteous even if circumstances forces them to be unrighteous. Until one gets power, one must be ruthless and if necessary evil; the prince must be both the "fox and lion." The ends justify the means. To those who would argue otherwise, Machiavelli would counter: "If the ends do not justify the means then what does?"[1]

The perspectives of Divine Right and Machiavelli assumed a just and right state, but as sensibilities changed, questions arose about what justified the state to take away a person's property in the form of taxes. How could a politician compel a young man into military service? How could government draw up laws and punishments? In short, what gave legitimacy to the government? Of course, the main justification had been that a just and virtuous state was presupposed as having been created under divine guidance. Both Divine Right and Machiavellian perspectives on justice and the state assumed that everyday citizens had no role in decisions made by the state, and that they *should* have no role. But as the Renaissance replaced the Middle Ages, more humanistic voices were heard.

THE SOCIAL CONTRACT

The basis of social contract theory is that states and governments are legitimate or illegitimate only to the degree that they are formed and supported by the mutual agreement of the citizens of that state. This presupposes that society exists before the state does. Following this line of thinking, America—its society and sense of community—existed before the United States came into existence. The Constitution created a structure of government but it did not form a society. England existed long before modern Great Britain appeared on the scene. This is true of most modern states. Humans, seeing that they would have to compromise some of their individualistic self-interests, created the modern state-ism through an unwritten contract or agreement among members of the society.

The first expression of this social contract was Thomas Hobbes's seventeenth-century book, *Leviathan* (1651). Before the formation of society and the state, there was brutish anarchy, according to Hobbes. The natural condition of man was animalistic and counterproductive to civilization. All humans are vane, and hostilities erupted over a person's desire for deference. Hobbes believed that humans are guided by self-interest and in the absence of political authority selfish motivation and natural inequality will degenerate into war and chaos. In this barbaric state, there is no justice or injustice. Therefore, a social contract is needed to protect humans from themselves. To ensure a modicum of liberty and tranquility, humans must give up total liberty. Justice then results when people in a society carry out the agreements implicitly made among its members.[2] Harkening back to the Greek notion of justice and righteousness, Hobbes declares,

> A just man . . . is he that takes all the care he can that his actions may be all just; and an unjust man is he who neglects it. And such men are more often in our language styled by the names righteous and unrighteous than just and unjust, though the meaning be the same. Therefore a righteous man does not lose that title by one or a few unjust actions that proceed from sudden passion or mistake of things or persons; nor does an unrighteous man lose his character for such actions as he does or forbears to do for fear, because his will is not framed by the justice but by the apparent benefit of what he is to do.[3]

John Locke came to the social contract, too, but with a different perception of human nature. In his *Second Treatise of Government* (1690), pre-political humans were seen as good and industrious, working to make society a better place. Humankind had natural rights to property, but some wayward people tried to take those rights away. Locke's social contract, therefore, was to protect man's property and fruits of his labor. Government was formed to do this. Political authority is instituted by contract to acknowledge and enforce these natural rights.[4]

Jean-Jacques Rousseau expressed a similar theme in his *Discourse on the Origins of Inequality* (1754) and *On the Social Contract* (1762). Rousseau sees primitive man as happy and healthy individuals too. But primitive men were indifferent to each other. As they slowly acquire property, they form law and government to protect their possessions, but in doing this, they lose their innocence. The invention of private property, and the inequalities that follow from it, result in the end of our primeval happiness and independence. All of our unhappiness arises from the institution of private property—the artificiality and competitiveness of contemporary society, the exaggerated differences between the rich and the poor. But there is no going back to the paradisal state. Therefore, a social contract is necessary, not to protect us from ourselves or our property, but to elevate us from mere humanity to the morally more important condition of citizenship.[5]

NATURE OF LAW

A very important part of the legitimacy of the state has to do with just laws and just lawmakers.[6] Where does law come from? Many philosophers, going back to the ancient Stoics, began to think in terms of natural law, a system of rules and principles of human conduct that were independent of enacted law or of the systems particular to one people. These laws preexisted humans, were fixed and unchangeable, and could be discovered by the rational intelligence of humans. The Stoic doctrine grew out of the proposition of a life ordered according to nature. Stoics believed in the existence in ancient times of a "state of nature," a condition of society in which people universally were governed solely by the rational and consistent obedience to the needs and impulses of true human nature before it was defaced by dishonesty, falsehood, and baser passions. In ethical terms, this consists of universal rules of conduct that had been established by the author of human nature as essential to the Divine purposes of an orderly universe.[7]

Such a concept became essential for justice. It became a way to determine just laws and just governments. Just societies, laws, and leaders are those who conform to natural law.

In the founding of America, with the proclamations made in the Declaration of Independence, the natural laws were articulated as principles for guiding state authority. As justification for throwing off the yoke of an unjust government, Thomas Jefferson alerted his readers that humans had inalienable rights. This declaration of individual rights of life, liberty, and the pursuit of happiness became the bedrock of a new nation and a statement of natural rights. Much like Locke, Jefferson declared that government was created by the people, and if it failed to live up to the desires of the people, it could be done away and another would replace it.

The Constitution of 1787 created a tripartite government with executive, legislative, and judicial carefully balancing each other so that no concentration of power would predominate. Initially, the Constitution did not address individual rights, and as an afterthought ten amendments were added to ensure the government did not overbear on the individual. The Bill of Rights indicates the restrictions placed on government, particularly in its police power. These natural rights were to override any development of government. Such a concern was important because the justness of law and governmental authority had other defenders.

Besides natural law, others advocated **positivism.** This school of thought felt that law came from those in power. It was not transcendental. Of course, it was very important to have just people in power or the state and its subjects would be enslaved by human greed and lust for power. Laws do change, but they change as those in power change. This was less offensive in a democracy than in a despotic state. In a democracy, it was presumed that those who came to power did so with the agreement of the citizens. Even the losers, as part of the social contract, agreed to abide by the will of the majority. Those who chose not to abide by the government had to prove the laws and the state unjust or suffer the label of outlaw.

Another group, identified as **sociological jurisprudence,** believed that changing conditions altered the law no matter who was in power. The evolving conditions of human society demanded laws to change. The end of slavery and granting women the right to vote are two examples. The creation of hate crimes is another such response (see Chapter 8). Public sensitivities have evolved, the argument might go, and the law has adjusted to them.

How law emerges has implications for how one views the state—the state as something that protects rights and promotes justice, or the state as something to be protected from. Natural law, positivism, and sociological jurisprudence provide very different perspectives on the link between justice and the state.

LIBERTY AND EQUALITY AND JUSTICE

A free society suggests liberty. But how much liberty? Can society interfere with a person's exercise of their freedom? Does justice imply that everyone is equal? That everyone be treated equally? But everyone is not equal; some are more intelligent than others, some have more talents than others, some are more attractive than others, some are healthier than others. Should people who are different be treated equally? Should two students be given the same grade when one studied hard and another cheated? Should two bank robbers be given the same sentence even though one did it to feed his hungry children while the other did it for fun? Should a person who has talent and courage to make a fortune in the free market be punished for his or her success? Should a person who is a failure because of the lack of intelligence and energy be rewarded with government-sponsored giveaways? A society that bases its ideology on equality and the freedom to pursue property finds itself in a bind. Capitalism and the free market, unlike socialism, do not guarantee equality. To the contrary, capitalism is based on the idea that many will fail while a few will succeed.

A central question for those concerned with a just society has to do with these notions of liberty and equality. This is particularly relevant in the last century where so many countries have moved to democratic societies. Ideally, a society would hope to maximize both liberty and equality. But these two principles may work at cross-purposes.

At one extreme, you have **libertarians**—those who place the highest values on liberty even at the expense of equality. They want unlimited liberty and freedom even if it results in inequality of conditions. The only equality they want is equality of opportunity because it encourages freedom of enterprise and a meritocracy based on talents and hard work. Vast inequalities will result and are acceptable because otherwise there would be a loss of individual liberty, which from this perspective is the highest value. To create an equality of conditions can be achieved only by the loss of individual freedom.[8]

In contrast to libertarians, **egalitarians** regard equality of conditions as the supreme value and are willing to achieve this by infringing on the liberty of others. To egalitarians, if individual freedom is unrestrained inequality of conditions—poverty, housing, privilege—will result, and this is to be avoided. Egalitarians hope to maximize equality of conditions even if individual liberty has to be sacrificed. Egalitarians as social activists are often in the forefront of social justice movements. They consider capitalism as a major problem unless it is socialized and the workers are given a stronger voice and share of the economic and political benefits of society.[9]

So how does one determine the proper balance between freedom and liberty? There are at least two sources of freedom and liberty. First, there is the freedom implicit to all humans because they are human. These may be called natural rights. They are life and the pursuit of happiness. These encompass other entitlements. For example, a human, in a just society, is entitled to enough economic goods to sustain life. Health and education are additional requirements to give humans access to humanity and humane treatment. Second, there are circumstantial rights and freedoms. These have to do with the freedom to exercise one's talents to the fullest and enjoy the benefits of such gifts.

This requires an environment, one regulated by justice, that allows the greatest pursuit of happiness without infringing upon the happiness of others.[10]

Of course, all people are equal in their humanity. But after that is a wide divergence in talents and skills. There is equality of conditions. Not all people have the same basic skills or intelligence. Then there is equality of opportunity. Mortimer Adler, in his book, *Six Great Ideas*, illustrates the difference using the foot race as an example. The race starts with everyone having an equal opportunity to win. There are no hidden barriers or obstacles for some and not others. When the race is over, these same individuals end up unequal; some come in first, second, third, and last based on their athleticism, training, and determination. This is equality of conditions. It is up to a just society to ensure the equality of opportunity. It is up to the individuals to succeed or not based on their conditions. Equality under the law is another example. Society cannot guarantee that some will or will not break the law. But in the law all should be treated the same, an equality of condition.[11]

Furthermore, when one abides by the laws, even if they curtail some freedoms, one does not lose his or her freedom. As Adler says in reference to America:

> The constitution to which the citizen has given consent by exercising his suffrage provides for a decision by the vote of the majority. He has accepted the principle of majority rule and, having done so, the citizen has also accepted, in advance, the results of majority rule, whether or not the voting places him in the majority or in the adversely affected minority.[12]

Although liberty and equality are important values that may appear to be in conflict, these conflicts need not lead to paralysis of thinking. A just society is one that balances these two competing values. Freedom and liberty cannot be exerted contrary to the best interests of the community.

WAR

Some of the most difficult issues of justice to be faced by nation-states concern the conduct of war. War has been a part of every nation's history.[13] It has been a means to acquire territory, resources, wealth, women, and pride. Early wars were localized to competing armies or navies; ordinary citizens were largely left alone. Soldiers were a professional class who were often not even emotionally attached to the nation for whom they were waging war. Sometimes war took on religious overtones. The crusades are an example of how Christian Europe attacked and fought to free the Holy Land from Moslem conquerors.

Modern war took on new attributes. First, many nations did away with mercenaries and professional soldiers, and ordinary citizens who had a more emotional interest entered the scuffle. Second, total war became common in which the land and lives of noncombatants were swept up in the destruction. Third, war became more mechanized and lethal with tanks, artillery, and bombs. By nature, war is cruel, but it is particularly true in modern times. People are killed and property destroyed. It is something that should not be entered into lightly.

To describe some wars as just and others as unjust, one must assume that some higher moral and legal standards can be used to make this distinction. In an earlier time, religious leaders and institutions provided such standards. St. Augustine, in his *The City of God*, was perhaps the first to articulate the concept of a "just war." Thereafter, the Catholic Church assumed the role of defining and guiding the use of force along Christian ethics.[14] In modern times, these standards are drawn up by an international community of nations[15] (see Chapter 14). These standards can be applied to the cause of the conflict, carrying out of war policy by the state, the manner of individual behavior in war, and treatment of the vanquished after the conflict.[16]

On the surface, the cause of war seems to be a simple assumption. A nation that aggressively attacks another has done an unjust thing. Consequently, the state that has been attacked must go to war in the name of self-defense. Such countries may posture themselves as morally superior—they did not start this war; they are victims fighting for survival. For nations whose international policies reflect this attitude, including America in the twentieth century, war is a necessary evil. Preventive war, going to war early to prevent a future aggressor, is wrong according to this perspective. The just nation would generally have a non-warlike posture. Diplomacy and treaties to negotiate disputes and deter aggression would be the first and most just approach. But a nation might create conditions that force another to be aggressive. For example, the Japanese attack on Pearl Harbor launched a just war for the United States. But America had numerous policies in the 1930s that threatened Japan's desires for oil supplies. Those policies maneuvered Japan into an attack, making the issue of justness more cloudy.[17]

Once an aggressor has started a war, the victim nation, in the name of military necessity, can be very aggressive and violent. The act of instigating a war changes things. However, there are some restraining considerations. One is based on the "evil few" concept. Even in the aggressor nation, only a few evil people are truly responsible for the act of war. The "many good" are simply brought along through patriotism and propaganda. Ordinarily, a just war policy tries to avoid citizen casualties. Of course, in the name of military necessity, total war—that in which many of the innocent majority are caught up in the violence of war—may occur and be justified. For example, the nuclear bombing of two Japanese cities in 1945 was argued to be necessary because of the many more Japanese and Americans who would have been killed and injured if an invasion of the country were forced. However, international rules dictate how combatants are to be treated (see Chapter 14). Proper prisoner of war camps and appropriate humane care need to be established. The Japanese role here, particularly in the death marches in Bataan, reaffirmed that the allies were fighting a just war. Nazi treatment of the Jews posed them in villainous roles so that certain leaders could be tried as "war criminals" at the Nuremberg trials after the war (see Chapter 14). Several German and Japanese war leaders were executed for their unjust waging of war.[18]

Even fighting a just war does not free individual soldiers to do inhumane things. Fighting for one's life can bring the individual soldier down. To see death and destruction all around is demoralizing. Being trained and forced to kill, which some argue is contrary to human nature, may blunt one's humanity. Such problems can emerge in any war. But in a particularly frustrating war, they may be greater. For Americans, such a war was Vietnam. Clearly defined goals and morally repressible enemies were not present. Moral support from home was tenuous. Issues of the enemy being the aggressor were elusive. Massive bombing and killing of people and destruction of the landscape were debatable. But two incidents point to the unjust behavior of individual soldiers. First, during the Vietnam War there was the patrol duty of Lt. Calley at My Lai in which numerous apparently innocent villagers were slaughtered. Calley was later convicted of a war crime. Second was the career of a navy seal who invaded and slaughtered a village of apparently innocent people. He won numerous medals and a U.S. Senatorial seat before exposure years later. These are just two of countless incidents in Vietnam. The nature of war suggests that countless other examples may be found in all wars.[19]

Finally, there is the treatment of the defeated after the conflict. This is a matter of no small consequence. Hitler used the treatment of Germany after World War I as a means to achieve power and bring on the Second World War. Forgiveness is not an easy thing to obtain, especially if the war was a particularly costly one. Simon Wiesenthal has beautifully captured this dilemma in *The Sunflower*. In that book, a young Jewish prisoner, while undergoing horrendous treatment in Nazi death camps, is summoned before a dying German soldier. The soldier, stricken with enormous pangs of guilt for what he and his comrades had done, pleads for forgiveness. Bewildered, the prisoner leaves only to be summoned again and given mementoes the soldier wants delivered to his mother. The prisoner takes the items but still finds it impossible to forgive the soldier and leaves, never to see the dying man again. After the war, the prisoner went to the soldier's mother and is told what a sweet, honest, peaceful young man the soldier had been. Now the old prisoner faced another dilemma, whether to tell the mother what a demon her son had really been. Thereafter, in the book, scholars, theologians, and philosophers were perplexed about the moral and ethical dimensions of *The Sunflower*. Clearly, issues of a just war have to do with events before, during, and after the conflict itself.[20]

In the last half of the twentieth century, a new type of war, terrorism, emerged. Here, a war is not officially declared, citizens become a main target, suicide warriors have no respect or regard for life, and gangster psychology is part of the aggressor's mindset. For many in the Western world, such aggression falls into the unjust war category. But terrorists assume this strategy because they are too weak to fight legitimate wars. They are the dispossessed, and they resort to outlandish tactics, having little to lose.

CRIMINAL JUSTICE

Very early justice was connected to the processing and punishment of criminals, and it remains so. In every human society, no matter what political and economic form it takes, some people violate the rules of society. Society's response is delivered through a system of criminal justice.

What constitutes a just processing of criminals? Processing of criminals might be defined as steps in the criminal justice system, including arrest, interrogation, charging, representation by an attorney, courtroom ceremonies, sentencing, and punishment (see Chapter 7). In this regard, justice is a process. On one level, this process needs to be fair. On another level, the system is guided by its own set of desires and agendas that shape the nature of this fairness. Two mind-sets exist about the appropriate processing of criminals. Herbert Packer has described these approaches as the **crime control** and **due process** perspectives.

Those who subscribe to the crime control mentality believe that a major problem of modern society is crime. The criminal justice system–the police, the court personnel, and those in corrections—needs all the power it can get to process criminals. Victims of crime are of the most concern. Efficiency overtakes fairness in their minds. The appropriate metaphor for the system is the assembly line. Justice is a smoothly operating efficient system run by professionals who should have the resources to do their jobs with little oversight by outsiders. Although not uttered, the presumption is that the accused person is guilty.[21]

Others approach criminal justice from a due process perspective. These people feel that along with criminals, the criminal justice system itself is a potential threat to justice. Although efficiency is a good thing, too much efficiency might define a police state in which citizens have no rights. Therefore, the just system is one in which the police and others in the system have controls on their behavior. Although respect toward victims is necessary, people accused of crime also need protections. The presumption here is of innocence. The appropriate metaphor for the system is the obstacle course. High standards of procedures, accountability of actions, and close scrutiny by outsiders characterize this perspective.[22]

These are not abstract concerns. They are bureaucratic ones as well. Criminal justice systems need to process large numbers of cases and to do so as efficiently as possible. The just society is one that strives to find a balance between these two perspectives.

A fundamental question remains, why do we deprive people of life or liberty? John Stuart Mill and Jeremy Bentham believed in punishment and defended it in terms of rational ideas. Mill and Bentham believed that societal good came from punishing its wrongdoers. Bentham, in his *Introduction to the Principles of Morals and Legislation* (1789), even believed that society should have a guiding principle for decisions made in society. That master rule was the principle of utility—does the good outweigh the bad? All actions, rules, and institutions are justified only to the extent that they bring about the greater overall good, or the maximum of pleasure and the minimum of pain. Punishment is the intentional infliction of something unpleasant or the intentional deprivation of something pleasant by the state. From this **utilitarian** perspective, society should determine the amount of punishment based upon a cost/benefit analysis of suffering inflicted versus social gains achieved.[23]

The classic alternative to the utilitarians was **retributivism.** Those guilty of crimes need to be punished because they deserve to be punished. Utilitarians would determine punishment based on the amount of good it would do society. Retributivists would rely on the idea that the punishment inflicted should be in proportion to the severity of the offense. Immauel Kant, in his *The Philosophy of Law* (1797), stated it most clearly. The reason to punish someone is only if he or she committed a crime. The crime should be punished according to the principle of equality; the severity of the punishment should equal the severity of the crime.[24]

Others have presented ideas outside the utilitarian and retributivist debate. For example, Georg Wilhelm Friedrich Hegel, in his *The Philosophy of Right* (1821), believed that punishment was self-chosen, that wrongdoers actually invite their own punishment. He distinguishes between injury to the state and injury to an individual, and injury to the state requires the punishment. For example, even if the victim forgave the offender, the state still needed to punish the offender. That is why, Hegel explains, punishment often does not fit the crime—for the seriousness of the injury to the person may have little relationship to the threat to society. The sanctity of the particular society is the main concern, rather than the interests of the various citizens or even the public good.[25]

Michael Moore, in *The Moral Worth of Retribution* (1987), defends retribution simply because wrongdoing deserves punishment. He gives several atrocious cases taken from newspapers and asks what should be done. In every case, a natural abhorrence arises demanding some kind of pain. Reform and rehabilitation are not considered; issues of utility fall to the wayside. A natural impulse demands retribution, or "just deserts." He asks us to imagine a situation:

> A murderer has truly found Christ . . . so that he or she does not need to be reformed; he or she is not dangerous for the same reason; and the crime can go undetected so that general deterrence does not demand punishment (alternatively, we can pretend to punish and pay the person the money the punishment would have cost us to keep his or her mouth shut, which will also serve the ends of general deterrence). In such a situation, should the criminal still be punished?

Moore believes that most of us still would favor some punishment.[26]

Robert Nozick, in his *Philosophical Explanations* (1981), distinguishes between retribution and revenge. Retribution is impersonal, he thinks, whereas revenge is personal. Retribution is for a wrong, but revenge sometimes is merely for a slight. Retribution is limited in its severity by the offense, revenge is not. He defends retribution because it sends a message to the offender and likely to the wider society as well.[27] Robert C. Solomon, in his *A Passion for Justice* (1990), addresses the issue of revenge and retribution. He argues that much of the supposed irrationality and excess of revenge has been overstated. In fact, seeking revenge lies at the very foundation of our sense of justice. The desire of vengeance seems to be an integral aspect of our recognition of evil. Uncontrolled vengeance might be bad but to deny it as a legitimate motive would be as wrong. Therefore,

> Justice is not forgiveness nor even forgetting but rather it is getting one's emotional priorities right, putting blame aside in the face of so much other human suffering and thereby giving up vengeance for the sake of larger and more noble emotions.[28]

Many philosophers do not like retribution (which has a close kinship to vengeance, according to Solomon) because it is "backward looking," undoing a past offense. These people argue for deterrence and reform as forward looking. But Solomon thinks this is wrongheaded. Why punish at all? Let us forget past misdeeds and move on to the future. In fact, carrying it further, why not punish innocent people as object lessons and warnings to future possible wrongdoers? Of course, that is ridiculous and even unjust. Vengeance can be dangerous (an old Chinese saying is that "if you seek vengeance, dig two graves"), which is why it must be left to the state and not individuals. Solomon claims, therefore, "vengeance deserves its central place in any theory of justice and, whatever else we are to say about punishment, the desire for revenge must enter into our deliberations along with such emotions as compassion, caring and love." Of course, it also explains why some countries still have capital punishment.[29]

Capital Punishment

Perhaps the most controversial of punishments society can inflict is death. Capital punishment, once so widely spread across the world, has been abandoned by much of Europe. Ironically, the country that has been such an exemplar to the world when it comes to politics and economics, the United States of America, still practices capital punishment.[30] Empirical evidence seems to suggest that capital punishment does not deter others from committing murder. However, in a Supreme Court case, *Gregg v. Georgia* (1976), the majority upheld the constitutionality of the death penalty in light of arguments of retribution and deterrence:

> The instinct for retribution is part of the nature of men, and channeling that instinct in the administration of criminal justice serves an important purpose in promoting the stability of a society government by law. When people begin to believe that organized society is unwilling or unable to impose upon criminal offenders the punishment they "deserve," then there are sown the seeds of anarchy—of self-help, vigilante justice, and lynch law.[31]

Justices representing the minority opinion in the case dismissed retribution as vengeance and deterrence as not supported by evidence. Thurgood Marshall, going back to arguments given by Socrates, believed that it was wrong to return evil for evil. There was no evidence, he felt, that capital punishment would have a greater deterrent effect than a life term in prison.[32]

Hugo Bedau, in his *Death is Different*, argues that capital punishment is an ineffective deterrent and unnecessary for finding appropriate retribution. Although criminals need to be punished and the punishment should fit the crime, capital punishment does not do so. Bedau points out that death is not administered to all killers. Furthermore, it is unjustly applied. Wealthy white murderers do not get it. A very large number of those executed are poor and members of minority populations. Furthermore, who gets sentenced to death frequently has more to do with aggressive prosecutors and incompetent defense attorneys than anything else. Capital punishment cheapens and degrades human life rather than enhancing respect for it, claims Bedau.[33]

In contrast, Ernest van den Haag supports the death penalty because it is better to err in favor of potential victims than in favor of convicted killers. He thinks that despite the rhetoric, rehabilitation and deterrence are not really part of the American penal system. To be sure, there is uncertainty about the death penalty's effect. But by executing real killers, we ensure they will never kill again. Furthermore, there is a slim chance future victims might be saved by the example of killing a killer. Van den Haag thinks it is worth it to them that execution goes on.[34]

CONCLUSION

As abstract as the notion of justice might be, its presence or absence in a society is most evident in the workings of government. The political environment has the greatest immediate affect on individuals and justice. Some totalitarian states only make rhetorical gestures toward justice. Democratic states are caught on the horns of a dilemma: They must practice justice as well as talk it.

The relationship between the people and their government raises all kinds of issues. Perhaps first is the issue of legitimacy. Is the government—its people and policies—a reflection of the people or is it imposed by force? Laws—those written or proclaimed statements by the government that bind the citizenry to order—directly affect the lives of citizens. Where do these laws come from and how are they to be interpreted? However, the activities of the government belie any philosophical or fundamental principles. When it comes to foreign policy and war, to what extent is the government just? No soldier wants to fight for an unjust cause. Internally, one of the most dramatic activities of government is the criminal justice system. If it is true that a society will be judged by how it treats those it hates most, the treatment of criminals tests a people's sense of justice. For those countries that retain the death penalty, issues of justice are even more vivid. This chapter has tried to introduce the reader to those areas of justice. But there are a variety of other issues of justice that need to be discussed; they can be categorized as social justice.

Discussion Questions

1. Why is it essential for the state to be involved in issues of justice?
2. Does the "Social Contract" allow for dissent and disobedience?
3. Do you believe in Natural Law, Positivism, or Sociological Jurisprudence?

Endnotes

1. J. W. Allen, *A History of Political Thought in the Sixteenth Century* (New York: Barnes & Noble's University Paperbacks, 1960), pp. 445–494.
2. Thomas Hobbes, *Leviathan: Or the Matter, Form and Power of a Commonwealth Ecclesiastical and Civil* (London: Collier Books, 1962), pp. 28–31. See also Johann P. Sommerville, *Thomas Hobbes: Political Ideas in Historical Context* (New York: St. Martin's Press, 1992), pp. 29–31, 57–63.
3. Ibid., p. 116.
4. John Locke, *Second Treatise of Government*, Peter Laslett (ed.) (Cambridge: Cambridge University Press, 1967), pp. 336–348, 368–371. Also see Ian Harris, *The Mind of John Locke: A Study of Political Theory in Its Intellectual Setting* (Cambridge: Cambridge University Press, 1994), pp. 36–39, 189.
5. Jean-Jacques Rousseau, *On the Social Contract and Discourse*, G. D. H. Cole (trans.) (New York: Dutton, 1959), pp. 176–282. Also see Lester G. Crocker, *Rousseau's Social*

Contract: An Interpretive Essay (Cleveland: Case Western University Press, 1968), pp. 43–101.

6. For an introduction, see Thomas W. Simon, *Law and Philosophy: An Introduction with Readings* (Boston: McGraw Hill, 2001).

7. Paul Hazard, *The European Mind, 1680–1715* (Cleveland and New York: Meridian Books, 1968), pp. 266–283.

8. Mortimer J. Adler, *Six Great Ideas* (New York: Macmillan, 1981), p. 137.

9. Ibid.

10. Ibid., pp. 164–173.

11. Ibid., p. 157.

12. Ibid., p. 148.

13. David Welch, *Justice and the Genesis of War* (Cambridge: Cambridge University Press, 1993), pp. 7–23.

14. Williston Walker, *A History of the Christian Church* (New York: Charles Scribner's Sons, 1959), pp. 160–172.

15. John Hagan and Scott Greer, "Making War Criminal," *Criminology,* Vol. 40, No. 2, 2002, pp. 231–264.

16. James E. Childress, "Just Wars Theories," *Theological Studies,* 1978, pp. 427–445.

17. Robert W. Tucker, *The Just War: A Study in Contemporary Doctrine* (Baltimore: Johns Hopkins University Press, 1960), pp. 18–30.

18. Ibid., pp. 27–30.

19. Kenneth W. Kemp, "Just War Theory: A Reconceptualization," *Public Affairs Quarterly,* Vol. 2, No. 2, 1988, pp. 57–74.

20. Simon Wiesenthal, *The Sunflower: On the Possibilities and Limits of Forgiveness* (New York: Schoken Books, 1997), pp. 3–98.

21. Herbert Packer, *The Limits of the Criminal Sanction* (Stanford, Calif.: Stanford University Press, 1968), pp. 154–163.

22. Ibid., pp. 163–173.

23. J. H. Burns and H. L. A. Hart, *An Introduction to the Principles of Morals and Legislation* (London: Athlone, 1970), pp. 11–15.

24. Edward Caird, *The Critical Philosophy of Immanuel Kant,* 2 vols. (New York: Kraus Reprint, 1968), pp. 315–378.

25. Georg Wilhelm Friedrich Hegel, *The Philosophy of Right* (Chicago: Encyclopedia Britannica, 1952), pp. 64–78.

26. Robert C. Solomon and Mark C. Murphy (eds.), *What Is Justice?: Classic and Contemporary Readings* (New York: Oxford University Press, 2000), pp. 236–245.

27. Robert Nozick, *Philosophical Explanations* (Cambridge, Mass.: Harvard University Press, 1981), pp. 363, 366–368.

28. Robert C. Solomon, *A Passion for Justice: Emotions and the Origins of the Social Contract* (Reading, Mass.: Addison-Wesley, 1990), p. 286.

29. Ibid., p. 285.

30. For a perceptive discussion of the problem of capital punishment in America, see Franklin E. Zimring, *The Contradictions of American Capital Punishment* (New York: Oxford University Press, 2003).

31. *Gregg v. Georgia,* 428 US. 153 (1976).

32. Ibid.

33. Hugo Bedau, *Death Is Different: Studies in the Morality, Law, and Politics of Capital Punishment* (Boston: Northeastern University Press, 1987), pp. 32–34, 238–247.

34. Ernest van den Haag and John Conrad, *The Death Penalty: A Debate* (New York: Plenum, 1983), pp. 28–35, 55–56, 67–70.

CHAPTER 3

SOCIAL JUSTICE

To most people discussions of justice become too abstract and academic. Social justice is a more practical topic. Because of religious, political, or economic differences, many people find themselves at a social and financial disadvantage. Social justice focuses on the redistribution of resources to ensure fairness in meeting the basic needs of people. Social justice has to do with distributing society's benefits and burdens. Thinkers and activists are concerned with the gaps in society. A just society tries to diminish significant disparities. Karl Marx made the classic social justice statement: "From each according to his abilities, to each according to his needs."[1]

John Stuart Mill's argument for social justice and utility forms a significant part of his *Utilitarianism* (1863).[2] It is just to respect and unjust to violate the legal rights of any person. Justice means adherence to law. However, sometimes there are bad laws. Humans have moral rights that transcend such laws. In addition, people should get what they deserve.

> Speaking in a general way, a person is understood to deserve good if he does right, evil if he does wrong; and in a more particular sense, to deserve good from those to whom he does or has done good, and evil from those to whom he does or has done evil.[3]

Impartiality becomes a keystone in Mill's definition of justice. And then in ringing terms, Mill sees a critical aspect in the name of social justice:

> The entire history of social improvement has been a series of transitions by which one custom or institution after another, from being a supposed primary necessity of social existence, has passed into the rank of a universally stigmatized injustice and tyranny. So it has been with the distinctions of slaves and freedman, nobles and serfs, patricians and plebeians; and so it will be, and in part already is, with the aristocracies of color, race, and sex.[4]

Thus, social justice focuses on fairness and equality of opportunity for **classes** of people, rather than focusing on the justice due to individuals.

Pcl#: 16245432   Typ:R4   Tm:WPK570 Order # 61417815SM   Ctn: 1 of 1

Pl#:   1203   Date: 11/13/03   Wve:001   Tote: 16257560   **SLA:7**

Location   ISBN   **Pieces   Description**
570-117-031 0534623913   1   PURSUING JUSTICE

The enclosed materials are compliments of
DENISE HETZ 800 876-2350X7086   #00009

SHC: 0   THOMSON LEARNING   Page: 1 of 1

HUMAN RIGHTS

Many issues of justice are closely connected to human rights, basic rights that everyone should enjoy simply because they belong to the human family.[5] Generally, human rights come from two perspectives: negative and positive rights. Those who advocate "negative rights" seek to protect the individual from others interfering with one's efforts to build a future of the individual's own choice. Negative rights guarantee the individual freedom from coercion. Much of the early discussion of political theory was concerned with **negative rights.** The Bill of Rights of the U.S. Constitution is one example of negative rights. In the Bill of Rights, citizens are protected from the power of the government.

The **positive rights** perspective believes that people also have rights to food, clothing, medical care, education, and housing. These rights are not protections but, rather, statements of entitlement. The assumption here is that human rights are a minimal requirement for full participation in the community with dignity.[6]

In 1948, the General Assembly of the United Nations adopted the *Universal Declaration of Human Rights* (see Chapter 14 and the appendix). This was a result of the violations of human rights by the Nazis during World War II. The *Declaration* announced that the dignity and equality of all members of the human family were the foundation of freedom, justice, and peace in the world. Everyone had the right to life, liberty, and security. Slavery and the slave trade were condemned. Punishment that was inhuman and degrading was prohibited. No one was to be subject to arbitrary arrest or exile. Strikingly similar to the United States' notions of due process, the signatory nations agreed on the basic humanity of all people. Problems of human rights remained, however, and the United Nation's authority was not enough to ensure compliance. Almost 20 years after the original *Declaration*, the United Nation's position was emphasized, clarified, and expanded. In 1966, the United Nations issued the *Covenant on Civil and Political Rights* and the *Covenant on Economic, Social and Political Rights.*[7]

JUSTICE AND ECONOMICS

Jesus Christ said that the poor would always be in the world. Slaves, serfs, and peasants dot the historical landscape to suggest the wisdom of Christ's declaration. However, poverty puts people at risk for many problems, including poorer health, shorter life spans, greater exposure to crime, and unfruitful life styles. In a country such as America—with all of its wealth and opportunity—the existence of poverty is perplexing. In fact, 17 percent of children in the United States live in poverty, a rate two to three times higher than that of most Western industrialized nations.[8]

Some philosophers have addressed this troublesome issue of economic disparity. John Locke, in his *Second Treatise on Government* (1690), believed that private property was a natural right: The earth belongs to all humans as a gift of God. One was entitled to the fruits of their labor. However, as a brake on future "robber barons," this acquisition did not go so far as to take and harm other humans or nature. "Nothing was made by God for man to spoil and destroy," declared Locke.[9]

Adam Smith, in his *The Theory of Moral Sentiments* (1759), acknowledged the importance of self-interests (greed) but insisted that it was balanced by something called moral sentiments. This meant that humans had feelings and sympathies for the suffering of others, which hold any desire to exploit or harm in check. Foremost of these feelings that prohibit us from harming is a sense of justice.[10] Therefore, justice is the desire not to harm others, a desire for approval from others, and all above a useful way to make society stable. Smith went on in *The Wealth of Nations* (1776) to argue the virtues of the free market system. Such a capitalist system, he believed, would ensure the greatest prosperity for all citizens. However, this free market, with its quest of private property, necessarily led to many inequalities between the few rich and many poor. The natural enmity between the classes made civil government necessary, he believed.[11]

Immanuel Kant, in his *The Philosophy of Law* (1797), also argues for some natural right to property. Property is so important, Kant believes, that the violation of a person's property is an attack on his or her freedom. G. W. F. Hegel's *The Philosophy of Right* (1821) sets forth that property is not just a right but, rather, an expression of the self. One can give away or sell the products of one's labor, and the institutions of contracts came into existence because of this. However, if one gives or is forced to give so much away that he or she loses a sense of self, this becomes an unjust situation. Marx later used such an idea to attack the entire capitalist wage system, which he believed reduced humans to slaves.[12]

Perhaps no other thinker has had such a profound impact as Marx. His influence on the political and economic landscape of the world cannot be denied. Marx felt that human society could be only understood through the ways its individuals obtained subsistence, in short their labor. His most fully developed ideas appeared in *Das Capital,* the classic denouncement of capitalism. History was the struggle between economic classes. The minority—the ruling class— was pitted against the vast working class that controlled very little. The working classes—first as slaves and serfs then as workers after the industrial revolution—were exploited by the capitalist. The proletariat produced much but received few rewards. Capitalists produced very little but received great rewards. Capitalism, and all class-oriented societies, were unjust. They not only violated human rights, but, because they were based on flawed notions of economic production, they made it necessary to consider the issue of justice. As one author noted, "The demands of justice cannot be satisfied in the circumstances which made concepts of justice necessary; thus efforts to achieve justice inevitably fail."[13] Marx believed economic justice could only be achieved when the means of production were turned over to the workers. History proved that dramatic changes could occur, such as the transformation from feudalism to capitalism. He called for a new revolution, one from capitalism to communism.

Not everyone subscribed to the notion of economic justice. The Social Darwinists of the nineteenth century were leery of perpetuating the weaker sorts, and poverty was seen as a sign that the person was not well equipped to compete in society.[14] In the 1970s and 1980s, these ideas found expression in a new form of conservatism. Friedrich von Hayek, in his *The Mirage of Social Justice* (1978), was a major exponent of this belief. Hayek believed that any effort to predetermine distribution of wealth required placing power in the hands of government and taking it away from individuals. For example, it would require taking wealth from a few and depriving them of their liberty. What is often overlooked, according to Hayek, is that the free market system does not always reward merit and talent. Strong elements of luck are involved. No one—the untalented who are deprived and the talented who are overlooked—likes to go unrewarded. "Level playing fields" and equal opportunity are impossible to attain and any attempt to do so only strengthens the government and encourages dangerous meddling making the free market less free, thought Hayek.[15]

GENDER JUSTICE

On a number of fronts, women have a unique standing that forces us to address justice. The issue of sex—in terms of rape, prostitution, and harassment—is very large. Furthermore, issues of childbearing, domestic violence, lesbian identity, economic equality, and standards of beauty, to name a few, address the issue of gender justice.

Traditionally, there have been two gender roles. First is that of man as macho, or masculine with certain male entitlements in economics, politics, and sex. Second, women have been classified as seductresses. As seductresses, women are responsible for the "Eve Problem," ever ready to exploit the sexual weakness of males. Some societies are so concerned with this that they desexualize the female in public with strict dress codes or seclusion. Others require surgical processes, such as clitoridectomy, to de-sensitize the woman's sexual organs. Centuries of foot binding in China, wife scalding in Lebanon, and sati (widow burning) in India are other examples of injustice directed at women.[16]

In most societies, women have not had an equal share of justice with men. Historically, women were the property of men; property first of their fathers then of their husbands. Although several exceptional women obtained commanding positions in dynastic politics, very few women had political rights in such patriarchal arrangements. Take rape as an example. Throughout history, the victim of a rape was seen to be the significant male in the raped woman's life—father, husband, king. Women had to demonstrate that they truly resisted. Furthermore, as the tale of Potiphar's wife in the Bible suggests, the female might instigate or claim a false rape. In that story, Joseph worked for a high official in the Egyptian government named Potiphar. Joseph became the focus of a seduction by his boss' wife. When Joseph refused, Potiphar's wife claimed a rape attempt and had him cast into prison. The word of the victim was suspect, especially if she had a bad reputation. For centuries, women had to demonstrate resistence and prove they were not "loose women."[17]

Prostitution, frequently called the "oldest profession" is a worldwide phenomenon. Often males are part of the industry as pimps and procurers, and of course, men predominate as the customer base. Prostitution takes many forms: call girls, strip club dancers, masseuses in massage parlors, escort service providers, and streetwalkers. Elaborate rings of criminals abduct women and enslave them into prostitution. The Russian Mafia has taken over much of this activity in eastern and southern Europe. Some countries legitimize prostitution, and in some cities such as Bangkok and Amsterdam, the "red light districts" are widely advertised tourist attractions. Regular "sex tours" are quite common in Asia. In the United States where prostitution is illegal, except in a few counties of Nevada, enforcement is slack. However, when crusades—frequently called "operation angels"—are implemented, they are gender biased. These police operations go after the prostitute and not her customer. In recent years, the problem of prostitution has been compounded by the increasing use of children as prostitutes, including females as young as nine.[18]

Sexual harassment has been a persistent problem in the work place. Women have been subject to sexual demands to secure a job or be promoted in it. Leering men making suggestive comments contribute to a hostile work environment. Title VII of the Civil Rights Act of 1964 addressed and forbade this problem of harassment in the work place. However, women have to determine harassment, confront the perpetrator, and face judgmental coworkers. One problem has been on university campuses where professors prey on vulnerable female students. But it goes on extensively in overt and covert ways. These problems seldom confront men at work.[19]

When it came to work in the agricultural economy, women's positions were as important as men's were. But, as industrialization occurred, women were forced out of most labor markets and relegated to domestic roles in the home. Many assumed that women, once given the opportunity to have a family, would not fully commit to any other profession or job. Of course, women have been hard at work throughout history. This "reproductive work," having to do with raising a family, has never been defined as real work. When allowed into the marketplace, most women were segregated into predominately female occupations such as secretaries, elementary education teachers, and flight attendants. Furthermore, women were paid far less than men for doing the same work and "glass ceilings" prohibited advancement. For example, one study found that women and men had these median annual earnings[20]:

	High School	College	Professional Degree
Women	$18,252	$27,840	$33,604
Men	$26,790	$40,624	$46,978

Childbearing suggests several issues of justice. For example, for a long time a woman had no paid leave to give birth and assume motherhood during those crucial first months. Child care after birth places a tremendous physical and economic burden on a woman. Finding appropriate child care facilities becomes very important. Negotiating flexible work arrangements adds new burdens. Of course, the entire debate about abortion has been framed along a woman's choice or lack of choice over her body.[21]

Women make up the majority of the population in most societies. India might be an exception because of the practice of aborting unwanted female fetuses. But having discrimination against more than 50 percent of a society raises many issues of justice.

RACIAL JUSTICE

Every people make judgments about others. Xenophobia, or the fear of the foreign and the strange, has been a part of most societies. The history of the United States shows many ethnic tensions. As each wave of immigration arrived, American reaction was swift and discriminatory. From the Irish, disparagingly called Paddies, to Eastern and Southern European immigrants, to Jews, to African Americans, to Latinos—we have a history of suspicion and segregation of newcomers. Many think that internment camps for Japanese Americans during World War II were unjust. Another example of such prejudice is the treatment of Arab Americans after the terrorist attacks of 2001.

Frequently, the marker of color is used. Whites or lighter colored indigenous people have achieved higher status than darker colored peoples. Slavery was one way to keep a people subordinate and achieve some economic benefits as well. Slavery has been part of human history for thousands of years. Much of America's economy before the Civil War was built on the slavery of Africans. Even after a bloody war to free the African American a system of Jim Crow segregation kept them "in their places" for more than 50 years. Lynching and the rise of the KKK helped to do this too[22] (see also Chapter 8).

One racially charged part of American history was the plight of those indigenous peoples already living on the continent. Native Americans posed an alien culture and an obstacle to western migration. The way they looked at history, ownership of property, religion, integrity, and other attributes of culture were very different from the way Anglo-Saxons viewed these things. Considered a "nation," these disparate tribes were given promises and treaties that were quickly broken. Numerous wars in the eastern sections of the country ended with either tribal annihilation or forced movement in "The Trail of Tears," as tribes were forced to move from Georgia and the Carolinas to an "Indian Territory" that one day would be called Oklahoma and Kansas. As precious minerals were discovered and land hungry settlers pushed westward, conflicts arose. Instead of protecting the indigenous populations from such intrusions, the government used the military to wage war on Native Americans. Two theaters of battle occurred, one on the northern plains and the other on the southern desert lands, both ending in massacres and decimation of cultures. To this day, most Native Americans reside on reservations, segregated from the dominant culture. Though there have been attempts at a civil rights movement for the Native Americans, called American Indian Movement or AIM, these attempts have been weak and unsuccessful. Frequently, large issues of different cultures, poverty, alcoholism, and crime have been overshadowed by debates about sports mascots.

In the 1960s and 1970s, following a civil rights movement, a national social policy aimed at ending discrimination in voting was implemented. Soon, other "equal opportunity" legislation was passed to end discrimination in hiring practices. According to some of these early social adjustments, various quotas were used to ensure ample representation of minorities. However, some claimed that injustices resulted in the name of justice. For example, some felt that reverse discrimination occurred when numerous white males were passed over in the name of having a racially diverse work environment. Enough pressure was exerted to scale back many affirmative action practices. Questions of racial justice continue to divide the United States.

ENVIRONMENTAL JUSTICE

Justice as it is applied to the environment assesses the earth, its resources, and purity (see Chapter 11). Ancient peoples even made the earth a god, Gaia, and any damage to her was sacrilegious. In his thoughtful book, *Ishmael*, Daniel Quinn has his hero, an ape, advertise for those who want to save the world. Ishmael instructs his pupil about two types of inhabitants of the world: the leavers and the takers. The former lived in harmony with the world. They took only what they needed and were not wasteful. They held the earth and nature in high regard. The takers were those who wasted natural resources. Like a man who jumps from a cliff and flaps his arms frantically, there is an illusion of flight until the ultimate crash to the canyon floor. If humans continue to consume and waste and spoil the earth, there may be an illusion of progress, but it will end in a crash of destruction, declared Quinn's ape.[23]

For much of world history, industry and population were small enough not to jeopardize the earth. Even in countries with large populations, such as India and China, people tended to use resources in a way that left little waste. But during the industrial revolution of Western society, concerns arose about the natural resources and the purity of the environment. Although this is a worldwide concern, particularly in developing countries, much of this discussion will be directed at the United States.

In the 1890s, two separate revelations were made: (1) the U.S. Census Bureau announced that the frontier, that line separating civilization from wilderness, had ceased to exist; and (2) a group of investigative journalists, called "muckrakers," began exposing the industrial and corporate world's exploitation of the nation's natural and human resources.

The closing of the frontier profoundly affected American society. Before, with open western lands available as a safety valve, individual success was thought to be ensured by just picking up and moving westward. Land, timber, water, minerals, opportunity were thought to be the right of every American citizen. With the closing of that frontier, though in reality ample land was still available, the symbol was gone; now people had to stay put and succeed. There was a growing sense of limitation.

At the same time, people and government became aware that industry was consuming resources in a wasteful way. In the era of the "Robber Barons," those industrialists who were revolutionizing the economic structure of America, capitalism in its basest form was seen. Minerals and timbers were extracted with little regard for nature. Smoke-filled skies were seen as a sign of progress rather than pollution. Ida Tarbell's *History of the Standard Oil Company* revealed in detail the practices that made that business the giant in the refining industry. Authors like Theodore Dreiser wrote about *The Titan* and *The Financier*, characters who had reckless disregard for human and natural resources.

Two distinctive strands can be seen in the rise of environmental justice in reaction to the closing of the frontier and the exposure of the industrialists. One is the **conservation movement.** Although there were some small concerns earlier, the major thrust of this movement came in the Progressive era, 1900–1914. Conservationists wanted to protect natural resources—timber, minerals, land—to ensure their quality for future generations. Conservationists are human oriented; they are concerned with the needs of future generations and their right to these resources. George Perkins Marsh, in his *Man and Nature: or Physical Geography as Modified by Human Action* (1864), argued that the decline and death of all past civilizations occurred because they destroyed their environment. Frederick Law Olmsted, creator of New York City's Central Park, thought nature was necessary in urban settings. He believed in land management and the creation of city and national parks. John Wesley Powell explored and mapped the western wilderness, and in his *Report on the Lands of the Arid Region of the United States* (1878) to Congress, he advocated a system of dams and canals to reclaim the land. The Reclamation Act of 1902 resulted.[24]

Under President Theodore Roosevelt, political leaders took up the conservationist cause. A variety of agencies were set up to safeguard the environment. Numerous acres of federal land were set aside as national parks. Actually, the first, Yellowstone National Park, had been created earlier in 1872. But now under Roosevelt, and presidents who followed him, 365 parks were created as a national park system. In 1916, the National Park Service was established. After the depression and the election of President Franklin D. Roosevelt, the economic and climactic devastations across much of the country were attributed to poor management of the lands and rivers.[25]

The **preservationist** movement comprised those who wanted to protect the environment for its own value. These people were nature oriented and were less concerned with human need and consumption. Some of the earliest preservationists linked nature to God. George Catlin, Henry David Thoreau, and John Muir (the first president of the Sierra Club) all believed that nature was necessary as an inspirational and spiritual place. Humans needed nature as a spiritual compass for their daily lives. Wilderness was needed to preserve human civilization. Today, much of their thinking has influenced the ecology movement and radical environmentalism. For example, Aldo Leopold, in his book *A Sand County Almanac* (1949), believed "the opportunity to see geese is more important than television, and the chance to find a pasque-flower is a right as inalienable as free speech."[26]

As the industrial, urban, and suburban expansions after World War II occurred, new environmental issues arose. The need for resources such as oil compelled many to side with business rather than the conservationists and preservationists. Politically, the conservatives were less environment friendly than were the liberals.

Perhaps the single most important book that kindled the modern environmentalist movement was Rachel Carson's *Silent Spring* in 1962 (see Chapter 12). Born in a small town in western Pennsylvania, she developed passionate interests in nature writing and scientific research. She took a job in the Bureau of U.S. Fisheries in the late 1930s and began a career writing about undersea life. *Under the Sea Wind* and *The Sea Around Us* showed her concerns for the harm being done to the sea. *Silent Spring* became immediately successful and controversial. Her theme was that pesticides were ruining the environment. She argued that public health and the environment were inseparable. The petrochemical industry reacted vigorously with its scientific experts. Carson advocated that this issue was too important to be left to the experts; it had to be a democratically grounded public issue. As one author noted, "The mission of *Silent Spring* became nothing less than an attempt to create a new environmental consciousness."[27]

A variety of environmental issues arose in the 1970s. Global warming and the problem of greenhouse gases became evident as ozone holes in the atmosphere were discovered. Disposing of nuclear waste became urgent. Traffic congestion and automobile pollution in large cities threatened the public health. Endangering the foods and soils with pesticides called many to action. Saving endangered species and the tropical rainforest became a rallying cry.

An environmental justice movement was the product of the early work of the conservationist, preservationists, and several "environmental presidents."[28] Some environmentalists were concerned that issues of class and race were part of the problem (see Chapter 11). Wealthier communities could prevent locally unwanted land uses (LULUs), whereas poorer communities lacked the political and economic resources to do so. As a result, low income, minority communities received unwanted facilities.[29] Numerous organizations—such as Greenpeace and Earth First!—arose to fight for environmental justice[30] (see Chapter 13). Others were afraid, in the quest for the "bottom line," that businesses would even break the law. Environmental crime became an important issue. Finally, the federal government created an agency, the Environmental Protection Agency (EPA) in 1970.[31] But all societies of the world are caught between satisfying the demands of an ever-increasing population and guarding the ever-diminishing supply of natural resources.

CONCLUSION

Rather than talking of justice as it applies to individuals, social justice looks to larger segments of society and nature. Four themes emerge in discussing social justice. First, **egalitarianism** suggests that everyone, as part of the human family, deserves to be treated equally. Second, **membership** demands a concern for the exclusion and inclusion of people who might not enjoy the benefits of society. Third, there are issues of **time:** not only the responsibility society has toward those in the future but also to those who suffered in the past. Fourth, social justice advocates have expanded the **scope** of justice to include animals and nature.

Increasingly, issues of social justice are making their way into policy discussions and into the public consciousness. The issues raised in this chapter are complex and cannot be covered thoroughly in this brief discussion. The purpose of this chapter has been to introduce the concept of social justice and to illustrate some of the many dimensions of the concept.

Discussion Questions

1. To what extent is it the government's responsibility to address issues of social justice—such as poverty, racism, and sexism?
2. In a society in which "majority rules," what rights should minorities have?
3. From the perspective of gender justice, what are the arguments for and the arguments against legalizing prostitution?

Endnotes

1. William Hefferman and John Kleining, *From Social Justice to Criminal Justice: Poverty and the Administration of Justice* (New York: Oxford University Press, 2000), pp. 1–21.
2. See F. L. van Holthoon, *The Road to Utopia: A Study of John Stuart Mill's Social Thought* (Assen, Netherlands: Van Gorcum, 1971), pp. 68–85.
3. John Stuart Mill, *Utilitarianism, Liberty, and Representative Government* (New York: Dutton, 1910), quote on p. 41, but see also pp. 38–60.
4. Ibid., p. 59.
5. For an overview of some of these issues, see Thomas W. Simon, *Democracy and Social Injustice: Law, Politics and Philosophy* (Lanham, Md.: Rowman & Littlefield, 1995).
6. Carol S. Robb, *Equal Value: An Ethical Approach to Economics and Sex* (Boston: Beacon, 1995), pp. 19–21.
7. David M. Smith, *Geography and Social Justice* (Oxford, England: Blackwell, 1994), pp. 41, 47.
8. UNICEF Innocenti Research Centre, Florence, Italy, *Innocenti Report Card*, No. 1, June 2000. A league table of child poverty in rich nations.
9. John Locke, *Two Treatises of Government*, Peter Lassett (ed.) (Cambridge: Cambridge University Press, 1967), pp. 288–290.
10. Robert L. Heilbroner (ed.), *The Essential Adam Smith* (New York: Norton, 1986), pp. 65–66, 91–97.
11. Ibid., pp. 248–257.
12. See Robert C. Solomon and Mark C. Murphy (eds.), *What Is Justice?: Classic and Contemporary Readings* (New York: Oxford University Press, 2000), pp. 151–154, 155–166.
13. Allen E. Buchanan, *Marx and Justice: The Radical Critique of Liberalism* (New Jersey: Rowman & Littlefield, 1982), p. 51.
14. Richard Hofstader, *Social Darwinism in American Thought* (Boston: Beacon, 1963), pp. 13–50.
15. Norman P. Barry, *Hayek's Social and Economic Philosophy* (London: Macmillan, 1979), pp. 124–150. For a classic statement of his views, see Friedrich A. Hayek, *The Road to Serfdom* (Chicago: University of Chicago Press, 1965), pp. 88, 181.

Also see Alan Ebenstein, *Friedrich Hayek: A Biography* (New York: Palgrave, 2001), pp. 217–226.

16. Sakuntala Narasimhan, *Sati: Widow Burning in India* (New York: Doubleday, 1990), pp. 61–78.
17. Susan Brownmiller, *Against Our Will* (New York: Simon & Schuster, 1975), pp. 16–30.
18. Kevin Bales, *Disposable People: New Slavery in the Global Economy* (Berkeley: University of California Press, 1999), pp. 43, 74.
19. Robb, pp. 51–71.
20. Ibid., p. 30.
21. Ibid., pp. 31–50.
22. Walter White, *Rope and Faggot: A Biography of Judge Lynch* (New York: Arno, 1969), pp. 19–39.
23. Daniel Quinn, *Ishmael: An Adventure of the Mind and Spirit* (New York: Bantam/Turner Book, 1995), pp. 151–184.
24. Sally M. Edwards, "A History of the U.S. Environmental Movement," in *Environmental Crime: Enforcement, Policy, and Social Responsibility,* Mary Clifford (ed.) (Gaithersburg, Md.: Aspen, 1998), pp. 36–37.
25. Ibid., pp. 37–41.
26. Ibid., pp. 34–36.
27. Robert Gottlieb, *Forcing the Spring: The Transformation of the American Environmental Movement* (Washington D.C.: Island Press, 1993), p. 84.
28. Jonathan P. West and Glen Sussman, "Implementation of Environmental Policy: The Chief Executive" in *The Environmental Presidency,* Dennis L. Soden (ed.) (Albany: State University of New York Press, 1999), pp. 77–111.
29. Patrick Novotny, *Where We Live, Work and Play: The Environmental Justice Movement and the Struggle for a New Environmentalism* (Westport, Conn.: Praeger, 2000), pp. 11–27.
30. Sally Edwards, pp. 44–50.
31. Bill Hyatt, "The Federal Environmental Regulatory Structure," in *Environmental Crime: Enforcement, Policy, and Social Responsibility,* Mary Clifford (ed.) (Gaithersburg, Md.: Aspen, 1998), pp. 115–141.

P A R T

two

FORMAL SYSTEMS OF JUSTICE

It is tempting to think of justice in terms of individual cases. Did the rapist or child molester get what was coming to him? Was an employee treated unfairly because of his or her race or gender? Justice at that level is important to the individual victim and to others similarly situated. Justice at the individual level is also important for society because long-term failures to address these forms of injustice can challenge the legitimacy of society as a dispenser of justice. Ultimately, the legitimacy of society itself is questioned.

Focusing on justice at the individual level, while pursuing larger societal goals, is one of the main reasons for creating and maintaining governments. Numerous government agencies attempt to deliver justice. Some bureaucracies deal with poverty, race relations, workplace safety, and environmental protections. Those agencies are worthy of discussion. Here, however, discussion will be limited to general systems of justice with specific reference to those agencies dealing with law and order.

There are two great justice systems throughout the world: common law and civil law. Common law systems are more familiar to Americans. They come from medieval England. The features of common law systems are discussed in Chapter 4. Chapter 5 provides an overview of civil law systems, as can be found in France and in many parts of South America. Civil law systems are the oldest, most widespread, and most influential. They come out of the ancient organizations of the Roman Empire and the Catholic Church. In addition to these two distinct systems, what might be called colonial systems are hybrids, drawing from both the civil and common law traditions. Countries that had been colonies of civil or common law countries often take those traditions and add a particular ideology or heritage that puts a unique stamp on their notions of justice. For example, some Communist countries have civil law structures but a Marxist or Maoist ideology that gives their systems distinctiveness. Many Islamic nations, such as Egypt, have legal systems based on a civil law tradition, but they are also influenced by the teachings of Islam and its scriptures in the *Qur'an.*

A small number of countries have opted to have their legal systems guided by Islamic law. Although such legal systems are not common, the rapid spread of fundamentalist Islam may give rise to more such systems. Chapter 6 describes Islamic law systems and the features that distinguish them from common law, civil law, or colonial systems. Finally, Chapter 7 provides a brief overview of the American justice system with a particular focus on the tension between handling cases quickly and respecting due process, an issue that was touched on briefly in Chapter 2 in the discussion of due process versus crime control.

CHAPTER 4

COMMON LAW SYSTEMS

T he common law is a body of principles and rules deriving their authority from usage and customs of "immemorial antiquity" or from the judgments and decrees of the courts recognizing, affirming, and enforcing such usages and customs. This body of law comes from judicial decisions rather than from legislative actions.[1] Common law is a specific justice system emanating from England after the Norman Conquest of 1066 C.E.[2] The common law system is distinctly different than the other great justice system called the civil law system, which will be discussed in Chapter 5.

The influence of the common law tradition is far flung because many of the most powerful countries today use it as a model for their systems of justice. Its distribution has occurred in one of three ways. Those countries "seeded," such as Hong Kong and India, were well developed before the arrival of the English and the system was imposed on them. "Settled" colonies, such as the United States and Canada and Australia, were not well developed when the English came. The English founders of those nations simply copied the system of the mother country. Finally, there were "conquered" colonies, such as South Africa, that were under the influence of another power before control was taken forcefully by England.[3] Most of the references in this chapter will be made toward England. However, on numerous occasions, the United States will be used to illustrate a point. The common law tradition in England developed from three historical sources: feudal practices, custom, and equity.[4]

HISTORY

After several centuries of Roman occupation, England was free of imperial control by the fifth century C.E. Though the Romans influenced the building of roads and language, unlike those countries on the continent, the law was largely absent. The next five hundred years were marked by invasions of various tribes, most notably the Angles, Danes, Jutes, and Saxons. Some Christian missionaries brought elements of canon law too, but otherwise tribal law predominated. There were monarchs, but the law of the land was localized with no set of laws common to the entire country.[5] Before the Normans invaded, disputes were settled by assemblies of freemen sitting in shire and hundred courts. These might be interpreted today as county and village courts.[6]

Feudalism

The invasion by the Normans and the rule of William (often called the Conqueror) are taken as the beginning of feudalism. This medieval concept required strict obedience and obligations based on a society arranged along superior/inferior class structures. Upper classes gave protection to the lower classes, and in return, they expected loyalty and public order.

Actually, two legal systems emerged, a very strong local one in the various counties and villages and a national one based at Westminster. These were called the "people's peace" and "king's peace," respectively. Many of the Anglo-Saxon traditions and institutions were kept at the local level with courts making decisions based on local customs. The lord of the manor, the main landholder of the locality, frequently was looked to for the settlement of differences. Royal courts, which sat at Westminster, were concerned with disputes between large landowners.

The king's power was limited to controlling the roads, protecting the forest preserves from poachers, securing the sanctity of religious sites, and ensuring peace on certain holy days. Crimes among the ordinary people were to be settled at the local level. Crimes against Norman royalty and lands called the king's courts into action. On occasion, when ordinary crimes or feuds threatened the peace of the land, the king would step in to restore order. For example, for centuries, rape was a crime against the father of the attacked girl, but family revenge often led to disorder. The king simply redefined the nature of the victim—transferring it from the father of the girl to the father of the land, the king.[7]

No separation of powers within government existed in feudal times. William and his successors ruled as executive, legislature, and judiciary. Royal courts (*Curia Regis*) often called the Courts of Westminster, became a centralized court system. This court evolved and reformed into three entities: the Court of the Exchequer focused on financial issues; the Court of the Common Pleas dealt with the common people, though the king's direct participation was limited; and the King's Bench was set up to hear cases with a direct royal interest. Slowly these courts replaced the local courts, which were heavily influenced by canon or church law.

Ecclesiastical or religious courts persisted as rivals to the royal courts. These church courts continued to be a challenge to the monarch. A showdown occurred in 1170 with the murder of a leading proponent of the church court system, Thomas à Becket, in the Canterbury Cathedral by henchmen of the king. Thereafter, the ecclesiastical courts diminished in power and influence.

The monarch held considerable power and began to centralize much of the system, taking away power from the local jurisdictions. For example, King Richard I appointed "Keepers of the Peace," knights commissioned to keep the peace in the local areas. Later these knights were called justices of the peace. Though representatives of the king, they were regarded as local persons and were readily accepted by the people. They were a means for the local people to gain access to the royal courts. Actually, being heard by the royal courts was not easy. A system of writs developed early whereby a person had to make formal request, providing proof of the necessary action, and pay a fee before the court would hear the case. Over time, the royal courts continued to expand and by the end of the Middle Ages, they were the only courts of justice.

Custom

The crusades of the twelfth century brought home returning soldiers who had seen the world. Dissatisfaction with conditions in England arose and disorder became an issue. Already a king's representative, the shire reeve or sheriff, existed as the king's man in the counties. But such outsiders were resented. Remember the story of Robin Hood, a crook who was a hero, and the Sheriff of Nottingham, who was portrayed as villain? To stabilize society and the legal system, Henry II (1154–1189), frequently known as the Father of the Common Law, set up the Constitutions of Clarendon in 1164, which listed 16 customs practiced for the past one hundred years that should be a basis for contemporary law.[8] Of course, much of Anglo-Saxon law for years had been based on custom. But various tribes and villages had different customs. Without some unifying thread, customs could lead to legal anarchy. Henry II attempted to define the process of a law based on these "immemorial customs." Several elements emerged:

1. *Ancient.* No one should be able to remember its beginnings.
2. *Continuous.* It has never been abandoned or interrupted.
3. *Peaceable.* There was common consent of those using it.
4. *Reasonable.* There was a legal logic behind it.
5. *Compulsory.* Everyone was obliged to recognize and respect it.
6. *Consistent.* One could not contradict another one.[9]

Although it took years of development, this notion of custom set the stage of precedent or *stare decisis.*[10]

Equity

Unlike civil law, common law made no distinction between private law and public law. Because the legal system was so closely tied to the development of the monarchy, by the end of the Middle Ages all law became the king's law. Earlier local barons and clergy, resenting the weakening of the local courts where they had considerable influence, banded together to force the king to sign a charter in 1215, called the Magna Carta. This was an attempt to halt the erosion of their power in the local courts. But the charter also contained certain guaranteed rights for ordinary citizens, and later it took on the force of a fundamental document in legal history.

However, the common law was often deficient and frequently did not satisfy individuals. By the fifteenth century, an appeal system grew up as a remedy. This was called *equity*, which was meant to be fairness or "just." A set of practices, known as equity procedures developed to help people bring their grievances before court without using the complex common law system.[11] And an entire set of rules and lawyers grew up that were distinct from common law. Some of these equity principles still exist. For example, much of the modern day writ system is based on equity. Such writs are documents ordering some element of government to do something. For example, a writ of *mandamus* required public servants to do their jobs. An *injunction* was an order to prevent harm that would occur if the case went through the system. A writ of *habeas corpus* required the government to present someone before the courts. Of course, the monarch could not hear all such claims and a chancery was set up to do so. The chancery courts did not make law that was binding on other courts. Common laws were honored—hence the saying, "Equity follows the law"—and equitable intervention was applicable in the name of morality. Chancery courts decided conflicts between law and morals based on morality. Decisions were based on the equity of the case without reference to procedural technicalities. Even the language of the courts shows the distinctions. The procedure before the chancery court was a suit, rather than an action. The chancellor granted a decree, not a judgment; compensations rather than damages were awarded. Procedures were more inquisitorial and were written and inspired by canon law. There was no jury present. Today, the common law comprises the criminal law and the law of contracts and torts. On the other hand, equity includes the law of real property, trusts, partnerships, bankruptcy, the interpretation of wills and the settlement of estates.

CHARACTERISTICS OF THE COMMON LAW

Definition of Crime

Definitions of crime have gradually become the function of the legislatures; that is called the "substantive law." In a democracy, like the United States, judges are an elite group. Legislatures made up of elected people who passed laws seemed more democratic. This statutory law became important in the early new nation period (1791–1835) with the rise of the "Republican Code movement." Severe blows were aimed at the common law tradition as the new states began to create statutory law. Murder, rape, and robbery were concepts coming from the common law. But different jurisdictions used slightly different definitions and punishments. Furthermore, in places like the United States, supreme courts made judgments on the constitutionality and appropriateness of the law [judicial review] and the procedures of the justice system. In addition, criminal procedure in the United States developed case law to deal with the appropriate practices of search and seizure, interrogation, legal defense for the accused, prison facilities and features, and the place of capital punishment in the justice system. This was called "procedural law." During the "due process" revolution of the Warren court in the 1960s, many of the restrictions placed on the federal criminal justice system by the Constitution were applied to the state and local justice systems. All these are examples of judge-made law and are part of the common law. Therefore, even though most common law countries have moved to create statutes, the ultimate arbiter of the appropriateness of those laws and the actions of the government in implementing those laws is a common law function.

Statute

England has no written constitution. Instead, a series of rules, sometimes in the form of statutes but most often judicial in origin, guarantee fundamental rights and liberties. In a democracy, the laws coming from a legislature—duly elected by the people—are given some respect. But in a strictly common law country, a legislature is not seen as the normal avenue for making law. Since World War II, the laws of Parliament in England have increased in number and in acceptance. But English law still is basically judge-made for two reasons. First, judicial decisions set the framework for the development of most statutes. Second, legislators still think in terms of judge-made law and make their statutes in the language of judges. Historically, only after a statute had been tested by a court decision did it achieve any legitimacy in English law. Today, statutory law has become increasingly important, but the courts still must test it before it is fully accepted.

Process as Justice

Procedure has primary importance in the common law. "Forms of action" characterize the common law system, and the successful completion of these procedures was necessary for a judgment to be rendered. Such a focus on procedure was necessary because the process had a single function; the procedures followed shaped the facts to be put before a jury. According to David and Brierley, "The Common law was not so much a system attempting to bring justice as it was a conglomeration of procedures designed, in more and more cases, to achieve solutions to disputes."[12] This was particularly evident in criminal law. The definition of crime was allowed to go to the legislature, the Parliament in England and the Congress in the United States. But common law dominated the procedural aspects of criminal justice. "Most of the criminal procedure rules that are set forth in the Fourth, Fifth, Sixth, and Eighth Amendments to the U.S. Constitution, as well as the rules about bringing the accused before a judge to question his incarceration (habeas corpus), were adapted from the Common Law rules and from Parliamentary decrees based on the Common Law."[13]

A review of some of these basic principles in the Bill of Rights might be useful because they are the starting point for so much common law development in the United States. Note how many times the Congress is warned away from creating statutory law and how often the issue of procedure is raised.

1. Congress shall make no law respecting an establishment of religion, or prohibiting the free exercise thereof; or abridging the freedom of speech, or of the press; or the right of people peaceably to assemble; and to petition the Government for redress of grievances. [1791]
2. A well regulated Militia, being necessary to the security of a free state, the right of the people to keep and bear Arms shall not be infringed. [1791]
3. No Soldier shall, in time of peace, be quartered in any house, without the consent of the Owner, nor in time of war, but in a manner to be prescribed by law. [1791]
4. The right of the people to be secure in their persons, houses, papers, and effects, against unreasonable searches and seizures, shall not be violated, and no Warrants will be issued, but upon probable cause, supported by Oath or affirmation, and particularly describing the place to be searched, and the persons or things to be seized. [1791]
5. No person shall be held to answer for a capital or otherwise infamous crime, unless on a presentment or indictment of a Grand Jury, except in cases arising in the land or naval forces, or in the Militia, when in actual service in time of War or public danger; nor shall any person be subject for the same offence to be twice put in jeopardy of life or limb; nor shall be compelled in any criminal case to be a witness against himself, nor be deprived of life, liberty, or property, without due process of law; nor shall private property be taken for private use, without just compensation. [1791]
6. In all criminal prosecutions, the accused shall enjoy the right to a speedy and public trial, by an impartial jury of the State and district wherein the crime shall have been committed, which district shall have been previ-

ously ascertained by law, and to be informed of the nature and cause of the accusation; to be confronted with the witnesses against him; to have compulsory process for obtaining Witnesses in his favor, and to have Assistance of Counsel for his defence. [1791]

7. In Suits at common law, where the value in controversy shall exceed twenty dollars, the right of trial by jury shall be preserved, and no fact tried by a jury, shall be otherwise reexamined in any Court of the United States, than according to the rules of the common law. [1791]

8. Excessive bail shall not be required, nor excessive fines imposed, nor cruel and unusual punishment inflicted. [1791]

9. The enumeration in the Constitution, of certain rights, shall not be construed to deny or disparage others retained by the people. [1791]

10. The powers not delegated to the United States by the Constitution, nor prohibited by it to the States, are reserved to the States respectively, or to the people. [1791]

The concern of the founders of the United States derives from the common law. Shortly after the creation of the United States, another event validated the role of the courts in the common law. The Judiciary Act of 1801 created numerous courts and judicial positions. President John Adams, as he was leaving office, quickly filled these offices. A new president, Thomas Jefferson, resented such action and tried to withhold the appointments. The Supreme Court, not yet tested and looking for direction, had a strong chief justice in John Marshall. In the case of *Marbury v. Madison,* Marshall addressed these appointments and established that the court could invalidate federal statutes that it deemed contrary to the Constitution. Such judicial review was a common law principle.

Procedure

Throughout the history of English law, procedure was most important. This raises the interesting dichotomy between "factual guilt" and "legal guilt." An individual may indeed be factually guilty of a crime; evidence has been gathered, witnesses assembled, and cogent arguments made. However, if the justice system has acted inappropriately, "legal guilt" might not be established and the defendant could be released.

Procedure was carefully developed to solicit the real points of disagreement between litigating parties. Unlike civil law systems (see Chapter 5), where the dossier (or case file) is most important, these distinctions must emerge in oral testimony with the answering of questions by "yes" or "no." This must be done in open court. Historically, this information was to be provided to a jury—a group of laypersons, many of whom were poorly educated—in the simplest of ways. Rules of evidence developed to exclude evidence not obtained through proper procedures. To the continental (civil law system) lawyer, it would seem that real justice was being thwarted by technicalities. The concept of justice for the common law practitioner was in the process rather than the outcome. English courts accept that the accused must have a fair trial. The strictly adhered-to procedure called due process must occur for justice to be met. Observing a regulated procedure, fair in all respects, will lead to a just solution.

The English tradition also pays considerable attention to the enforcement of judicial decisions. Unlike the continental systems, where there is considerable disregard for judicial decisions, in common law countries the disregard of a court's decision becomes a crime itself. The courts can issue orders to other parts of the government. Therefore, the administration of justice becomes a critical activity of the common law courts. For example, courts can require certain administrative steps be taken with a writ of *mandamus*. The police can be ordered to release a person through *habeas corpus* writs. Refusal to follow the orders of the court can result in contempt charges and sanctions.

Lawyers: Education and Practice

Of course, such an emphasis on procedure affected the practice of law. In common law systems, knowledge of the law was not as important as courtroom performance. For example, in America, in the early history of the profession of law, the reading of the law as an apprentice to a practicing lawyer was quite enough. Law schools were slow to develop, many rising in the late nineteenth century. When they appeared, they had a distinct common law orientation. For example, Christopher Columbus Langdell—Dean of the Harvard Law School from 1870 to 1895—introduced the case method. This pedagogy required the student to read decisions made by judges to discover the points of law and understand the process of legal reasoning. In 1871, Langdell published the first casebook on contracts. It was largely made up of English decisions because he felt law and legal thought should be most like that of England. Before, instructors of law were practicing lawyers who shared their experiences. Langdell wanted to give students grounding in legal logic and principles and left the practical stuff to be learned on the job. Langdell's model became the standard for the elite law schools of America.[14]

However, a counter model developed in the "sundown schools." At the beginning of the twentieth century, many immigrants, in the name of economic upward mobility, wanted to go to law school. Because of finances or ethnic prejudices, most of these people could not go to a standard law school. In response, numerous "proprietary" law schools arose. These were not connected to a university, their entrance requirements were minimal, and classes were conducted in the evening so that students could hold down jobs during the day. These "sundown schools" did two things. First, with little interest in legal reasoning, they taught the student to pass the local bar. Second, they emphasized courtroom techniques and tactics. In short, both the university law school and the proprietary school in their own ways demonstrated an ongoing connection to the common law.[15]

Furthermore, in America the common law emphasis placed a premium on courtroom style with oratory and persuasion being of greater importance than legal thinking. The great courtroom lawyers in U.S. history were skilled orators. John Adams, Daniel Webster, Henry Clay, Abraham Lincoln, Clarance Darrow, and William Jennings Bryan, to name a few, were known for their oratory and theatrical skills more than for their knowledge of the law. All one has to do is remember the ability of Johnny Cochran in the O. J. Simpson trial. Simpson had been asked to try on a bloody glove that was a key piece of prosecutorial evidence. He had struggled to put it on but failed. In his brilliant summation, Cochran reminded the jury, "If it does not fit, you must acquit." The jury found Simpson not guilty.

Also, it is no small wonder that in most common law countries, but most notably in the United States, the law became a means for establishing a career in politics. At no time in their education or practice of law do lawyers learn to make laws. However, the skills of oratory and public performance are those most easily translated into a career in politics.

Decisions of the Courts

In most common law countries, the court structure today is largely divided between superior and inferior courts. The inferior courts hear most of the cases, but the judge-made decisions of the superior courts have the greatest strength because of the principle of precedent or *stare decisis*. Precedent means that decisions in court are influenced by past court decisions.

In the continental (civil law) systems, legal principles have always been derived from a body of rules, a legal code. Court decisions do not contain rules of law. Common law countries are quite different. The purpose of judicial decisions is not to just apply but to define legal rules. This simply means that a decision of one court is binding on all courts equal to and less power in the court hierarchy. Earlier English judges did not have to give reasons for their decisions. However, judges soon did begin to explain why the decision was made to instruct future lawyers, students who received most of their education by attendance at court. Soon these decisions were published for larger numbers of students to ponder. They would appear thus

   Landauer v. Asser [1905] 2 K.B. 184

Landauer would be the plaintiff, Asser the defendant. This case could be found in the law reports published in 1905 of the King's Bench series in the second volume on page 184.

Legal Literature

If law was unwritten, not put in statutory form, it was important to record the decisions of the judges. Making judicial decisions widely available to other courts became more common in the nineteenth century. These records became more formalized in England by 1865 with judicial reports being published as the *Law Reports*. This case law became a basis to study and understand the law. Several scholars began to write about the law too. These authors became important for the aspiring student of law. Perhaps the most famous and influential was Sir William Blackstone (1723–1780). Written when the common law was at its zenith, his *Commentaries on Laws of England* describes law in the late eighteenth century and became a major source of information and instruction for American lawyers and nation builders.[16]

Public and Private Law

Unlike the civil law systems, the common law jurists rejected any distinction between public and private. The English law as it developed made the trial a public and not a private matter. Thus, the royal courts enlarged their jurisdiction by developing the idea that all intervention was justified in the interest of the crown and kingdom. Technically, criminal violations were not against people, but against the state. The courts emerged as independent branches of the Curia Regis or king's courts and were political rather than judicial organs because they were intended to resolve problems involving the interests of the king and the kingdom—the general interest—and not principally the private interests of individuals. Unlike the systems on the continent, the English legal system's development was tied to the rise and strength of the centralized government.

Jury

England had two competing trends. One was the growth of the central government and its monopolization of the court system. The other was the historic suspicion of the monarchy as seen in the Magna Carta. Because so much of the law was going to be judge-made and there was no clear distinction between public and private law, it was necessary to have representatives in the court who were not part of the court. Judges remained the keepers of the law, but juries became assessors of the facts. Of course, in such a stratified society, these juries were not meant to be gatherings of the lowly sorts. Qualifications and checks were needed to ensure that neither the monarchy nor the peasantry gathered too much strength. Ideally, these juries were to be made up of one's peers. Those present at the signing of the Magna Carta would be like those who found their way into juries.[17] In a real way, juries reflect the basic nature of the common law. Law was not as absolute as in the civil law systems; it was being "discovered" by judges as they went along. So the juries, with their ability to upset the law by nullification, also made law. Nullification is when a jury, despite overwhelming evidence of guilt, refuses to convict.

An important question may be to what extent juries and judges agree or disagree in trial decisions. Some researchers have examined more than 3500 criminal trials in which a jury played a part. Evidence indicates that juries and judges agree about 75 percent of the time. One study suggests that juries do tend to be more lenient; the conviction rate of juries was 64 percent whereas judges did so at a rate of 83 percent.[18]

Another attribute of common law that arose because of the jury's presence was guarding these laypeople from hearing things from crafty lawyers that might unduly sway their opinions; these were called "rules of evidence." A classic example was hearsay, or second-hand information. Only dying declarations and excited utterances were exceptions to prohibitions of testimony based on hearsay. Another rule of evidence had to do with the common law notion of privilege. Wives could not be forced to testify against husbands, priests against confessors, doctors against patients, or writers against sources of information. Therefore, both judges and juries were reflectors of the common law system.

MODERN DAY STRUCTURE OF THE LEGAL SYSTEM

England is perhaps the best single example of the modern day common law country. Of course, historical forces are such that there is no pure common law country. But because England started it and continues in the tradition today, England is a good place to look for a contemporary example.

Atop the political structure of England sits the monarchy. At first, this institution was very powerful, but today it is more symbolic—it represents the unity of the country. More important is the Parliament, which comprises the House of Lords and House of Commons.

The House of Lords, the most ancient division of Parliament with roots as deep as the monarchy, has diminished in power, too. Today, the House of Lords consists of about 1,200 members who fall into one of three groups. First are the religious lords, consisting of the archbishops of York and Canterbury and the several bishops of the Church of England. In addition, this group consists of the law lords, to be discussed later. Second are the hereditary lords, about 800 of them, who hold seats because some past monarch had knighted an ancestor as a duke, marquess, earl, viscount, or baron. Third are life peers, those knighted for public service or some other achievement and whose peerage lasts only during their lifetimes.

The House of Commons is the most important branch of the Parliament. Created in the thirteenth century but not prominent until the sixteenth, today it is the major legislative body in England. There are 658 elected members, and it is the most representative body in Parliament. Two political parties predominate: the Conservative and the Labour. The leader of the country, the prime minister, and the cabinet sit in the House of Commons on the front bench. They are the leaders of the party that won most seats to the House. Across from them, the opposition sits with a shadow cabinet, the officials who would assume office if the existing administration government should receive a vote of no confidence.

Even the police are part of this common law tradition. The police organization is centralized. A cabinet member, the home secretary, administers the police. Under the Home Office, an Office of Inspectors of Constabulary ensures efficiency and effectiveness. Under the inspectors are 41 provincial police forces, the City of London Police, and the Metropolitan Police of London. Each of these 43 committees consists of 17 members, 9 of whom are politicians from the local area covered by the police. The common law heritage of the police was reaffirmed by A *Report of the Royal Commission of Police Powers,* in 1929:

> The police of this country have never been recognized, either in law or by tradition, as a force distinct from the general body of citizens. Despite the imposition of many extranious duties on the police by legislation or administrative action, the principle remains that a policeman, in the view of the common law, is only "a citizen paid to perform, as a matter of duty, acts which if he were so minded he might have done voluntarily."[19]

The court structure most reflects the common law traditions in England. The courts in England can best be understood by highlighting three officials. The first is the lord chancellor, who is appointed by the monarch on the prime minister's recommendation. Although this a political appointment, the lord chancellor comes from the prime minister's political party, and it is customary to select someone who is distinguished as a lawyer or jurist. He is given peerage and a seat in the highest court of the land, the House of Lords. The lord chancellor heads the entire judiciary and has five duties:

1. Participates in judicial appeals that reach the House of Lords.
2. Recommends all appointments to the courts.
3. Performs day-to-day administration of the courts.
4. Oversees the legal aid system.
5. Takes an active role in law reform.[20]

The second key figure is the attorney general. This cabinet member, with his or her subordinate the solicitor general, are the legal officers of the Crown and Parliament. These law officers are responsible for the criminal process in the courts. The attorney general answers all questions pertaining to law reform that come before the House of Commons.

The third figure is the director of public prosecutions. This person administers a large staff of lawyers who specialize in criminal law. In addition, since 1985, this office has taken the power to prosecute from the police and instigates all prosecutions. This group also watches over the police to see that investigations are carried out appropriately.

The organization of the English courts is thus:

- *House of Lords.* The oldest common law courts are Parliament. The House of Lords handles this function. Within the House of Lords are a small number of distinguished law lords (the number varies from 9 to 11), who act as the supreme court of the land. Their work is limited to hearing appeals on civil and criminal matters from the Court of Appeal.
- *Court of Appeal.* This intermediate appellate court is broken into two divisions: civil and criminal. The presiding judge of the civil division is called the Master of the Rolls. The presiding judge of the criminal division is the Lord Chief Judge. Twenty judges make up the Court of Appeal.
- *High Court.* This single court has both original and appellate powers. It is divided into three divisions: Chancery, Queen's Bench, and Family. The Chancery is largely concerned with property, trusts, wills, and estates. The Queen's Bench, the largest division, is concerned with civil and criminal matters and has both original and appellate powers. The Family Division is concerned with matters of matrimony, guardianship, and adoption. All together, the High Court has 80 judges selected by the lord chancellor.
- *Crown Courts.* These deal with major crimes and handle appeals coming from the magistrates' courts. Three kinds of judges preside in these courts. Some justices from Queen's Bench handle the more serious cases. Approximately 400 circuit judges preside over the less serious. Then 500 recorders [part-time judges] help the circuit judges with their caseload.
- *Magistrates' Courts.* These are the workhorses of the court system. There are more than 500 of them, and they handle 96 percent of the criminal cases in England. Two types of judges make up this court. Stipendiary or professional magistrates are trained in the law and are paid for their services. In addition, nearly 27,500 magistrates, called justices of the peace, are laypersons providing services without compensation.

Legal Profession

Since medieval times, the legal profession in England has been divided into two branches, solicitors and barristers. There are now about 50,000 solicitors in England. Most are office lawyers who rarely appear in court. Instead, they are the legal advisors to the public. They help write wills and contracts, set up land and commercial sales, and deal with divorce issues. A person becomes a solicitor in one of two ways. They can complete a university law degree, which is a three-year undergraduate education, followed by a two-and-one-half-year apprenticeship with an established solicitor. The other approach is to attend a college of law for one year and then serve a four-year apprenticeship. After their training, solicitors can apply to be members of the Law Society, the professional society for solicitors.

Barristers are a second category of lawyers. Barristers present cases before the court. Oral advocacy becomes the greatest quality of the barrister. Solicitors may actually prepare the case, but the barrister argues it before the judge and jury. There are about 8500 barristers in England. They operate under a very strict code of conduct. For example, they cannot advertise their services. A solicitor must bring cases to the barrister. The bar is organized into 270 chambers or offices out of which the barristers operate. In each chamber, barristers are divided into two groups: Queen's Counsel (QC) and juniors. Junior barristers are those who have been practicing law for less than 15 years. Once the junior barrister has accumulated 15 to 20 years of practice, he or she can apply to the lord chancellor for appointment as Queen's Counsel. This is called "taking the silk" because they can then wear a silk rather than a cotton robe in court. In addition, they can have the initials QC after their name. Every barrister is a member of one of the four ancient organizations called the Inns of Court. They are Gray's Inn, Lincoln's Inn, the Inner Temple, and the Middle Temple. Any person who wants to be a barrister must join one of these Inns, take occasional meals there, receive instruction on the more practical aspects of court procedure, and develop a fraternal spirit with his or her fellow members.[21]

Judges are not a separate entity in the legal system. They are appointed by the lord chancellor from the ranks of the barristers. There is no popular election or confirmation hearings, as in the United States. There is no legislative input. It is purely ministerial with the lord chancellor in complete control of appointments.[22]

Juries are the critical indicator of a common law system. Today, however, the jury system is used sparingly in England. The Grand Jury was abolished in 1948. Juries are no longer used in civil cases. They exist in criminal cases but only 1 in 20 defendants selects a jury trial. To serve on a jury, one must be between 18 and 70, be a registered voter, and have resided in the United Kingdom for five years. A person can be disqualified from jury duty if he or she had been convicted of a crime. Anyone who has been sentenced to more than a five-year prison term is disqualified for life. Those who work in the justice system are disqualified. So are members of Parliament, health care officials, and military personnel.[23]

The role of the university in shaping the law and legal structure is quite different in England from that of the continent. As will be discussed later, the civil or continental systems were developed largely through the universities and academic thinkers. All training was received in the university and emphasis was placed on history, reason, and logic. In England, however, law was not even taught at Oxford until 1758. Cambridge did not teach law until 1800. The most important aspect of the legal profession was procedure, so university training was less important in England. One could learn the job "practicing" under an experienced lawyer. English law was not a product of the universities, or a law of principles. It was the law of practitioners interested in procedure more than principles.

> It has never been the tradition for English lawyers to be educated in universities; even today to be the graduate in law of a university is not mandatory in order to become a barrister, a solicitor, or a judge. Traditionally, these persons were educated in legal practice in which no mention was ever made of Roman law and in which attention was constantly focused on matters of procedure and evidence upon which the success and indeed the receivability of the action depended.[24]

Conclusion

Common law systems are not widespread throughout the world, but their influence has been great, mainly because several of the common law countries—particularly England and the United States–have assumed important roles on the world stage in the past two centuries. Of course, today there is no pure common law country. Instead, these countries have adjusted to historical forces and made compromises. The United States is a classical example; it has maintained common law principles in many areas but also made room for the decidedly democratic institution of statute. Nonetheless, even in America procedural law and judicial review maintain the power and influence of the common law. Civil law countries far outnumber any other, and we now turn to them. As we will see, civil law systems take a very different approach to justice.

Discussion Questions

1. How does the Bill of Rights reflect the common law origins of the United States?
2. Why is procedure or process so important in a common law country?
3. There is a saying, "If you are guilty of a crime it is better to be in a common law country, but if you are innocent it is better to be in a civil law country." How can that be?

Endnotes

1. Henry Campbell Black, *Black's Law Dictionary,* 6th edition (St. Paul, Minn.: West, 1990), p. 276.
2. The designation c.e., standing for "Common Era," instead of a.d., Latin for Year of our Lord, is itself an issue of justice. This designation considers the multitude of readers who are not Christian.

3. Mary Ann Glendon, Michael Wallace Gordon, Christopher Osakwe, *Comparative Legal Traditions: Text, Materials, and Cases on the Civil Law, Common Law and Socialist Law Traditions with Special Reference to French, West German, English and Soviet Law* (St. Paul, Minn.: West, 1985), p. 279.

4. Philip Reichel, *Comparative Criminal Justice Systems: A Topical Approach* (Englewood Cliffs, N.J.: Prentice Hall Career & Technology, 1994), pp. 95–98.

5. Rene David and John E. C. Brierley, *Major Legal Systems in the World Today: An Introduction to the Comparative Study of Law* (London: Free Press, Collier-Macmillan, 1968), p. 288.

6. Reichel, p. 95.

7. Susan Brownmiller, *Against Our Will: Men, Women and Rape* (New York: Simon & Schuster, 1975), pp. 24–30.

8. Theodore Plucknett, *A Concise History of the Common Law* (Boston: Little, Brown, 1956), pp. 17–18.

9. Reichel, pp. 96–97.

10. Melvin Aron Eisenberg, *The Nature of the Common Law* (Cambridge, Mass.: Harvard University Press, 1988), pp. 50–61.

11. Erika Fairchild and Harry R. Dammer, *Comparative Criminal Justice Systems* (Belmont, Calif.: Wadsworth Thomson Learning Series, 2001), p. 52.

12. David and Brierley, p. 295.

13. Fairchild and Dammer, p. 53.

14. Kermit L. Hall, *The Magic Mirror: Law in American History* (New York: Oxford University Press, 1989), p. 220.

15. Jerold S. Auerbach, *Unequal Justice: Lawyers and Social Change in Modern America* (New York: Oxford University Press, 1976), pp. 74–99.

16. Roscoe Pound, *The Spirit of the Common Law* (Francestown, N.H.: Marshall Jones, 1921), pp. 193–216.

17. Plucknett, pp. 106–138.

18. H. Kalven and H. Zeisel, *The American Jury* (Boston: Little, Brown, 1966), pp. 55–65.

19. Richard Terrill, *World Criminal Justice Systems: A Survey* (Cincinnati: Anderson, 1999), p. 21.

20. Ibid., p. 33.

21. Ibid., p. 40.

22. Ibid., p. 41.

23. Ibid., pp. 41–42.

24. David and Brierley, p. 313.

CHAPTER 5

CIVIL LAW SYSTEMS

Among the modern systems of justice, the civil law tradition is the oldest and most widespread. Western Europe, all of Central and South America, many parts of Asia, and a few places in North America [Louisiana, Puerto Rico, and Quebec] have civil law systems.

This could cause some semantic confusion. The term *civil law* has particular meaning, especially for students in the United States. In the United States, civil law connotes a branch of the law, distinct from the criminal law, that deals with conflicts between individuals (see Chapter 12). Divorce, contracts, house closings, alimony payments, estate planning, to mention a few. That is not what is being referred to in this chapter. This chapter concerns a family of justice systems. Other phrases that might be used when studying the civil law systems are the continental or Napoleonic systems of justice. In this chapter, the three terms will be used interchangeably when discussing civil law traditions. Like the common law systems, this family is a product of historical development.

HISTORY

Rome

The civil law system comes from ancient Roman law. Early in the Roman Republic, two legislative bodies, the *comitia centuriata* and the *comitia tribta,* enacted statutes called *lex* or collection of laws. The earliest form of this law occurred in 450 B.C. when a council of 10 men created the Twelve Tables that set forth the rights of a Roman citizen. In the Empire period, magistrates called *praetors* issued edicts that had the force of law. But the most important development was the codification of the law by Emperor Justinian in Constantinople. His *Corpus Juris Civilis* placed the law in written and codified form and became the sole authority on the law for hundreds of years. In the eleventh century, the first European university opened at Bologna with the civil law as its main curriculum.[1]

Canon Law

When the Roman Catholic Church assumed ascendency in Rome and later in Europe, its canon or church law was based on Roman models. Reichel believes, "As the Roman civil law comprises the universal law of the worldly empire, canon law was the universal law of the spiritual realm."[2] Papal pronouncements, called *decretal* letters, had the force of law on Christians. Soon conflict arose between emperors and popes about who was the main source of the law. By the time of Pope Gregory I (590–604), canon law had a secure place coming out of the law of the Roman Empire. However, canon law placed religion and religious institutions in the forefront of the system. In fact, many refer to the medieval church system as *inquisitorial*. As the Roman Empire died, canon law continued to have an influence throughout the Middle Ages. However, as nation states emerged and the Reformation of the Protestant churches arose, the idea of a national law free from the history of Rome and the edicts of the Catholic Church became important. The French Revolution addressed that.[3]

French Revolution

The French Revolution was one of the greatest revolutions—equaled perhaps only by the Bolshevik Revolution of Russia—in world history. It not only disrupted the ruling structure of France but also made way for profound changes in the law with the Napoleonic code. This codification movement was fundamental to the civil law tradition. First, it removed many of the religious laws that had carried over from the dominance by the Catholic Church. Second, besides being anti-clerical, the Revolution was anti-feudal. Dislike of the aristocracy became intense. Judges and the judicial process, remnants of past elitism, were attacked as feudal and isolated. Third, a strict separation of powers in France led to a system of specialized courts and restrictions on judicial review. Power was taken from the courts and the lawyers and placed in the hands of the people in legislatures. Fourth, codification or written laws became important. One student of the civil law system declared, "Codification gives civil law a revolutionary character and written format that adds to its separate identity among legal families."[4] Written law was legitimate and binding on all because it was enacted by a recognized authority, generally a legislature, that followed formal procedures.

United States

Conventional wisdom, and the preceding chapter, accepts that the United States is a common law country. However, there are strong historical antecedents of the civil law tradition in America. For example, though the thin strip of colonial America was attached to England and its common law, France and Spain actually settled much of the continent. The French were eventually eliminated and their influence narrowed down to parts of Canada. However, the Spanish had a much greater impact. The first permanent white settlement in America was established by the Spanish in St. Augustine, Florida, in 1565. Santa Fe, New Mexico, was settled in 1609 by Spaniards, and it became the first continuing capital city in America. Therefore, the Spanish—as representatives of Spain and later Mexico—were in America early and had profound impacts in California, Texas, and New Mexico. Early legal development in these areas brought both the common law and civil law into proximity and shaped the debates on the direction of the law in the United States. The French also settled many parts of the American continent, bringing their civil law tradition with them. Today, Louisiana state law is primarily a civil law system.[5]

CHARACTERISTICS OF THE CIVIL LAW

Definitions of the Law

The idea of a "Divine source" of law, essential to canon law, gave way during the French Revolution. Law came from the people or the state, particularly from the legislatures. Law did not come from external or local sources. Nationalism dictated that law come from the central government. Only statutes enacted by legislative power could be the law. Neither judicial decisions nor discussions by legal scholars had the force of law. The law was in the code.[6]

A legal code is the compilation of all the statutes of a country. Common law countries have codes. But civil law countries have a distinct ideology when it comes to their codes. The purpose of the code is to weaken the role of the lawyer and the judge. The code needs to have no gaps or loopholes. There should be no conflicting provisions allowing judicial discretion. There should be no ambiguity that would allow for individual interpretation. If gaps and ambiguities are found, a special court, frequently called a Constitutional Court, assesses the problem and sends the law back to the legislature for clarification if necessary. Such an approach to law shapes the role of the judge, the legal training of lawyers, and the role of the prosecutor.[7]

Statute

In the civil law system, substantive law, a written statement defining what is a crime, becomes most important. As Reichel says, "Even though common law jurisdictions have moved toward statutory crimes and procedures, the civil law holds more closely to the principle that every crime and every penalty must be embodied in a statute enacted by the legislature. The civil lawyer sees common law courts violating this principle every time people are convicted of common law crimes and whenever judges prohibit relevant evidence and make rules regarding criminal procedure."[8]

A very important distinction in statute in a civil law country is between private and public law. First, public law deals with relations of people to public officials and agencies. It allows citizens to complain and hold accountable the agencies of government. Strictly speaking, public law is more interested in administrative issues than legal ones. In France, a series of Administrative Courts was put in place to deal with these issues. Early in the history of the civil law tradition, a problem arose. Crime was originally a private matter; victims or families of victims were expected to bring people to court. However, as time went by, society began to recognize that crime affected more than the primary victims—it affected all of society. So civil law countries had to decide whether to move crime into the public law. Most of these countries decided to leave such matters in the private law category.[9]

In private law, the government enforces individuals' private rights. The government is a referee in such matters. In public law, the government is much more active. Crimes fall under the category of private law. The two primary documents in criminal law are the Code of Criminal Procedure and the Penal Code. The former deals with the justice system's procedure; the courts are not left to decide such weighty matters as in the common law countries. The Penal Code is the substantive law.

Typically, the Penal Code of a civil law country will have four sections or books. Book one will define the available punishments. Book two will explain criminal liability and responsibility. Book three will define the various offenses. Book four will do the same for lesser offenses, called violations. Criminal offenses will be divided into three categories: crime (serious offenses that we might call felonies), delit (less serious felonies and misdemeanors), and contraventions or violations. Such distinctions address the seriousness of the act and indicate the kind of court to which they will go. For example, in France, crimes are punishable with imprisonment from more than five years to life and are heard at the highest level of courts called Assize Courts. Delits are punishable by a fine or a prison term of two months to five years and are heard in a Correctional Court. Contraventions may result in a fine or a jail term as long as two months and are heard before a Police Court.[10]

The Judge

In civil law systems, the judge is a civil servant, a functionary of the government. Decisions of the judge are different from the common law system. The decisions of the court are procedural, and though they affect individual cases, their decisions are not binding on other cases. There is no concept of precedent in a civil law country. The solution to a case is found in the written law; the judge has to show that any decision made is based on the provisions already declared in the code.[11]

Becoming a judge is a quite different process from that of common law systems. After graduation from university, a student must decide on one of several career paths. A person who decides to become a judge must take a state test. If the individual passes this rigorous test, he or she will then attend a special school for prospective judges. Upon completion of the academic training, the individual will be appointed a junior judge, without ever having practiced law in court. Civil law countries do not have juries. Instead, a judge will have two or more subordinate judges that form a panel.[12]

The judge is to only use the written law; there is no *stare decisis* or precedent. Any unclear, incomplete, conflicting, or confusing legal issues will be sent back to the legislature for authoritative interpretation. The legislature might even create a "special court" to handle constitutional issues. These Constitutional Courts [in France they are called Cassation Courts, *cassation* meaning to quash] are established by the legislature because ordinary judges are not given the power to interpret the law. Thus, the supremacy of the legislature is protected from judicial usurpation.[13]

The concept of certainty is important to all legal systems. Common law countries achieve this inductively, the accumulation of many cases to develop a legal principle. When it is not clear how a law is to be applied to a particular case, common law courts rely on what has been decided before to determine what to do in the current case—the principle of precedent. Thus, the general principle arises from individual cases. For example, a Supreme Court decision about a case will help establish a more general legal principle. Civil law countries achieve this deductively. There is a legal syllogism in civil law traditions. The major premise is the statute. The minor premise is made up of the legal facts of the case. The conclusion follows logically. In other words, individual case decisions emerge from general principles rather than general principles emerging from individual cases.

Equity is a principle used to make the law fit the incident and person justly. In common law countries, the judge, using principles of mitigation or aggravation, may change the nature of the substantive law. This could not happen in a civil law system. The judge would not have such power.

Legal Scholars

Legal education in civil law countries is different than that in common law countries. Because case law is unimportant in civil law countries, the entire curriculum and pedagogy is different. Generally, legal education is an undergraduate activity that is very general and interdisciplinary. Universities have law departments and students can specialize in law as undergraduates. Further-more, emphasis is given to studying the code, its history, and philosophical foundations. Argumentation and moot court practice are not essential.[14]

Civil law systems use and have greater respect for legal scholars and schol-arship than other systems do. The teacher-scholar is the real power in the civil law tradition. This is very old, going back to the Roman *jurisconsult,* an aca-demic expert on the law who advised the legislature and the judge. In civil law jurisdictions, scholars look at the law in high levels of abstraction, relegating the facts to a minor place. Principles are taken out of their factual and historical context. As one scholar has said, "The legal scientist is more interested in de-veloping and elaborating a theoretical scientific structure than he is in solving concrete problems."[15] Theories from the social sciences are notably absent in what is called "conceptual jurisprudence." These academic lawyers are very powerful because they mold and direct legal thinking. A retinue of docents and disciples cluster around their professor and "schools of thought" develop that influence legislators.

Lawyers

Other members of the legal profession have unique characteristics. For exam-ple, there are distinct legal careers. People in one area think of themselves as different and unconnected to other branches. There is a high degree of com-partmentalization and immobility.

Public prosecutors, often called procurators in civil law countries, pre-pare and present the case to court. In addition, they have a greater role in the investigative process. Recently graduated law students may move directly into the field of prosecution. They may take a special governmental examination, then begin at the bottom of the ladder and build a career based on seniority. Actually, there are three types of prosecutorial roles, each of which may be cho-sen by the recent law graduate: the judicial police, the procurator, and the ex-amining judge. The judicial police investigate cases and see that this is done legally. Procurators determine appropriate charges against the accused, prose-cute minor crimes, and direct the judicial police. Examining magistrates, cho-sen from the court judges, direct all investigations.[16]

Advocates are defense lawyers. They meet with clients to give advice and representation in court. In most civil law systems, the defense has a much more subdued role than in the common law systems.

Civil law notaries draft all important legal instruments such as wills and contracts. Notaries act as public records offices, keeping all original documents and providing bona fide copies to the public on request. The typical civil law country is divided into a number of notary districts, and the total number of notaries is limited. Therefore, it is a very competitive and cherished civil law position.

Civil Procedure

Civil law procedure owes its origins to ancient Rome and canon law. Three separate stages are in the procedure. Generally, common law countries have an adversarial system. On the other hand, civil law countries may be called inquisitorial. The single most distinctive attribute of this inquisitorial system is the importance of the judge. In all stages of the process in civil law systems, the judge plays a prominent role while the lawyers play passive ones. Unlike the adversarial's competition between opposing sides, a trial in the civil law country is an ongoing investigation. The common law system places an emphasis on the trial, but civil law countries emphasize the preliminary screening process.

First is the preliminary stage. This stage is very brief. Pleadings are submitted and a hearing judge, usually called an instructing judge, is appointed.

Second is the evidence-taking stage. At this point, the instructing judge takes all the evidence and prepares a summary written report.

Third is the decision-making stage. New judges consider the report from the instructing judge. They then hear arguments and render a decision.

Trials and hearings in a civil law system may be thought of as "trials by files." Word trials, with elaborate speeches and summations are rare. Typically, adjudication is a series of isolated meetings and written communications between lawyers and the judges. The appearances of witness and lawyers are brief and constitute a small part of the total case. Cross-examination is particularly foreign to a civil law system. Lawyers who want to question witnesses must first prepare a written statement of "articles of proof," which describes the matters on which he wants to question the witness. This document goes to the judge and opposing council in advance. Therefore, witnesses know in advance the types of questions that will be asked. This procedure is long and arduous, frequently taking as much as two months. First, the lawyer asks in writing for a witness to be called; a copy of this request goes to the other lawyers. The instructing judge sets a date for the lawyers to present their reasons for calling the witness. Finally, a judge will decide and issue his ruling. Only then can the witness be called in to the trial. Then the witness testifies and the judge takes notes. There is no verbatim record kept in the trial.[17] In the adversarial setting of common law courts, opposing lawyers decide which witnesses will be called, what they will be asked, and what evidence will be introduced. In civil law systems, judges take on these responsibilities.

Criminal Procedure

Substantive criminal law—the definitions of particular crimes in statutes and fixing the appropriate punishment—is not very different in common law and civil law countries. But criminal procedure, the process by which cases are handled, is very different.

There are three basic parts to the civil law criminal procedure. First, the **investigative phase** is under the direction of the public prosecutor. In some countries, the detectives operate directly under the prosecutor. Of course, the investigation ultimately is under the judiciary, so there is little worry about the legal appropriateness of the investigation. The prosecutor compiles large files or dossiers of evidence at this stage. Inquisitorial systems assume that all persons are seeking the truth. Therefore, the expectation is that the defendant will cooperate. This means providing information before the trial and at the trial, and it means that defendants are not fully protected from self-incrimination. In the adversarial set up of a common law country, there is no such expectation, which puts an added burden on the prosecutor.[18]

Second, the **examination phase** is under the direction of an examining judge. Though the prosecutor is still active, the weight of the proceedings has shifted to judges. This phase can be described as "trial by file" and is not very public. The main purpose is to see if there is sufficient cause and evidence to move to the next phase. There is no system of plea bargaining. Even if a person were to plead guilty and offer a confession, a trial—which is a fact-finding rather than an adjudicating ceremony—would go on. The confession and plea would simply be treated as evidence.

Third, the **official trial** finalizes an already developed system. That is why it is commonly felt that rather than a "presumption of innocence," as found in common law countries, a "presumption of guilt" is attributed to civil law justice systems. The evidence has been collected. Judges—seeking fuller understanding of the file of evidence—ask questions of the defendant and witnesses. At this stage with a presumption of guilt, the burden of proof shifts to the defendant. Any refusals to testify are taken as elements of culpability and held against the accused. Prosecutors and especially defense attorneys play minor roles. For example, there is no system of cross-examination of witnesses as might be found in a common law country. Though juries sometimes exist, they are rare. Particularly in those countries with wide economic or ethnic divisions, there is a distrust of popular participation in the justice system. These systems exist in highly bureaucratized countries where there is a belief in the efficiency and thoroughness of the system. Any resemblance to a jury is found in the existence of the lay judges.

Most trials do not have a single judge. Instead, there is a panel of at least three—a main judge and two assistant or lay judges. Together these three listen to the proceedings, then leave to deliberate and render a verdict. Theoretically, the lay judges can outvote the main judge, but they rarely do.[19]

Scholars point out that there is a real difference between the civil and common law systems. If a person were guilty of a crime, he or she would have a better chance in a common law country where the process would be filled with rhetoric, argumentation, and emotion. With its emphasis on procedure, common law systems are more likely to allow the guilty to "get off on a technicality." If a person were innocent, however, he or she would have the advantage in a civil law proceeding. In short, judgment in a civil law system—with its logic and strict adherence to unemotional bureaucratic proceedings—is more likely to distinguish factual rather than technical guilt and innocence.

MODERN DAY STRUCTURE OF THE LEGAL SYSTEM

Political Structure and Background

France is perhaps the best example of a modern-day civil law country. For centuries, the government was headed by a monarch. That ended with the French Revolution of 1789. Since then, the French have been guided by two ostensibly different goals. They have a profound desire for personal freedom and independence. At the same time, they have enormous respect and faith in authority, especially if it is wielded by a hero who unifies the country.[20] Throughout the nineteenth century, France was guided by a series of emperors. In the twentieth century, this shifted to presidents. The one common characteristic of these executives was their use of power and authority.

Today, the French government is organized according to the Constitution of the Fifth Republic developed by Charles de Gaulle in 1958. The president of the republic is elected for a term of seven years to be head of state, but there are no limits to the number of terms the president may serve. The president appoints the premier or prime minister who is head of government. The premier is a link between the national legislative body and the president. The premier must explain and defend the president's policies. The premier selects a cabinet called a Council of Ministers, members of which are career civil servants, university professors, or technical experts. Very few are politicians.[21]

The Parliament is made up of two houses: a Senate, which is the upper chamber, and a National Assembly, or lower chamber. The National Assembly is the more powerful, and its delegates are elected directly by the people for five-year terms.[22] Each delegate represents one of the numerous political parties. For example, there is the National Front, representing the extreme right of the political spectrum. The Movement for France is also a very conservative party. The Rally for the Republic (RPR) is a conservative party that owes its origins to the Charles de Gaulle era; it favors a market economy and regulation by the central government. The Union for French Democracy (UDF) is a center-right party that attracts the moderate voters. The Socialist Party had not been strong until Francois Mitterand revived it and won the presidential election in 1981. Throughout the 1980s, this party dominated French politics. The Communist Party (PCF) has declined as the Socialist Party has ascended. Most of the trade unions abandoned the PCF for the Socialist Party. Three parties specialize in ecological issues: the Greens, the Ecological Generation, and the New Environmentalists. The French believe in "proportional representation," which means that in the Parliament all these parties will be present in number in proportion to the vote they got in the election. Such a proliferation of political ideologies—all subscribing to some measure of ideological purity—makes coalition building very difficult. But in the name of political justice, it does ensure that large numbers of people with drastically different political views have representation in government.[23]

Administration of Justice

Unlike England and America, with their desires for local input into government administration, the French have a history of highly centralized and bureaucratized government. Even in the 95 "departments," local levels of administration comparable to counties in America, strong ties remain to the central government.

Police   Throughout the history of France, the police had been highly centralized in the national government. A pronounced military connection is prevalent with the police. Unlike England and America where the police were kept distant from the military, the French police grew out of the military. This meant they were quickly uniformed and those costumes were very similar to those worn in the military. Unlike in England and America, French police were quickly armed. Another characteristic of the French police is the extent to which they can interfere in the lives of ordinary citizens. This is quite common in civil law countries and is the result of the notion that the collective needs of society are more important than individual rights. Historically, the French police—and this is also true of other civil law systems—have a close relationship with the judiciary. In fact, many of the earliest leaders of the French police, called lieutenant generals, were magistrates.[24]

There are two police systems in France. The **National Police** is the largest, employing more than 133,500 people. It is responsible for policing cities and towns with populations greater than 10,000. The National Police is under the Ministry of Interior, one of the most important members of the Council of Ministers. The director of the National Police is a civilian career bureaucrat who is concerned with the central administration of the National Police. The head of each local "department," the administrative subdivisions of France, is a prefect. The prefect is linked to the director general but is the liaison to the local department.

To accomplish its mission, the National Police has several subunits. First is the Office of Inspector General of Police, whose job it is to make sure the police are not too brutal or corrupt. Second, the Judicial Police, divided into 18 regions throughout the country, carry out all criminal investigations. Third, the General Intelligence Directorate, sometimes referred to as the "political police," collects all kinds of intelligence to safeguard the security of the nation. Fourth is the Public Security Directorate, which consists of the uniformed branch of policing, that is, urban uniformed patrol. Fifth, the Territorial Surveillance Directorate is a specialized unit concerned with protecting those at risk from terrorist attacks. Vital industrial, scientific, and technical industries fall under its protection. Sixth, the Directorate for the Control of Immigration and Illegal Employment, created in 1994, has an air and border patrol to handle security at the airports and along the borders. Finally, there is the Republican Security Company (CRS) or riot police. This directorate is highly militaristic and is encamped throughout the country to quell public unrest such as student demonstrations and union strikes. This group protects the president of France and visiting dignitaries.[25]

The **National Gendarmerie** is the other principal police organization of France. Administratively, the National Gendarmerie falls under the Ministry of Defense and does three tasks. First, it acts as the military police for the French army, navy, and air force. Second, it provides law enforcement services for the French overseas territories. Third, the Gendarmerie provides policing in France for all those communities with a population less than 10,000.[26]

The police of France are highly centralized and have much expanded powers and authorities compared with the typical common law police. In this regard, the French police are quite typical of all civil law justice systems.

Judiciary   There are two kinds of courts in the French legal system. Administrative Courts supervise the government. They try to regulate and balance any conflict between the general interests of the state and individual rights. The other branch is the Ordinary Courts, which handles all civil and criminal cases. The Ordinary Courts are of most interest to us because they deal with most questions of justice.

The Ministry of Justice, a cabinet position in the Council of Ministers, is the governmental overseer of the Ordinary Courts. This minister is concerned with administering the correctional system, selecting and appointing magistrates (judges and prosecutors), and generally administering the law.

France's court structure is typical of civil law countries. In America, the Supreme Court can rule on the constitutionality of the laws and practices of government agencies. Such a judicial review does not exist in France in the court system. Instead, a special council is established to do this. This Constitutional Council is composed of nine members who serve terms of nine years; one-third of the council is appointed every three years. The president of France and the presidents of the Senate and National Assembly share in this appointment power. All former presidents of the Republic serve as *ex officio* members. The council has two responsibilities: One is addressing complaints about elections. Second, the council determines the constitutionality of legislation passed by the parliament. This second activity occurs before a piece of legislation is

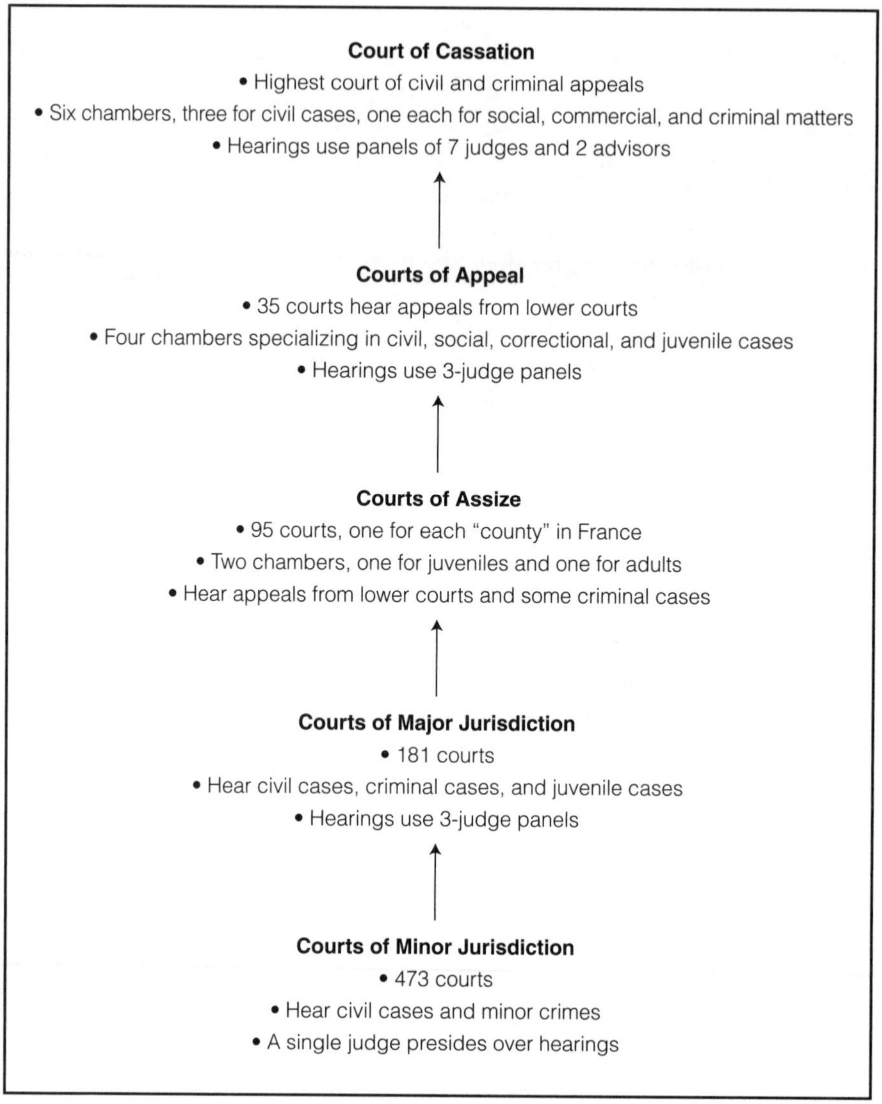

Court of Cassation
- Highest court of civil and criminal appeals
- Six chambers, three for civil cases, one each for social, commercial, and criminal matters
- Hearings use panels of 7 judges and 2 advisors

↑

Courts of Appeal
- 35 courts hear appeals from lower courts
- Four chambers specializing in civil, social, correctional, and juvenile cases
- Hearings use 3-judge panels

↑

Courts of Assize
- 95 courts, one for each "county" in France
- Two chambers, one for juveniles and one for adults
- Hear appeals from lower courts and some criminal cases

↑

Courts of Major Jurisdiction
- 181 courts
- Hear civil cases, criminal cases, and juvenile cases
- Hearings use 3-judge panels

↑

Courts of Minor Jurisdiction
- 473 courts
- Hear civil cases and minor crimes
- A single judge presides over hearings

FIGURE 5.1

Structure of French Courts

signed into law. Such scrutiny occurs only when the president of the republic or the premier makes a special request, or the presidents of the Senate or National Assembly.[27]

As shown in Figure 5.1, there are five layers of court in France. The Court of Cassation is the highest court of civil and criminal appeals in France. The word *cassation* comes from the French verb *casser,* to shatter. This court listens to appeals on the interpretation of the law by the lower courts. The court has six chambers, three of which handle civil cases. The other chambers listen to issues concerning social, commercial, and criminal matters. More than 120 judges sit in this court. Eighty-five are senior permanent judges. About 40 are career judges, called "advisors," who are appointed for ten-year terms. Each case that is heard by the court will have a minimum of seven judges and two advisors.[28]

Thirty-five Courts of Appeal deal with civil and criminal appeals from the lower courts. These courts consist of four chambers, each specializing in civil, social, correctional, or juvenile cases. A three-judge panel will hear each case. Two types of issues will bring an appeal to these courts: cases that involve a point of law needing clarification and cases that deal with some factual issue. In the latter case, this court's decision is the final decision.[29]

Ninety-five Courts of Assize, one for each of the departments (counties) of France, sit to hear appeals from lower courts and have original jurisdiction in criminal matters. These courts are divided into two chambers, one for juvenile cases and one for adult cases. Three judges sit as a panel to hear civil cases. For criminal cases, three judges and nine lay jurors preside.[30]

Courts of Major Jurisdiction serve as the next layer of courts. There are 181 Courts of Major Jurisdiction. Each court is divided into three chambers. When it hears civil cases, they are called civil courts. When they hear criminal cases, they are called correctional courts. This court also sits a juvenile court, and three-judge panels make up each of these courts.[31]

Courts of Minor Jurisdiction are the lowest courts in the hierarchy of courts. Each of these 473 courts is divided into two tribunals. They are civil tribunals when they hear civil cases. A police tribunal hears minor crimes, called contraventions. These courts are the only ones in the French system that have a single judge presiding.[32]

Legal Profession   The law professor is at the pinnacle of the legal profession. Legal education in France is an undergraduate interdisciplinary field of studies. French universities are public institutions administered by the Ministry of National Education. Legal education takes four years, divided into two phases. In the first two years, the student studies history, economics, political science, sociology, and finance. Students are to obtain a general broad education in this initial phase. In the second phase, the student concentrates in law. At the end of the third year, the student is given a license in law, equivalent to a bachelor of law degree. At the end of the fourth year, the student is given a master of law degree. Instruction is highly theoretical and philosophical. Law professors operate in the realm of ideas and are little concerned with the practical aspects of the law or legal profession. As Terrill notes, "Their responsibility is to train people to think like jurists, not to produce legal practitioners."[33]

Judges are part of the judicial bureaucracy. Unlike the United States where judges are elected or appointed, French judges are civil servants. They tend to start and end their careers as magistrates. They are called *magistrates du siege* or sitting magistrates. Their training and career path is very different from that found in England and the United States. To become a judge, one needs to receive a license in law then attend a National School of the Judiciary in Bordeaux. A person learns to be a judge at this school. This three-year training is divided between very theoretical course work and an apprenticeship. The first appointment is as an assistant judge in a Provençal city. From that point, judges slowly work their way up the career ladder. Judges are committed to theoretical purity and tidiness. Their decisions and writings are clear and brief, usually no longer than a page. Their thought processes are deductive. The general principle in the written law is the major premise. The facts of the case are the minor premise. The conclusion flows smoothly and logically. Any decision must show how it is in accordance with the code.[34]

Procurators, called prosecutors in the United States, are another important part of the French judiciary. They are called *magistrates debout* or standing magistrates. Procurators also attend the National School of the Judiciary but opt for a different career path than judges do. Unlike the United States' prosecutor, the procurator's job is not to secure a conviction. Rather, procurators seek to achieve justice and serve the interests of society—they are not attorneys for the state. For example, in a civil case where the state is one of the litigating parties, the government must hire its own lawyer; it cannot use a procurator. There are two types of procurators: First, the public procurator represents the general public, and second, every lawyer who appears in court for a victim serves a procurator's role, too.[35]

Before 1971, the defense council was divided into two groups, *avocats* and *avoues,* similar to the British solicitor and barrister. Then they merged so now they are *avocats* only. *Avocats* need to obtain a license in law from their universities, pass an examination, and register at a local bar association, of which there are 180 in the country. During a three-year probationary period, the new *avocat* attends a specialized training school set up by the court of appeal in the region of residence. Historically, these lawyers practiced alone. However, legislation has been passed by the Parliament allowing small partnerships to form. This has become the favorite form of legal organization in the last generation.[36]

Unlike many civil law countries, France does have a jury system. It is used only in the Courts of Assize. To serve on a jury, a person must be a citizen, be at least 23 years old, be able to read and write, and be on the voting lists. Before a court session is opened, the names of 35 jurors and 10 alternates are listed. On the day of a trial, names are drawn from an urn. *Avocats* can challenge 5, and the procurator can reject 4. Reasons for challenges and rejections need not be given. Nine jurors are finally selected and are seated on either side of the three judges. Jurors are to decide issues of guilt or innocence, but are at a disadvantage. They are not provided any written record of the trial nor are they provided any summing up of the law before the trial begins. In other words, in the name of the revolutionary spirit of the Napoleonic era, juries were added but they are powerless compared with the judges.

CONCLUSION

The civil law family is an important part of the justice systems of the world. Many argue that truly impartial justice can only be had by the rational, logical, and coldly bureaucratic civil law system. To these advocates, the common law system is too arbitrary and unscientific. Civil law systems tend to arise in highly centralized civil-servant countries. The system of justice mirrors the political environment in which it finds itself. Most of Europe, Latin America, and South America have such systems. Even some former socialist countries, such as Russia, resemble the civil law structure. Some countries may have an ideological orientation that on the surface makes them seem different. For example, China, with its Communist background, still looks like a civil law system. Although there are exceptions, these differences seem to be at the legal end of the spectrum. China's structure still looks very much like the continental model explained here. One such example of a civil law system with ideological influences might be those countries with a strong ideological base in religion, such as Islam. We must now turn to that example.

Discussion Questions

1. How do civil law systems of justice differ from common law systems of justice?
2. How have some civil law traditions affected the United States?
3. Which is more efficient: a civil law or a common law justice system? Explain.

Endnotes

1. Philip Reichel, *Comparative Criminal Justice Systems: A Topical Approach* (Englewood Cliffs, N.J.: Prentice Hall Career & Technology, 1994), p. 100.
2. Ibid., p. 101.
3. Erika Fairchild and Harry R. Dammer, *Comparative Criminal Justice Systems* (Belmont, Calif.: Wadsworth Thomson Learning Series, 2001), p. 48.
4. Reichel, p. 102.
5. Ibid., pp. 103–106.
6. John Henry Merryman, *The Civil Law Tradition: An Introduction to the Legal Systems of Western Europe and Latin America,* 2nd ed. (Stanford, Calif.: Stanford University Press, 1985), pp. 19–25.
7. Ibid., pp. 26–33.

8. Reichel, p. 141.
9. Ibid., pp. 118–122.
10. Ibid., p. 142.
11. Merryman, pp. 34–38.
12. Richard Terrill, *World Criminal Justice Systems: A Survey* (Cincinnati: Anderson, 1999), pp. 227–229.
13. Ibid., p. 225.
14. Ibid., pp. 232–234.
15. Merryman, p. 64.
16. Reichel, p. 225.
17. Merryman, pp. 111–123.
18. Reichel, pp. 149, 152–153.
19. Merryman, pp. 124–132.
20. Terrill, p. 193.
21. Ibid., pp. 195–196.
22. Ibid., p. 197.
23. Ibid., pp. 197–200.
24. Ibid., pp. 203–204.
25. Ibid., pp. 206–208.
26. Ibid., pp. 209–210.
27. Ibid., p. 234.
28. Ibid., p. 225.
29. Ibid., pp. 225–226.
30. Ibid., p. 226.
31. Ibid.
32. Ibid.
33. Ibid., p. 233.
34. Ibid., pp. 227–228.
35. Ibid., pp. 229–230.
36. Ibid., pp. 230–231

ISLAMIC LAW SYSTEMS

C ommon law and civil law systems form the basis for most Western images of how a formal justice system should be structured. For people living under such systems, they seem quite natural, and it may be difficult to imagine alternatives for dispensing justice. Islamic law provides a good illustration of a very different way of formally addressing the issue of justice. As the name suggests, Islamic law is based on the principles of Islam, a set of religious principles, and followers are called Muslims. Western systems of justice tend to make a distinction between religion and government, but that distinction disappears under an Islamic system of justice. In countries governed by Islamic law, the head of state is also the head of the church, government proclamations are also religious proclamations, and criticism of the government is viewed as a criticism of Islam, and ultimately, of God. The religious leader of the country appoints judges in Islamic courts, and Islamic trials are conducted in mosques. Thus, it is impossible to understand Islamic law without first understanding the religion Islam.

ISLAM

Among the world's religions, Islam is relatively young. Its origins can be traced to the city of Mecca, Arabia, where the word of God was revealed to the prophet Muhammad in the early 600s A.D.[1] Those revelations were written in the book known as the *Koran*, or as it is called in the Muslim world, the *Qur'an*. Islam shares many of the ideas found in the Old Testament of the Bible. For example, Muslims believe in a single god, whom they refer to as Allah, and they believe in many of the Old Testament prophets, including Abraham and Moses. In fact, Muslims, Christians, and Jews all worship the same god, the god of Abraham.[2] Muslims also believe in Christ. "Jesus is one of the most important and prominent figures in the *Qur'an;* he is mentioned 93 times by name in the sacred scripture of Islam."[3] Muslims view Christ as simply another prophet.

Although it began in the Middle East, Islam spread quickly throughout the world and is presently the second largest religion in the world.[4] Today, the largest numbers of Muslims are in Asia and in parts of Africa, but there is also a large Muslim population in the United States. A study by the Council on American-Islamic Relations found that between 1994 and 2000, there was a 25 percent increase in the number of mosques in America and a 300 percent increase in the number of Muslims participating in religious activities in mosques.[5] The study estimates that the number of Muslims in America is between six and seven million and is growing rapidly.

ISLAM IS NOT THE SAME EVERYWHERE

Although Christians may follow the same Bible, there are large variations across denominations in their interpretation of the Bible and in the behaviors they expect of believers. Similarly, there are large variations in the practices of Muslims and in the application of Islamic law. Many countries with large Muslim populations do not operate under Islamic law, some countries have partially adopted Islamic law, and among countries that formally recognize Islamic law are large variations in how that law is interpreted. For example, under the Taliban, Afghanistan was an Islamic law country in which there was a strict interpretation of the *Qur'an.* Police there arrested and punished citizens for behaviors that would have been ignored or viewed as minor indiscretions in other Islamic countries. When the Taliban was in power, the Islamic government in Afghanistan forbid both native and foreign women from working or from driving automobiles.[6] Other Islamic governments may forbid Muslim women to work but allow work by non-Muslim women. Still other Islamic governments may not place restrictions on women's work, or they may discourage it, but not ban it.

There are also variations over time within individual Islamic countries. For example, officials in Pakistan and Egypt have become more restrictive in the behaviors they allow, whereas those in Sudan have become more tolerant.[7] Perhaps the most common situation is for a country to adopt a civil or common law system and integrate key elements of Islamic law into that system.[8] Under these blended systems, behaviors considered essential to following Islam are regulated under Islamic law, whereas other behaviors are regulated by secular law and processed through secular courts, similar to courts in much of Europe.[9] Islamic law is often applied to what are considered moral issues, and more secular law is applied to other areas of behavior.[10]

And, just as there are wide variations in how Christians interpret and follow the Bible, there are wide variations in the religious practices of Muslims living in non-Muslim countries. Muslims living in the United States, for example, generally recognize the criminal justice law of the United States but refer to Islamic law to guide moral behaviors, such as sex, gambling, and the use of alcohol and drugs. This reminder of variation is to caution that the description that follows is what some social scientists have called an ideal type—a picture drawing on the essential elements of Islam, the exercise of which may vary from one country to another.

SOURCES OF ISLAMIC LAW

Collectively, the laws of Islam are known as the Shari'a, which can be translated as "the path to follow." There are four sources of Islamic law (Table 6.1), but the *Qur'an* is the primary source with which all other sources must be in accord.[11] Muslims believe the *Qur'an* is a sacred document and as such is infallible. Thus, there are variations from one Islamic community to the next in the interpretation of the *Qur'an*, but there is never a challenge to the *Qur'an* itself. As we will see later, such challenges are among the most serious of offenses in Islamic law. This also means that compared with legal scholarship in the United States and Europe, scholars of Islamic law take a less critical approach to the subject. American law journals are filled with articles criticizing particular laws or punishments, but Islamic legal scholars never question laws or penalties spelled out in the *Qur'an*, only the interpretation of those laws.

Although the focus of this discussion is on the Islamic approach to criminal law, the *Qur'an* provides legal guidance on a variety of life issues, including religious obligations, commerce, family relations, and diet. In fact, of the 6,237 verses in the *Qur'an*, "only about 200 verses deal with legal issues in the strict sense of the term."[12] This means that the *Qur'an* does not explicitly cover many areas of criminal behavior. To deal with such problems, Muslims turn to three other sources of Islamic law. These are the Sunnah, consensus of the Muslim community, and analogical reasoning.[13]

Second in importance to the *Qur'an* are the Sunnah, the words and actions of Muhammad which have been written down and whose authenticity has been verified by religious scholars.[15] These ideas are thought to be from God through Muhammad as an extension and clarification of the *Qur'an*. Violating the rules established in the *Qur'an* or in the Sunnah means not simply violating the rules of society but violating the rules of God.

Consensus of the Muslim community is also a source of Islamic law for issues not included within the *Qur'an* or the Sunnah. In some cases, religious leaders may issue a religious edict or order that does not have the weight of law, but that might solidify public opinion on an issue and lead to a new law. For example, a Muslim cleric in Lebanon issued an edict banning Muslims from

TABLE 6.1	SOURCES OF ISLAMIC LAW[14]
Primary Sources	
Qur'an:	The Muslim holy book
Sunnah:	Customs sanctioned by Muhammad
Secondary Sources	
Consensus:	Agreement among members of the Muslim community
Analogical Reasoning:	Applying existing rules to a new situation that is similar to an existing situation

smoking tobacco.[16] It was expected that most of the cleric's followers would obey the order, although it did not have the weight of law. In societies guided by Islamic law, should there be general agreement among his followers that smoking should be banned, the edict might well become law.

Analogical reasoning is the fourth source of Islamic law. Through analogical reasoning, the law can adapt to new situations while remaining true to the spirit of the Qur'an and the Sunnah. For example, the Qur'an specifically prohibits fornication but does not mention sodomy. Some scholars have argued that by analogy, sodomy is comparable to fornication and should result in the same legal punishment.[17]

CRIME AND PUNISHMENT UNDER ISLAMIC LAW

There is an image of Islamic law as harsh and unyielding, but this is not entirely accurate. Although the penalties for some offenses are much harsher than in many non-Islamic systems, strict enforcement of these laws is often difficult given the strict criteria that must be met under Islamic law. Further, some offenses that are considered among the most serious in Western law are, by comparison, treated less harshly under Islamic law. Islamic law also differs from Western law in that, technically, only God and the individual can be seen as victims—there are no crimes against the state. Further, there is no provision in Islamic law for recognizing corporations as individuals or entities capable of being either an offender or a victim. Charges may be brought against individuals who control the corporation, but not against the corporation itself.

TABLE 6.2	**CATEGORIES OF ISLAMIC LAW**

Hudud Offenses:	These are offenses against God and the public good. Hudud offenses and their corresponding penalties are specified in the *Qur'an*.
Quesas Offenses:	These are offenses against individuals, either resulting in death or in serious physical harm. These offenses and their corresponding penalties are specified in the *Qur'an* and the Sunnah.
Ta'zir Offenses:	These are offenses that harm society or individuals but for which the punishments are not specified in the *Qur'an* or Sunnah. Religious authorities decide these offenses and a judge decides their corresponding punishments.

Although common law and civil law systems tend to categorize crimes by the relative harm that results, Islamic law categorizes crimes according to the nature of the punishment that follows a conviction. In general there are three categories of crime under Islamic law: hudud offenses, quesas offenses, and ta'zir offenses (Table 6.2).

Hudud offenses are those for which the offense and the penalty are explicitly defined in the *Qur'an*. Quesas offenses include crimes against the person, and punishments are designed to provide victims with a formal mechanism for retribution. Finally, ta'zir offenses are offenses not specifically listed in the *Qur'an* or Sunnah, for which the penalty is left to the discretion of the judge with a focus on correction or rehabilitation of the offender.[18]

Hudud Offenses   There are seven hudud offenses and their respective penalties listed in the *Qur'an*. The punishments for hudud offenses are presented in Table 6.3, along with the standard of proof that must be met before conviction. These offenses are the following:

- *Apostasy:* This refers to followers of Islam who voluntarily renounce Islam or its beliefs.
- *Armed Rebellion:* This refers to attacks against the state with the intention of overthrowing it, or giving aid to its enemies.
- *Theft:* Theft refers to taking the property of another in a secret manner. The object must have been in a secure place and the thief must have full possession of the property.
- *Highway Robbery:* This includes both robbing highway travelers and, in some jurisdictions, murdering highway travelers.
- *Extramarital Sex:* This includes both adultery and sexual relations between individuals who are not married to each other.

- *Slander/Defamation:* This refers to accusing someone of extramarital sex without being able to meet the necessary standard of proof.
- *Drinking Alcohol:* At the time the *Qur'an* was written, the ban on alcohol appeared to refer to drinks made from grapes, but some Islamic scholars have interpreted the law to refer to any alcoholic beverage.

Strictly enforced, the required punishments for hudud offenses can be quite harsh. Although these offenses and their punishments are technically not subject to negotiation, in reality it is a common practice for Islamic officials to find ways to justify lesser penalties. For example, theft may be reduced from a hudud offense to a lesser offense if it can be shown that the thief was hungry or needy, "for in this case the blame is attributed to the injustice of society or the ruler."[19] Similarly, having sex outside of marriage is made more difficult to prosecute because of the requirement that there be four witnesses. However, the pregnancy of an unmarried woman may be such a visible and undeniable violation that religious leaders feel compelled to carry out the proscribed punishment.[20]

TABLE 6.3 HUDUD OFFENSES, STANDARD OF PROOF, AND PROSCRIBED PENALTIES

Offense	Standard of Proof	Punishment
Apostasy	2 witnesses or a confession	Death by beheading for males, imprisonment until they repent for females
Armed Rebellion	2 witnesses or a confession	Death if captured while fighting; a lesser punishment if the person surrenders
Theft	2 witnesses or a confession	1st offense: amputation of hand at wrist
		2nd offense: amputation of second hand at wrist
		3rd offense: amputation of foot at ankle or imprisonment until the person repents
Highway Robbery	2 witnesses or a confession	Amputation of right hand and left foot, execution, crucifixion, or exile
Extramarital Sex	4 witnesses or a confession	Married offenders are stoned to death. Unmarried offenders receive 100 lashes
Slander/Defamation	Failure to prove adultery	80 lashes across the back of the offender
Drinking Alcohol	2 witnesses or a confession	80 lashes across the back of the offender

Although hudud offenses are not usually punished fully, such punishments are always possible. In 1989, the Iranian government offered a bounty for the death of author Salman Rushdie because his novel *The Satanic Verses* was ruled to be an affront to Islam and thus a form of apostasy. Before they were removed by American troops, Afghanistan's Taliban rulers announced they would carry out the death penalty against any Muslim who converted from Islam to another religion.[21]

Quesas Offenses   These are commonly referred to as offenses against the person and include murder, voluntary killing, involuntary killing, intentional physical injury or maiming, and unintentional physical injury or maiming. The manner in which quesas offenses are handled and the punishments that accompany them make Islamic law quite distinct from either common law or civil law traditions. Although by Western standards the punishments for hudud offenses may seem harsh, the punishments for quesas offenses can be comparatively mild, depending on the wishes of the victim. Unlike common law and civil law, neither homicide nor battery is a crime against the state or against society. Instead, they are seen as personal matters between individuals in which the state acts only as a neutral mediator.[22] Thus, the victim has the option of seeking either retaliation or compensation. In the case of willful murder or manslaughter, the victim's family may choose among death to the offender, financial compensation, or a complete pardon. In the case of an accidental killing, the victim's family may seek compensation or may pardon the offender. For inflicting bodily harm, the victim may seek to have the same harm inflicted on the offender, compensation, or a complete pardon. In most modern Islamic states, the victim's family's wish to have a killer executed is carried out by the state, acting as a representative of the victim's family. Quesas offenses are crimes against individuals, whereas hudud offenses are crimes against God. Consequently, hudud offenses are viewed as more serious. As a result, "A proven murderer thus has, at least in principle, a better chance of averting punishment than does the proven sexual offender."[23]

One provision of Islamic law that is unusual and controversial by Western standards is the practice of not punishing "a father or a teacher who kills a child in the course of correction."[24] This same provision allows for the killing of a female who has harmed the family name by having sex outside of marriage or by marrying a man unacceptable to the father or male guardian. According to a report by the United Nations, the number of these so-called "honor killings" is increasing worldwide, as is the number of countries in which it is practiced.[25] Within Islamic societies, the practice of honor killing is controversial. Some argue the *Qur'an* requires it, but others argue the *Qur'an* prohibits the practice. In reality, honor killing was practiced in the Middle East long before Islam came into being and is more accurately a reflection of tribal custom than of a religious practice. Honor killing is also practiced in countries that do not follow Islamic law, such as Lebanon, where the practice is technically illegal. Often authorities choose to look the other way, but in doing so they are violating the law.

Ta'zir Offenses   These offenses concern behaviors that are not specifically outlined in the *Qur'an* or the Sunnah, and for which neither the *Qur'an* nor the Sunnah specifies penalties for violators. Religious scholars, guided by the principles outlined in the *Qur'an* and Sunnah, determine which acts will be defined as crimes. The judge, acting as a representative of the ruler will decide the punishment, considering the specifics of the case, the offender's background, the likelihood that a particular punishment will bring about reform in the offender, the best interests of the society, and the range of punishments allowed by the *Qur'an* or the Sunnah. Ta'zir offenses include behaviors that do not rise to the level of a hudud offense, such as petty theft or unlawful cohabitation. This category of crime also includes behaviors that threaten the stability of society, such as bribery, or that violate important religious principles, such as the prohibition against eating pork.[26] For ta'zir offenses, more than for hudud or quesas offenses, there is an emphasis on using punishment to reform and rehabilitate the offender.

CRIMINAL PROCEDURE UNDER ISLAMIC LAW

The crimes and punishments emphasized by Islamic law are often very different from those in Western justice systems, but the procedures followed to carry out the law have much in common with those in both civil and common law systems. There is, for example, a strong sense of privacy underlying Islamic law. Consequently, authorities must obtain a search warrant based on probable cause from the minister of complaints (not from a judge) or they must obtain consent of the owner before they may search the owner's home, person, or letters.[27]

Islamic law also operates under the presumption that the accused is innocent until proven guilty beyond a reasonable doubt.[28] Consistent with this belief, in some Islamic societies, people accused of crimes under Islamic law are not held in confinement while waiting for trial. In modern Islamic societies, authorities are forbidden from using torture to force a confession from the accused. Further, the accused has the right to withdraw his confession any time before the sentence is carried out. For hudud offenses, the accused also has the right to remain silent and his silence cannot be used against him in court.[29]

The presumption of innocence is accompanied by an emphasis on fairness of the proceedings. Consequently, many procedural steps that Western societies would consider essential to fundamental fairness can also be found in Islamic systems:

> The accused and his attorney are to be informed of the charges and the supporting evidence, and of any evidence in the possession of the prosecution that indicates the defendant's innocence. The accused has the prerogative of being present at all proceedings relating to the charges, is to be informed of what occurs at any proceeding that he or his attorney fails to attend, and is to be provided the opportunity to present rebuttal evidence to investigators.[30]

At trial, the accused has the right to a fair and impartial trial, to present a defense, to have an attorney to assist in his defense, and to appear before a competent judge.[31] In fact, it is a crime for a judge to intentionally issue an erroneous judgment, and the accused is entitled to damages in such cases.[32]

There is also a belief in equality before the law. The *Qur'an* requires that the law treat everyone equally, regardless of their income or whether they are Muslim or non-Muslim.[33] The concept of equality of the law is compromised in some jurisdictions in which non-Muslims may testify against other non-Muslims, but they may not testify against Muslims.[34] The concept of equality before the law does not always apply to equality between the sexes. In some Islamic systems, women are prohibited from being witnesses in criminal cases. An exception to this is that two women may testify in the place of one man where the charges involve extramarital sex.[35]

Affirmative Defenses   Those familiar with Western legal systems are also familiar with a number of defenses in which the accused admits to having done the criminal act, but denies legal responsibility. For example, the defendant who claims to have killed in self-defense admits to the killing but argues that the circumstances absolve him of criminal responsibility. Islamic law allows for many of the same affirmative defenses that are allowed under Western law, including insanity, intoxication, infancy, coercion, necessity, mistake, and self-defense.

1. *Insanity:* Islamic law recognizes the defense of insanity, which, like Western law, is generally based on the individual's ability to distinguish right from wrong. Some schools of thought will postpone a trial if the person is thought to be insane at the time of the trial, but for others the only issue is whether the person was insane at the time of the offense. Islamic law gives special consideration to the issue of mental retardation. In general, mentally retarded offenders are treated according to their mental age, not their physical age. That is, a mentally retarded adult with the mind of a 6-year-old, will be treated in the criminal law as if he were 6 years old.[36]
2. *Intoxication:* Although consuming alcohol, and by analogy drugs, is against Islamic law, there are different schools of thought about the criminal responsibility of someone who commits a crime while intoxicated.

Some Islamic scholars believe the individual is fully responsible for any acts committed while intoxicated, others believe the individual is only responsible if the intoxication is voluntary, and a third group believes the intoxicated person cannot be held criminally responsible because he or she lacks the necessary criminal intent.[37]

3. *Infancy:* Like nearly all legal systems, Islamic law holds that someone under the age of seven cannot have criminal intent and cannot be held criminally responsible for his or her acts. Between the ages of seven and puberty, the child has the same status as someone who is mentally retarded. Children at this age can be expected to make monetary compensation for damage they cause, but they will not receive the full legal punishment of adults. In many cases, children's families will be held accountable for their crimes. Finally, children who have reached puberty or older are treated as fully responsible for criminal acts.[38]

4. *Coercion:* Someone who is threatened or coerced into committing a crime will not be held legally responsible providing the threat is real to them and the person making the threat is capable of carrying it out.[39]

5. *Necessity:* Islamic law, like Western law, does not hold someone legally responsible for violating the law if that violation was necessary to prevent some greater harm. Bahnassi cites the example of cutting off someone's leg to stop the spread of gangrene.[40]

6. *Mistake:* If someone injures or kills another by mistake, the person is generally not held criminally responsible for the injury or death. If that person mistakenly damages property, he or she may be required to compensate the victim for damages or to pay a fine.[41]

7. *Self-Defense:* The Islamic view of self-defense is very similar to that in most Western systems. Under Islamic law, self-defense is a natural right, but there are limits on its use. Self-defense can be used to prevent a crime when it is not possible that public authorities will be able to respond and when the person claiming self-defense uses only the force necessary to stop the crime.[42]

CONCLUSION

In practice, there are many variations of Islamic law. The *Qur'an* and Sunnah specify some offenses and penalties that to the outsider might appear to be both harsh and inflexible. However, the harshness of these penalties is generally tempered by the strict evidentiary requirements needed to obtain a conviction and in the day-to-day applications of these rules. Judges routinely find ways to reduce the penalties. For example, the hudud offense of extramarital sex requires four eyewitnesses, a difficult standard to meet. However, the judge may reduce the charge to cohabitation, a ta'zir offense with a substantially milder penalty.

Also, Islamic societies differ in how strictly the laws will be interpreted. For example, some interpret the prohibition against alcohol to include only that made from grapes, whereas others include any form of alcohol.

This variation among Islamic societies and within the same societies over time can make it difficult to provide a simple description that is both accurate and captures the essence of Islamic law. It is easy to get lost in the details that differentiate the laws of one Islamic nation from another. Even those who live under an Islamic law system may find themselves confused about what is allowed and what is forbidden. The situation is so complex that some Islamic nations have begun telephone hotlines on which people may call Islamic clerics with specific questions about what behaviors are allowed under Islamic law in their country.[43]

Although Islamic law can be interpreted and applied in many ways, some basic ideas guide Islamic law and make it more understandable to the outsider:

- *All law ultimately flows from the* Qur'an *and the Sunnah and must be consistent with the teachings of Muhammad.* Thus, laws are a direct reflection of religious beliefs. Violating the law is not simply violating the will of the people, but it is a violation of the will of God.
- *Although many passages in the* Qur'an *and Sunnah spell out offenses and punishments, these documents also emphasize compassion and forgiveness.* This compassion and forgiveness not only tempers the apparent harshness of many Islamic laws, but also provides a religious justification for routinely making exceptions to administering the harshest of penalties.
- *Under Islamic criminal law, when judges are allowed discretion in sentencing, they must give the greatest weight to punishments that consider the general public interest.* Punishments are not simply imposed for demonstrating harshness, but should ideally be used for the betterment of society. This may happen in a variety of ways, such as through compensation to victims or by serving as an example to others. For this reason, imprisonment is a possible penalty under Islamic law, but is not frequently used because it places a financial burden on the society, keeps the individual from contributing to society, and exposes the individual to more hardened offenders.[44]
- *There is a considerable emphasis on the rights of individuals and on fundamental fairness in the process of justice.* Even at its harshest, Islamic law also strives to be fair and to provide those accused of crime a number of due process protections, including the right to be free from unreasonable searches, the right to an attorney, and the presumption of innocence.

Perhaps the most difficult aspect of Islamic law to accept without question is its treatment of women in general and in the criminal law in particular. Even within the Islamic community, this issue is a contentious one. Some view the treatment of women as oppressive, whereas others argue that the restrictions placed on women are for their own protection. In criminal law, Muslim women are forbidden from testifying in court for most crimes.[45] They are allowed to serve as witnesses in cases involving sex outside of marriage, but even here, the testimony of two women is given the weight of the testimony of one man. In other matters of daily life, the restrictions on women are much more severe. Under strict Islamic law, women are not to work outside the home, are not to venture outside of the home without their husband or a male relative, are to cover all parts of their bodies except for their palms and faces when in public to avoid arousing sexual desires in men, and are even to worship in a separate area of the mosque.[46] Further, women are only allowed to inherit half of the value of any estate that would have been left to a man.

Some suspect that the influence of Western models of justice on the legal systems of Islamic nations will continue to grow, and as that happens, that Islamic criminal law will fall into disuse. Such a transformation would leave the *Qur'an* and Sunnah to serve as moral guides for behavior without the weight of formal law behind them.[47] However, there is nothing inevitable about this scenario. From the time of the Iranian revolution in 1979, which led to the creation of an Islamic republic, fundamentalist Islamic groups have grown in influence. In some countries, they have come to dominate all levels of the justice system. Although these fundamentalists represent a minority of Muslims worldwide, there is nothing to suggest that movement will disappear in the near future, or that other nations will not come to fully embrace Islamic legal principles. In Afghanistan, for example, the defeat of the fundamentalist Taliban by American forces led to an immediate loosening of restrictions on women, but over time, many of those restrictions have returned because they reflect the deeply held beliefs of many citizens there.

For Americans, understanding Islam and Islamic law is important for several reasons. With the emergence of a world economy, it becomes increasingly important that we can work with other nations and other cultures, and that requires the ability to work with other countries to pursue justice. That, in turn, requires being able to come to common understandings about what justice means and how it is to be pursued. As one example, U.S. efforts to reduce violence in the Middle East requires being able to understand both Jewish and Muslim perspectives on the problem and on their respective approaches to the dispensing of justice.

In addition, as the number of Muslims in the United States grows, it will be increasingly important to understand their perspective on justice. Non-Muslim Americans often have an incomplete and distorted view of the Islam religion and of the nature of Islamic justice. The absence of such an understanding sets the stage for prejudice, discrimination, and eventually acts of violence against Muslims.

Discussion Questions

1. Islamic law views murder very differently from the way murder is viewed in either common law or civil law systems. In what ways might the Islamic perspective be a more just way of viewing murder and in what ways might it be a less just way of viewing murder?

2. Islamic law lists seven hudud offenses. If you were to create a list of the seven most serious crimes that threaten the long-term existence of a society, how would the crimes on your list differ from those considered hudud offenses?

3. When you consider both crimes and procedures, which system would you consider more just—an Islamic law system or a common law system? Specifically, what makes one system more just than the other?

Endnotes

1. John L. Esposito, "Islam," in *The Oxford Encyclopedia of the Modern Islamic World,* John L. Esposito (ed.) (New York: Oxford University Press, 1995), pp. 243–254.
2. Charles Kimball, *When Religion Becomes Evil* (San Francisco: HarperSanFrancisco, 2002), p. 50.
3. Ibid.
4. Ibid.
5. Ihsan Babgy, Paul M. Perl, and Bryan T. Forehle, *The Mosque in America: A National Portrait.* Report from the Mosque Study Project by the Council on American-Islamic Relations, Washington, D.C. (accessed online at www.cair-net.org/mosquereport on 26 June 2001).
6. "Taliban Forbids Foreign Women to Drive, Defends Hindu Ids," *Chicago Tribune,* 1 June 2001, p. 3. After the September 11, 2001, attack on the World Trade Center in New York, American forces invaded Afghanistan and overthrew the Taliban. Despite this, many of the tenets of Islamic law persist in Afghanistan.
7. Philip Smucker, "Sudan Shows Signs of Erasing Its Enforcement of Shari'a," *Christian Science Monitor,* 14 May 2001, p. 7.
8. Farhat J. Ziadeh, "Criminal Law," in *The Oxford Encyclopedia of the Modern Islamic World,* John L. Esposito (ed.) (New York: Oxford University Press, 1995), pp. 329–333.
9. Ibid. For a general overview of the Islamic criminal law, see Matthew Lippman, Sean McConville, and Mordechai Yerushalmi, *Islamic Criminal Law and Procedure* (New York: Praeger, 1988).
10. Bernard Weiss, *The Spirit of Islamic Law* (Athens: University of Georgia Press, 1998).
11. Lippman, McConville, and Yerushalmi.
12. Ibid., p. 29.
13. Ibid.
14. Ibid., p. 29. Adapted from Table 2.
15. Norman Calder, "Law," in *The Oxford Encyclopedia of the Modern Islamic World,* John L. Esposito (ed.) (New York: Oxford University Press, 1995), pp. 450–456.
16. Hussein Dakroub, "Muslim Cleric in Lebanon Bans Faithful from Smoking," *Chicago Tribune,* 7 June 2001, p. 3.

17. Taymour Kamel, "The Principle of Legality and Its Application in Islamic Criminal Justice," in *The Islamic Criminal Justice System,* M. Cherif Bassiouni (ed.) (New York: Oceana, 1982), pp. 149–169.
18. See Ziadeh.
19. Aly Aly Mansour, "Hudud Crimes," in *The Islamic Criminal Justice System,* M. Cherif Bassiouni (ed.) (New York: Oceana, 1982), pp. 196–201.
20. For example, see Agence France Presse, "Nigerian Girl to Be Lashed 180 Times," *Christian Science Monitor,* 4 January 2001, p. 7.
21. "Taliban to Execute Converts from Islam," *Christian Science Monitor,* 9 January 2001, p. 7.
22. See Weiss.
23. Ibid., p. 156.
24. Lippman, McConville, and Yerushalmi, p. 50.
25. "UN Aide Says 'Honor Killing' of Women on the Rise Globally," *Chicago Tribune,* 8 April 2000, p. 8.
26. Ghaouti Benmelha, "Ta'zir Crimes," in *The Islamic Criminal Justice System,* M. Cherif Bassiouni (ed.) (New York: Oceana, 1982), pp. 211–225.
27. Osman Abd-el-Malek al-Saleh, "The Right of the Individual to Personal Security in Islam," in *The Islamic Criminal Justice System,* M. Cherif Bassiouni (ed.) (New York: Oceana, 1982), pp. 55–89.
28. Ibid. Also see Ma'amoun M. Salama, "General Principles of Criminal Evidence in Islamic Jurisprudence," in *The Islamic Criminal Justice System,* M. Cherif Bassiouni (ed.) (New York: Oceana, 1982), pp. 109–123.
29. al-Saleh.
30. Lippman, McConville, and Yerushalmi, p. 65.
31. al-Saleh; Awad M. Awad, "The Rights of the Accused Under Islamic Criminal Procedure," in *The Islamic Criminal Justice System,* M. Cherif Bassiouni (ed.) (New York: Oceana, 1982), pp. 91–107.
32. al-Saleh.
33. Muhammad Salim al-Awwa, "The Basis of Islamic Penal Legislation," in *The Islamic Criminal Justice System,* M. Cherif Bassiouni (ed.) (New York: Oceana, 1982), pp. 127–147.
34. Lippman, McConville, and Yerushalmi.
35. Ibid.
36. Ahmad Fathi Bahnassi, "Criminal Responsibility in Islamic Law," in *The Islamic Criminal Justice System,* M. Cherif Bassiouni (ed.) (New York: Oceana, 1982), pp. 171–193.
37. Ibid. Also see Lippman, McConville, and Yerushalmi.
38. Bahnassi.
39. Ibid.
40. Ibid.
41. Ibid.
42. Ibid.
43. Sarah Gauch, "Need to Know if Koran Allows Soccer? Call Islam Line," *Christian Science Monitor,* 6 April 2001, p. 7.
44. Benmelha.
45. Lippman, McConville, and Yerushalmi.
46. Weiss.
47. Ibid.

CHAPTER 7

JUSTICE AMERICAN STYLE

A ny discussion of pursuing justice must consider the criminal justice system. The previous three chapters have presented very different approaches to structuring a criminal justice system—common law, civil law, and Islamic law. The systems outlined in these three chapters represent ideal types—models of justice that, in practice, are modified to fit the particular needs of a society. In any society, the institutions, procedures, and personnel that make up the criminal justice system reflect the character of that country. A close look at a single system reflects the values that shape that country and highlights many contradictions that system must face.

This chapter focuses on the justice system in the United States because America holds itself out as a beacon to the world when it comes to freedom, compassion, and justice. Our discussion begins by providing a brief overview of the system, then turns to two examples of a contradiction built into the system. How the contradiction is resolved changes over time, reflecting changing concerns about justice.

As discussed in Chapter 4, the United States originally was close to England and had strong ties to the common law tradition. However, by its nature common law is elitist. A small number of judges, none of whom were elected, made the law with their decisions. This was contrary to the democratic experiment fermenting in the late eighteenth and early nineteenth centuries. Shortly after the new nation was established, a "republican code movement" arose in the majority of states.[1] New constitutions were written that placed greater emphasis on law making in popularly elected institutions called legislatures. This movement led the United States to drift away from a pure common law system and to draw in elements of a civil justice system, but many common law traditions remain. For example, the American system relies heavily on precedent, using decisions in prior cases to make decisions where the written law might be vague, and appellate courts operate much as they did under common law. The American system, like other common law systems, is based on an adversarial system in which the prosecution and defense battle it out in court, while the judge sits as a referee, making sure each side follows the rules.

Elements of the civil law tradition emerged as law came to be defined in statutes, a movement largely completed by the 1830s. Today most laws are now written down in statutes passed by the legislature, and courts are expected to follow these statutes. Judges may interpret the law, but if legislators don't like the interpretation, they may change the wording and compel judges to adhere to their wishes.

The contradiction inherent in the American system of justice reflects the basic definitions of justice: process versus outcome. America has historic antecedents in the common law tradition that emphasized procedure. The focus on procedure reflects a belief that orderly, predictable, fair processing will guarantee justice. This might be called "bureaucratic justice." Others care less for the process but appeal to higher law demanding a "transcendent justice," the righting of some wrong no matter how it is done. When President Reagan stood before a press corps and jokingly pointed his finger and declared, "Go ahead, make my day!," he was quoting a pop cultural character in police movies who believed that "the ends justifies the means." As a rogue cop in San Francisco, "Dirty Harry" Callahan made his own justice outside the formal justice process. America's long tradition of vigilantism characterizes this mind-set. When all else fails, citizens should take justice into their own hands, proclaim hundreds of historic examples. Hollywood latched on to this feeling when it produced a series of films, the first being *Death Wish* (1974), of an ordinary man taking guns and killing criminals after his wife and daughter had been attacked. Such transcendent or abstract justice appeals to high emotions. The loved ones of victims of homicide might not feel justice is done or emotions laid to rest until they have witnessed the murderer's execution. Process becomes secondary to other feelings. A too-slow process—say, 20 years and countless appeals before the execution takes place—might get in the way of their conception of justice. Before we consider other examples of important contradictions, it is useful to first provide a framework and an overview of the system.

EFFICIENCY VERSUS INEFFICIENCY AND JUSTICE

The criminal justice system is part of a larger political system. Fair and efficient processing of offenders provides justice to the offender and to society. But the structure of the government does not always allow efficiency. First, a case can be made that the founding fathers did not want an efficient system. Many procedural obstacles were set up, largely in the Bill of Rights and subsequent case law, to keep the government from becoming too efficient. Further, most of the founders of the United States justice system saw a diminished role for the national government. They believed government and justice systems were better at the grassroots level.

Second, the nature of government in the United States shapes the justice system. America is a federal republic, which means there is a national government, with its federal law, police, courts and prisons; 50 state governments, with their state law, police, courts, and prisons; hundreds of county entities, with their ordinances, sheriff, police, courts, and jails; and thousands of towns and cities, with their ordinances, police, courts, and lockups. Unlike a more unitary or a national system of justice, America appears to be fragmented into countless justice systems. Sometimes these different federal divisions cooperate; often they do not, and jurisdictional quarrels result.

Third, within various government levels, there are many checks and balances. The cornerstone of the American political system is the system of checks and balances in which the executive, legislative, and judicial branches have relative independence and in which each is expected to monitor the behavior of the other two. This system was designed to limit the power of the government and to make government actions tedious and, in effect, to make the government inefficient. The executive branch might appoint high criminal justice officials, such as police administrators or prison wardens, but the legislative branch holds the purse strings and allocates or withholds money, and the judicial branch might determine the propriety of criminal justice actions.

Fourth, local criminal justice systems are constantly checked and held accountable by the larger system. Consider the following examples:

- Courts may limit the power of the criminal justice system by creating procedural law that regulates the process. The Miranda warning and various restrictions on search and seizure are examples.
- The police, who are part of the executive branch, must go to the courts for warrants, and the courts ultimately decide if the procedures followed by the police will be allowed in the prosecution of an offender.
- The legislature may curtail the power of judges to make decisions and to exercise discretion in sentencing by requiring mandatory minimum sentences.
- Governors and presidents can override decisions of the courts by granting pardons to people they believe wrongly convicted of crimes or whose punishments were thought to be too harsh.

Finally, citizens in the United States have a large voice in the way the criminal justice system works, though they might not always fully exercise their authority. Citizens elect mayors, governors, and presidents. They vote for legislators as well. More specifically, voters elect most prosecutors and judges in America. Citizen review boards, watchdog groups that hold agencies of criminal justice accountable, may threaten civil suits against the system. Membership on a grand jury or trial jury ensures laypersons' check on the system. As this discussion suggests, justice in America is complicated. Attempts are made to have a fair process, one halted and obstructed by principles that guarantee some inefficiencies in the system. A look at the flow of the criminal justice system and several examples of tension between the quest for efficiency and the fear of it will be illustrative.

OVERVIEW OF THE AMERICAN CRIMINAL JUSTICE PROCESS

The official criminal justice system adheres to a process. As long as that process is fair and impartial, symbolized in the figure of a blindfolded goddess holding a book for reason and a sword for power, justice will be done. Such a methodical processing ensures justice and adheres to principles of efficiency. On the surface, the procedure seems to be simple—a flow chart is always produced in standard introductory criminal justice textbooks—but a number of procedural checks to ensure accountability actually creates inefficiency.[2] What follows is a simple outline of the justice process in America. Some basic contradictions will be noted.

1. *After a crime has been reported, an investigation occurs.* Crime scene investigators and forensic scientists play an important part here. Rules of evidence dictate that search and recovery of evidence be done in appropriate ways. This notion of the "fruits of the poisoned tree," the idea that evidence obtained in wrongful ways taints that evidence, might lead to it being excluded at trial. Such a doctrine is a check on the police. Judicial permission, called warrants, might be required, adding to the labor of the police. Protection from unlawful search and seizure was so important to the framers of the Constitution that it was written into the Bill of Rights more than two hundred years ago. However, in the name of efficient process, numerous warrantless searches have been allowed. Consent searches, searches incidental to an arrest, and most automobile searches are a few examples of warrantless searches. A considerable amount of law has evolved because of the tension between bureaucratic and abstract justice when it comes to search and seizure.
2. *Disposition of the case follows.* This is a decision about how many resources are going to be put forth on a case. Some high profile cases such as murder will get considerable attention, but others such as robbery might not. The police want a high degree of success but to still be economical with their resources. This means not all cases will be given the same work effort. Sometimes this has to do with resources. Other times it has to do with the amount of publicity surrounding a case. Some departments frequently "unfound" a case they do not want to work on. This

means that they make a bureaucratic judgment that this crime did not actually occur. Such disposition decisions highlight the differences between process and outcome. Working hardest on the easiest cases because that effort will most likely result in success is contrary to the position that all crimes should be given equal treatment.

3. *Follow-up investigation might lead to surveillance and arrest.* Surveillance is spying and seems contrary to the American way of life. But it is an efficient way to collect evidence for search warrants, information to be used in interrogations later on, arguments to force a plea bargain, and to curtail further crime. Although ordinary surveillance is intrusive, using electronic devices is even more so. Initially, there were restrictions on such technology (the Constitution protects people not places, proclaimed the Supreme Court in *Katz v. U.S.* in 1967), but as crime became more prevalent, many restrictions were lifted. Another example has to do with arrests. Unless an officer sees a crime being committed or otherwise has strong probable cause to arrest someone, an arrest warrant is needed. This is official judicial permission to make an arrest. Historically, in conducting an arrest, it was important to make an "announcement." Officers had to proclaim who they were and the purpose of their presence. All citizens, even possible criminals, had the right to fair warning. Of course, this took the element of surprise away from law enforcement officers and might put them in harm's way. Under dangerous circumstances, a judge may give a "no knock" privilege in the original warrant, which allows officers to forgo making an announcement.

4. *The interrogation is another critical stage in building a case.* Along with search and seizure, interrogation processes have generated considerable case law. In the name of efficiency, the police would like a confession. The entire system would operate more swiftly if only the suspect would confess and face his or her punishment. Historically, officers used physical force, the infamous third degree, to obtain admissions until the courts (*Brown v. Mississippi,* 1936) banned it. Then prolonged custody without access to friends or legal council was used until it was banned in the 1940s. In the 1960s, the U.S. Supreme Court defined interrogation as any questioning after an arrest was made even if the questioning occurred at the crime scene or in the back seat of a police squad car. Recently, considerable debate has arisen about the televised recording of interrogations, an innovation many police officers resist.

5. *The case then goes to the prosecutor.* In some jurisdictions, prosecutors are called state's attorney or district attorney. The prosecutor decides to accept it and proceed or deny it (*nolle prosequi*). The prosecutor acts as a check on police procedure, holding the police accountable for their activities. At the same time, as a bureaucrat, the prosecutor seeks to have

cases where the odds of success are greatest. The decision to refuse a case because it might jeopardize the prosecutor's "conviction rate" might seem contrary to our notions of justice.

6. *Initial appearance before a magistrate occurs next.* Under the common law, a principle of *habeas corpus* requires a person to be brought before a magistrate to determine the lawfulness of the detention. Issues of bail and right to council are addressed at this hearing. Justice requires that a person be protected from excessive bail. Of course, what is excessive for some might not be for others. Poor people are at a distinct disadvantage when it comes to bail. A person who cannot make bail and spends time in jail has a greater likelihood of being convicted later. Some people are considered so dangerous they are denied bail; this is called preventative detention. In the name of process, propriety, and fairness, if a person cannot afford a lawyer, a court-appointed lawyer will be selected. This is achieved in several ways. Some jurisdictions have a public defender's office, whereas others appoint private attorneys. In an adversarial system, it is important that the defense attorney be at war with the prosecution. However, public defenders actually are a part of the system and the fees for a contracted lawyer come from the state.

7. *A grand jury or preliminary hearing occurs.* During this, the prosecutor seeks permission from a lay body (grand jury) or magistrate (preliminary hearing) to proceed. This is an attempt to have laypeople or a judge check the system and hold it accountable. The prosecutor does not have to reveal all the state's evidence but must present enough to convince the jury or magistrate that the case should go forward.

8. *Arraignment comes next.* The defendant stands before a judge and is told of the charges and asked to plead. Most pleas at this time are guilty based on a plea bargain, a bureaucratic way to get a conviction and avoid a trial. Plea bargaining is one of those points in the system that reveals the gap between procedure and outcome. The defendant, if truly guilty, might get a reduced punishment in the name of keeping the system smoothly running. In *Santobello v. New York* (1971), the Supreme Court declared plea bargain as constitutional and necessary. If everyone had his or her day in court, the system would grind to a halt. If the offender pleads not guilty, a trial results.

9. *Before the trial begins, pretrial motions are given.* These might be motions to dismiss the charges, to suppress evidence because it was illegally obtained, to change the venue or location of the trial because of adverse pretrial publicity, or for a delay of the trial called a *continuance.* Continuances, most often applied for by defense council, account for the largest number of delays in the adjudication process.

10. *A bench or jury trial occurs.* In this highly ritualized ceremony, the state offers its case and the defense rebuts it. Then the defense offers its case

and the prosecution rebuts it. Closing arguments by both sides summarize their cases. Historically, this process has lent itself to lawyers with oratory and theatrical talents more than to the importance of the evidence.

11. *The judge offers instructions to the jury, and they retire to deliberate.* In most felonies, the jury's decision must be unanimous. On many occasions, the jury is unable to decide, and the case will be retried. On other occasions, the jury might nullify. Jury nullification occurs when the jury finds the defendant innocent despite overwhelming evidence to the contrary. The jury might do this because of collective ignorance or because jury members believe the person should not have been charged.

12. *If there is a finding of guilt, a presentence investigation is conducted.* The presentence report helps the judge make the most appropriate sentence. Historically, judges had considerable discretion in sentencing. Sometimes this led to sentence disparity, a process under which different judges looking at the same case give different sentences. Attempts to regulate such sentence disparity have met with resistance from the judicial establishment; however, legislatures might require mandatory sentences as a way to limit such discretion and resultant disparity.

13. *People found guilty receive punishment.* As punishment, most convicted offenders will be required to pay a fine or be released into the community on probation. Probation usually requires they follow certain rules, such as paying child support and abstaining from alcohol consumption. Serious offenders, or those with many previous convictions, will face incarceration in prison. Deprivation of liberty is painful to all those imprisoned. Here, too, there is a tension between bureaucratic and transcendent justice. Historically, incarceration was intended to reform the inmate. Old-style penitentiaries and reformatories were set up to rehabilitate. Programs—religious, work, or educational—were created to treat and change inmate behavior. However, overcrowding made most of these programs and conditions ineffectual. Over time, "truth in sentencing" laws demanded prisoners serve substantial parts of their sentences no matter the degree of reform, "three strikes" laws sought to get at habitual offenders, and "civil death" principles permanently took away many of the prisoners' rights as citizens, such as voting or holding public office.

14. *After sentencing, the convicted person can appeal to higher courts to examine the procedure of the system.* Should a convicted person win the appeal, the case will be retried.

This brief overview of the process shows how the system is supposed to operate, as well as some of the obstacles that slow the process. Now let us look at two issues in American justice that further highlight the tension between bureaucratic efficiency and due process, what was described in Chapter 2 as a tension between due process and crime control.

ISSUES IN AMERICAN JUSTICE

The American justice system must accommodate strong, contrasting forces that require speedy justice and full attention to due process. Although there are dozens of examples of this tension, our discussion will focus on two: racial profiling by police and wrongful convictions.

The Police and Profiling

The strongest and most powerful expression of government in civil society is law enforcement. The police have the power to inconvenience, take away liberty, and under certain circumstances, take life. Discretion, the necessity of making independent decisions on the street, to tailor-make justice, is an important part of policing. Ironically, the hallmark of any "profession" is the use of discretion. Lawyers decide which strategies to use in litigation, doctors decide which therapies to use in treatments, and professors decide what kinds of tests to give in their classes. Police administrators try to eliminate or at least control independent officer discretion, but sometimes discretion is allowed by policy in the name of efficiency. This is best seen in the issue of profiling.

Informal profiling has been around as long as the police have existed. Individual officers, with years of experience, developed "gut instincts" when crimes or suspicious behavior confronted them. But such profiling was unsystematic and inefficient. When a veteran officer retired, all that occupational wisdom vanished too. In the 1960s, a more formal profiling emerged, which used its scientific credentials to establish legitimacy.

On the surface, formal profiling seems to be scientifically based. It is the **theory** that a group of characteristics—behavioral, physical, or psychological—when brought together predict a person's actions or establish someone as the most likely perpetrator of a crime. This is based on the assumption that criminal activity reflects the personality of the offender and that the offender cannot or will not change his or her personality. Criminal profiling takes attributes associated with a group of crimes, **empirical** information, to develop a portrait of a likely culprit. Studying past offenses and behavioral patterns allows the profiler to **predict** the future. This makes the police process appear to be very efficient; it bases suspicion about a potential offender on science rather than hunch.

Formal profiling began in the 1960s with the problem of commercial airline piracy and hijackers taking planes to Cuba. In 1968, 18 American planes were hijacked, the next year 40 attempts were made, 33 of them successfully. "Sky marshals"—specially trained U.S. Marshals—were put on planes, but hijacking continued. A government task force developed a profile of potential hijackers. Using information on known hijackers, they developed a picture of a potential pirate. It was hoped that the criminal would be identified before boarding the plane. This did not work, so instead all boarding passengers were required to undergo mandatory electronic screening before they boarded. By 1976, the number of hijackings of U.S. commercial airplanes decreased to 4, a 90 percent decline from those of 1969.[3] Electronic screening rather than profiling caused this decline.

The more famous profiling has to do with serial killers. In the late 1970s and early 1980s, the Federal Bureau of Investigation's (FBI) behavioral sciences unit began to study violent people. The first attempt at profiling was in the case of Wayne Williams, the Atlanta-based killer of two young black men. He fit the profile, although the profile itself did not lead to his arrest and conviction. The police believed he was responsible for 20 other killings, but he was never convicted of those. In 1983, the Violent Criminal Apprehension Program was established. In 1987, the National Center for the Analysis of Violent Crime was begun, and profiling was formalized. A serial killer profile was based on interviews of those who had already been caught. In addition, officers who captured serial killers were interviewed. Based on these interviews, the FBI created a profile to help apprehend serial killers as they became active.[4] Such a police technique captured the imagination of popular culture, but there is little evidence to prove its effectiveness. For example, such serial killers as John Wayne Gacy, Joel Rifkin, Jeffrey Dahmer, and Theodore Bundy were captured without any notable input from profiling. In the Seattle area, the Green River Killer murdered 49 persons from 1984 to 1988 but was not captured for more than a decade. The capture finally came from a relative's tip.[5] Actually, one would be hard pressed to find a single serial killer who was caught because of a profile.

Also in the 1980s, profiling came into much wider use with the development of the "drug-courier" profile at airports. These profiles were much closer to those aimed at hijackers rather than serial killers. Those profiles were less designed to describe a perpetrator and more intended to predict criminal activity. Many of these profile characteristics could be a base for terrorist profiling today, so it might be instructive to isolate them. A drug courier most likely would (1) pay for an airline ticket with a large amount of cash; (2) travel under a name different than the one under which his or her telephone was listed; (3) make a round-trip to a so-called drug-source city such as Miami; (4) stay in the destination city for a very short time; (5) appear nervous; (6) not check any luggage.[6] Over time, many drug profiles emerged, often based on contradictory criteria. A person could fit a profile if he or she were (1) the first to leave the plane, the last to leave the plane, or if he left in the middle group; (2) appeared too nervous or appeared too calm; (3) had too little luggage or had too much luggage; or (4) bought a one-way ticket or bought a round-trip ticket. A new government report in 2000 concluded that black women were nine times more likely than were white women to be x-rayed or forced to endure other intrusive searches. However, black women were less than half as likely to be carrying drugs.[7] Of course, the possibility of an innocent person being inconvenienced and

embarrassed is great. The U.S. Supreme Court upheld these profiling techniques in 1989 in *U.S. v. Sokolow,* although there are no reliable statistics to
prove the technique's effectiveness.

Profiling on the highways has become particularly widespread and controversial. This practice began in Florida in the 1980s to curtail the flow of drugs
out of that state. Drugs had come into Florida from South and Central American countries and were transported to other states by highway. Florida highway
patrol officers made numerous successful stops and noticed "cumulative similarities" among the drug couriers. After a driver was stopped on a traffic offense, these cumulative similarities were brought into play to justify a broader
search. Some characteristics were the driver's demeanor, the vehicle not being
registered in the driver's name, an overly cautious driver, things that look out of
place like a spare tire in the back seat, the use of a large, late-model car, early
morning hour driving, and drivers and occupants who avoided eye contact with
officers. Unfortunately, this criminal profiling became racial profiling because
one significant attribute was one's race or ethnicity. Numerous state police systems began to use the Florida model. Even the Drug Enforcement Administration was impressed and began to fund and encourage the Florida model in
something called Operation Pipeline.[8]

Just how successful is this highway profiling? Law enforcement officials
think it is very efficient. But statistics indicate that "hit rates," the number of dis-
coveries of contraband versus the number of stops, are not significant. For example, in Florida, where it all started and was touted as most successful, the
number of minorities stopped was astonishing. Research has shown that African
Americans and Latinos made up only 5 percent of the drivers who used the I-95
in Florida. However, videotapes connected to trooper's cars indicate that stops
of minorities were more than 70 percent of all those detained. When searches
of the automobile occurred, 80 percent were directed toward to a minority.[9] In
Maryland, African American drivers made up 17 percent of all drivers, but were
70 percent of those searched.[10] In both Maryland and New Jersey, black motorists were five times more likely to be stopped on the highways than were
whites.[11] A 1999 report by the American Civil Liberties Union (ACLU) found
that 30 percent of the motorists stopped by Illinois state police were Hispanic,
even though less than 8 percent of the state population was Hispanic.[12] Studies of Philadelphia found that the police singled out minorities at least 71 percent of the time.[13] In Dallas, Texas, for every 50 white motorists stopped, 1 was
searched. With blacks, the figure rose to 1 in 22. Hispanics underwent the most
searches, 1 in 20. The "hit rate" for both blacks and whites was 10 percent. The
hit rate for Hispanics was 6.5 percent.[14] Troopers found evidence on minorities
they searched 28.4 percent of the time but found evidence on white drivers 28.8
percent of the time.[15] Under a federal consent decree, the Los Angeles police
department began recording and reporting their traffic stops in 2003. Blacks and
Latinos were more likely to be stopped and searched. Of those stopped, 7 per-

cent of the whites were asked to step out of their cars, compared with 22 percent of Latinos and 22 percent of African Americans.[16] The unstated argument was that minorities fit a profile of likely offenders, but "hit rate" information suggests otherwise. Minorities complained that they were stopped for the crime of "driving while black" or "driving while brown." Justice—both bureaucratic and transcendent—seemed not served by highway profiling.[17]

Another form of profiling has to do with stopping people walking the streets. As early as the late 1960s, the Supreme Court allowed the police to stop and frisk—a pat down of the outer clothing of some suspected persons—for weapons in the name of officer and citizen safety (*Terry v. Ohio*, 1968). However, when policy makers adopted more severe measures, like that in New York City in the 1990s, this stop-and-frisk technique became widespread and questionable as racial profiling. Using the social science concept called the "broken windows theory," the police went aggressively after low-level crime and disorder to minimize bigger crime.[18] Extensive stops and frisks of ordinary citizens, mostly aimed at minority populations, in the name of efficient preventive police work occurred. Strictly speaking, these were informal profiles, based more on an officer's intuition rather than on a checklist of characteristics.[19] Officials would claim that New York City became a safer city because of such practices. Many minorities did not think the city so safe, however, especially after a young black immigrant, Amadou Diallo, was shot and killed by New York City police. In 2003, the ACLU brought civil suit against the Chicago police department for making racially biased stops.[20]

The gap in trust between the police and the minority population widened as blacks were more likely to be stopped and frisked than were whites. Rational policing would expect a higher percentage of arrests of African Americans for carrying weapons since they are stopped more often. Researchers found that police made 1 arrest for every 15 whites stopped on a suspicion of a weapons offense. Blacks had a ratio of 1 arrest for every 17.4 stopped; Latinos had a 1 for every 18 weapons stops ratio.[21] In other words, the "hunch" or racial profile was ineffective. Whites were less likely to be stopped but were actually more likely to be carrying weapons. Courts have been reluctant to curtail police discretion and profiling. Still, five states have passed "DWB" (driving while black) laws, and 24 others are considering such laws to limit the use of racial profiling by police.[22]

September 11, 2001, saw the attacks on the World Trade Center Buildings in New York City and the Pentagon. Most of the hijackers were Arab. The hysteria that followed focused on a new victim of profiling, the Arab American. As might be expected, this ethnic profiling was widely accepted by the white population. In a new irony, however, the victims of previous racial profiling joined in to support the new racial profiling. Some African Americans remembered that Arab American taxi drivers often passed them by just because they were black. One black professional woman remembered how "Arab taxi drivers have passed me by too many times for me to feel much sympathy for them. Let them find out how it feels to be profiled."[23] A Gallup poll conducted in Boston found that 71 percent of the black respondents favored special and more intense security checks for Arabs, including those who are U.S. citizens. Fifty-seven percent of whites favored such a policy.[24] This issue is a key test of how many civil liberties Americans are willing to give up in the name of security. As noted in Chapter 8, nearly three-fourths of terrorist acts that occur in the United States are committed by "home grown" terrorists, so the wisdom of profiling Arab Americans is further questioned. Focusing on Arabs will lead police to miss some very dangerous people.

Profiling is a difficult issue, particularly in a country like America. When President George W. Bush was pressured to do something about the problem, his spokesperson, Ari Fleisher, commented, "It's not as if there's one federal police force, that the president can wave a magic wand and make a very very difficult problem go away. It involves a lot of local jurisdictions that the United States government does not have direct control over. If it could be so easily done, I suggest that it would have been done a long time ago."[25] Profiling has some appeal because it appears to be a scientific way to spot offenders—a tool for improving efficiency. Although very popular, the success of profiling has been very limited, and there are serious questions about whether the continued use of profiling can be justified. The efficiency it claims has not been proven, and it has shaken many citizens' beliefs in the fairness of the system.

Wrongful Convictions

The American system of justice, with its emphasis on process and providing legal rights to the accused, can be incredibly slow. Trials can drag on for months, lawyers argue for hours about the smallest of details, and appeals may take years before the case is finally resolved—all in the name of making sure that justice is done. For the public, the emphasis on process can be frustrating. Some question why people who are obviously guilty should be provided a lawyer, why the convicted should be allowed an appeal, and why the entire process cannot move more quickly. They argue, "Justice delayed is justice denied." In addition, the large number of cases they face each year put pressure on police and prosecutors to quickly arrest and convict, and the pressure is particularly acute in high profile cases. Public defenders also face heavy caseloads and are under pressure to resolve cases as quickly as possible. Thus, actors in the system face the competing pressures of resolving cases quickly while following procedural safeguards.

Legal rights and procedural safeguards exist to make certain that innocent people are not convicted, and overall, it probably works quite well. There are exceptions, however—times when innocent people are sent to prison, or even executed. How often does this happen, and how is it possible?

How often does it happen? No one knows with any certainty. On the one hand, there are almost daily accounts of individuals who have been convicted and later exonerated, suggesting the actual number of cases may be quite large. On the other hand, the American criminal justice system handles millions of cases each year, and the percentage of cases in which someone is wrongfully convicted is probably quite small. One study conservatively estimated that wrongful convictions occur in only about one half of one percent of all criminal cases (0.5%), but given the large number of cases handled each year, this tiny percentage translates into about 10,000 wrongful convictions per year.[26] Whatever the actual numbers, the steady stream of revelations about wrongful convictions shakes public confidence in a system in which extensive due process and a strong presumption of innocence are intended to prevent such errors.

The case of Illinois shows the impact that wrongful convictions can have on confidence in the criminal justice system. Republican Governor George Ryan, who personally supported the death penalty, first declared a moratorium on the death penalty and later commuted the sentences of all death row inmates in Illinois after 13 individuals on death row had been released because of new evidence of their innocence.[27] Death penalty cases undoubtedly represent only a tiny portion of wrongful convictions, but such cases stand out because of the brutality of the original crime and the harshness of the sentence. Such cases also represent the extreme in the conflict between due process and speedy justice. In death penalty cases, police and prosecutors are often under extreme pressure to solve the case, but we expect the full range of procedural safeguards to be in place for death penalty cases. Even with such safeguards, between 1973 and 2001, 107 death row inmates were exonerated.[28]

How does it happen? There are a number of ways in which people who are innocent might be found guilty, but a few of the more common reasons include witnesses are mistaken, witnesses lie, police coerce suspects to falsely confess, laboratory technicians falsify reports, and prosecutors conceal evidence of innocence from the defense. Underlying all these reasons is a failure of the system and an eagerness to bypass procedure to achieve justice as quickly and as easily as possible. As Huff, Rattner, and Sagarin observed,

> If we had to isolate a single, "system dynamic" that pervades large numbers of these cases [of wrongful conviction], we would probably describe it as police and prosecutorial overzealousness: the anxiety to solve a case; the ease with which one having such anxiety is willing to believe, on the slightest evidence of the most negligible nature, that the culprit is in hand; the willingness to use improper, unethical, and illegal means to obtain a conviction when one believes that the person at the bar is guilty.[29]

As Westervelt and Humphrey persuasively argue, however, wrongful convictions are seldom the result of just one error. More commonly, mistakes at one stage ripple through the rest of the process:

For example, a poorly managed police lineup can lead to a mistaken eyewitness identification, which in turn can be used by police to pressure an innocent suspect into a confession. A prosecutor, relying heavily on the eyewitness and the confession, may choose to ignore or overlook evidence of the suspect's innocence and, believing that he or she has the correct person in custody, may choose to withhold that potentially exculpatory evidence from the defense. A jury, then, will hear only the flawed and incriminating evidence, not the potentially exculpatory evidence, and will most likely return a guilty verdict.[30]

A compounding of errors is even more likely when the defendant is represented by inadequate counsel, such as death penalty cases in which lawyers sleep through significant parts of the trial, are obviously intoxicated in court, or in which lawyers never bother to interview witnesses or examine evidence.[31] Shockingly, the courts have generally held that such behaviors are not the basis for challenging a conviction.

The most common reason why an innocent person is convicted is *eyewitness error*, which probably accounts for slightly more than half of all wrongful convictions.[32] Although the general public has a tendency to believe that eyewitness testimony is the best kind, eyewitnesses are notoriously unreliable. Witnesses can rather easily be persuaded to wrongfully identify a suspect and to genuinely believe this false identification. Anyone who has played any one of many popular memory games knows how easily details can be forgotten, witnesses often have only a brief look at the offender, and the trauma that accompanies a crime may further cloud a witness's memory. Consider the following example:

> After serving more than 25 years in prison for the rape and murder of a 9-year-old girl, two Chicago men were released in January of 2003 after DNA evidence cleared them of the crime. They were convicted primarily based on the eyewitness testimony of a woman who swore she saw the girl being attacked just after 6:30 P.M. The girl's mother had said the girl left home at 8:00 P.M., but changed her testimony to say the girl left home at 6:30 P.M. She later said she changed her testimony to be consistent with the witness. The witness now says she never pointed detectives to the two men, who were teenagers at the time. Rather, she says police kept insisting the two teens were the offenders and she finally relented and agreed they must have been the boys she saw.[33]

Experts often point to suggestive police interviews as a source of witness error.[34] In other cases, police act properly but witnesses simply mis-remember. Whenever a false identification is made, the image of the falsely accused becomes reinforced in the mind of the witness, so that as time passes, witnesses become more and more confident in their (false) identification.

Another situation in which witnesses provide false information involves informants who provide information to the police in exchange for their testimony. Jailhouse informants, for example, are individuals who share a cell or otherwise have contact with the defendant while in jail and then testify that the defendants admitted their guilt to the informants. The use of informants has been harshly criticized because they are nearly always people of questionable moral character who have everything to gain and nothing to lose by providing false information.[35] "Of the 13 Illinois death row inmates found to be wrongfully convicted and released from custody . . . five, or nearly 40 percent, were prosecuted using testimony of jailhouse informants."[36] Others estimate that as many as 21 percent of wrongful convictions are the result of lying informants.[37]

Official misconduct also plays a role in many cases of wrongful conviction, sometimes subtly, but sometimes blatantly, as when police or prosecutors hide evidence of an offender's innocence. For example,

- A police laboratory technician in Oklahoma City is accused of giving testimony falsely implicating defendants in a number of cases. In one case, the defendant was executed before the misconduct was discovered, and in another, a man served 15 years of a 45-year sentence before being freed.[38]
- In March 2003, the Justice Department revealed that as many as 3,000 cases were being reviewed because the convictions may have been based on false testimony by technicians in an FBI laboratory.[39]
- Four county sheriff's deputies and three prosecutors in suburban Chicago were charged with conspiracy, perjury, and obstruction of justice in the wrongful capital convictions of two men, Rolando Cruz and Alejandro Hernandez.[40]

Finally, a surprising number of wrongful convictions occur because the individual *falsely confesses* to the crime. Sometimes police pressure people to confess through long and grueling interrogations or even brutality.[41] Children, those with mental health problems, and those with low IQs are particularly susceptible to such pressure. On other occasions, innocent people confess because they are facing long prison sentences and don't want to risk going to court and losing. In Los Angeles, more than 70 cases were overturned after police admitted planting evidence and lying in court. Of these more than 70 cases, the accused had entered guilty pleas in 55 cases.[42]

There are even cases in which a suspect is coerced into confessing to a crime that never occurred. In Texas, for example, a man confessed to killing his ex-girlfriend, who later turned up alive in Arizona. In Arizona, a woman confessed to killing her three-month-old infant by letting another woman inject heroin and cocaine into the child. The child had died, but toxicology tests showed there were no drugs in the infant's system and that the cause of death was more likely pneumonia.[43] In Alabama, a mentally retarded woman was charged in the murder of her sister's baby, although no body was ever found and no one ever reported having actually seen a child. She had her sentence reduced (but not overturned!!) when it was discovered that her sister had been sterilized several years earlier and could not have become pregnant.[44]

Further, after a confession has been made, it is difficult for others to believe a recantation, or even to believe other evidence supporting innocence. In Illinois, a man confessed to a grisly double murder. When he recanted and provided proof that he could not have committed the crime because he was in jail at the time of the offense, prosecutors proceeded with the case and persuaded a jury to convict.[45]

Just as disturbing as wrongful convictions is the official response when the error is discovered. Some prosecutors have worked hard to correct their errors, but a disturbingly large number work hard to keep the wrongfully convicted in prison, or worse. In Missouri, for example, prosecutors argued before the state Supreme Court that new evidence proving the innocence of a convicted death row inmate should not stop the execution[46] because proper procedures had been followed leading to the conviction.

Taken together, the many examples of wrongful conviction rather dramatically demonstrate the dilemma of balancing expedient justice with a respect for due process. Too much attention to due process can bog the system down and make it almost impossible to convict the guilty. At the same time, too much emphasis on the quick and efficient resolution of cases can make it much too easy to convict the innocent.

Honest errors can occur in any system of justice, but the likelihood of error is also shaped by the structure of the justice system. Part of the problem of wrongful convictions is the adversarial process that characterizes the American system of justice.[47] In an adversarial system, the emphasis for both prosecutors and defense attorneys is on victory, not on truth seeking. Prosecutors are rewarded for winning convictions, not for pursuing the truth.

CONCLUSION

The American system of justice draws heavily on the adversarial process characteristic of common law systems. One characteristic of such systems is a tension between expediently handling cases and affording the accused the full range of due process procedures. Because the tension between expediency and due process are built into the system, this tension can never be resolved. Over time, the American system of criminal justice moves between an emphasis on expediency and an emphasis on due process, never completely showing allegiance to either. For example, many Americans bristled at the sacrifice of due process that resulted from racial profiling, but those same Americans were quick to embrace racial profiling after the September 11, 2001, attacks. Should fears of future terrorist attacks decline while abuses of profiling accumulate, public sentiment will likely again drift away from expediency and in favor of due process restrictions on racial profiling.

Similarly, after a long period of restricting the rights of defendants and limiting appeals for those sentenced to death, the problem of wrongful convictions has led many to rethink the emphasis on expediency and move toward granting more due process rights. At some point, with enough examples of how due process has been abused, the pendulum will undoubtedly swing again in the direction of expediency.

In the end, justice comes neither from expediency nor due process alone, but from a careful balancing of the two. The numerous checks and balances on police, prosecutors, and judges are the mechanisms by which the system is fine-tuned. The swing from one to the other over time represents an effort to reach that balance. Thus, the effort to create a just system of justice in America will never lead to a finished product, but will always be a work in progress.

Discussion Questions

1. What are the advantages and disadvantages for justice of having citizens play a large role in regulating the justice system—such as by serving on juries, electing judges, and electing prosecutors?
2. What kinds of obstacles keep the American justice system from being too efficient?
3. Is using race to profile offenders always wrong? Are there any circumstances under which race-based profiling might be justified? Is there any way to stop police from using race as a factor when they decide which cars to stop on the highway?
4. What might be done to reduce the chances of a wrongful conviction while still providing swift justice?

Endnotes

1. See, for example, William Nelson, *The Americanization of the Common Law: The Impact of Legal Change on Massachusetts Society, 1760–1830* (Cambridge, Mass.: Harvard University Press, 1975); and Charles Cook, *The American Codification Movement: A Study of Ante-Bellum Legal Reform* (Westport, Conn.: Greenwood Press, 1981).
2. The number of introductory textbooks is considerable. We have listed just a few here: Jay S. Albanese, *Criminal Justice* (Boston: Allyn & Bacon, 2000); George F. Cole, *The American System of Criminal Justice* (Belmont, Calif.: Wadsworth, 1995); Larry K. Gaines, Michael Kaune, and Roger Leroy Miller, *Criminal Justice in Action* (Belmont, Calif.: Wadsworth, 2000).
3. David A. Harris, *Profiles in Injustice: Why Racial Profiling Cannot Work* (New York: New Press, 2002), pp. 17–18.
4. See as examples John Douglas and Mark Olshaker, *Mindhunter, Inside the FBI's Elite Serial Crime Unit* (New York: Scribner, 1995); and Robert Ressler, Ann W. Burgess, and John Douglas, *Sexual Homicide, Patterns and Motives* (Lexington, Mass.: Lexington Books, 1988).
5. Carlton Smith and Thomas Guillen, *The Search for the Green River Killer* (New York: Onyx, 1991).
6. Harris, pp. 19–21.
7. "Report: Customs Targeted Black Women Unevenly," *USA Today,* 10 April 2000.

8. Harris, pp. 21–23.

9. Ibid. p. 63.

10. Ibid. p. 79.

11. "Why Some Get Busted—And Some Go Free," *New York Times,* 10 May 1999.

12. American Civil Liberties Union, *Report: Police Practices, Illinois,* 17 January 2000.

13. "ACLU: Racial Profiling Threatens Justice System," *USA Today,* 2 June 1999.

14. "Police Sensitive About Being Profiled," *Chicago Tribune,* 28 March 2001.

15. Harris, p. 80.

16. "LAPD Offers 1st Data on Traffic Stops," *Los Angeles Times,* 7 January 2003.

17. Gary Webb, "DWB," *Esquire* 131(4), April 1999.

18. James Q. Wilson and George L. Kelling, "Broken Windows: The Police and Neighborhood Safety," *Atlantic Monthly* 249(3), March 1982.

19. "Why Some Get Busted—And Some Go Free."

20. "ACLU to Bring Suit," *Chicago Tribune,* 25 March 2003.

21. Harris, p. 82.

22. "Courts Balk at Limiting Racial Profiling," *Christian Science Monitor,* 6 July 2001.

23. "My, Oh, My, Look Who's Profiling Now," *Chicago Tribune,* 3 October 2001.

24. Ibid.

25. "President: Profiling Will Be Under Review," *Chicago Tribune,* 10 February 2001.

26. Ronald C. Huff, Arye Rattner, and Edward Sagarin, "Guilty Until Proved Innocent: Wrongful Conviction and Public Policy," *Crime and Delinquency* 32, 1996, pp. 518–544.

27. "Ryan: 'Until I Can Be Sure,'" *Chicago Tribune,* 1 February 2000.

28. "Innocence and the Death Penalty," Death Penalty Information Center, 2003 (accessed online at www.deathpenaltyinfo.org on 25 March 2003).

29. Ronald C. Huff, Arye Rattner, and Edward Sagarin, *Convicted But Innocent: Wrongful Conviction and Public Policy* (Thousand Oaks, Calif.: Sage, 1996), p. 65.

30. Sandra D. Westervelt and John A. Humphrey (eds.), *Wrongly Convicted: Perspectives on Failed Justice* (New Brunswick, N.J.: Rutgers University Press, 2001), p. 10.

31. Adele Bernhard, "Effective Assistance Counsel," pp. 220–240 in ibid. See Barry Scheck, Peter Neufeld, and Jim Dwyer, *Actual Innocence* (New York: Doubleday, 2000); Steve Mills, "Texas Case Highlights Defense Gap," *Chicago Tribune,* 19 June 2000; Henry Weinstein, "Judge Refuses to Intervene in Texas 'Sleeping Lawyer' Case," *Los Angeles Times,* 29 October 2002;

32. Ronald Huff, Arye Rattner, and Edward Sagarin, "Guilty Until Proven Innocent," pp. 518–544; Rob Warden, "How Mistaken and Perjured Eyewitness Identification Testimony Put 46 Innocent Americans on Death Row," Center on Wrongful Convictions (accessed online at www.law.northwestern.edu/depts/clinic/wrongful on 20 March 2003); and Scheck, Neufeld, and Dwyer.

33. "When Jail Is No Alibi in Murders," *Chicago Tribune,* 19 December 2001.

34. George Castelle and Elizabeth F. Loftus, "Misinformation and Wrongful Convictions," pp. 17–35 in Saundra D. Westervelt and John A. Humphrey (eds.), *Wrongly Convicted: Perspectives on Failed Justice* (New Brunswick, N.J.: Rutgers University Press, 2001).

35. Clifford S. Zimmerman, "Back from the Courthouse: Corrective Measures to Address the Role of Informants in Wrongful Convictions," pp. 199–219 in Saundra D. Westervelt and John A. Humphrey (eds.), *Wrongly Convicted: Perspectives on Failed Justice* (New Brunswick, N.J.: Rutgers University Press, 2001).

36. "Ryan: 'Until I Can Be Sure.'"

37. See Scheck, Neufeld, and Dwyer.

38. "Prosecutors See Limits to Doubt in Capital Cases," *New York Times*, 24 February 2003.

39. "3000 Verdicts Involving FBI Lab Reviewed," *Los Angeles Times,* 17 March 2003.

40. "Trouble for Officials in Cruz Case," *Chicago Tribune*, 10 December 1996.

41. "Cops and Confessions: Coercive and Illegal Tactics Torpedo Scores of Cook County Murder Cases," *Chicago Tribune*, 16 December 2001; Richard A. Leo and Richard J. Ofshe, "The Consequences of False Confessions," *Journal of Criminal Law and Criminology* 88(2) 1998, pp. 429–496.

42. David Harris, "Driving While Black: Racial Profiling on Our Nation's Highways," *ACLU Report*, 2003 (accessed online at http://archive.aclu.org/profiling/report/index.html on 23 October 2000).

43. Leo and Ofshe.

44. "Woman Freed Amid Doubt 'Victim' Existed," *New York Times,* 18 July 2002.

45. "When Jail Is No Alibi in Murders."

46. "Prosecutors See Limits to Doubt in Capital Cases."

47. Daniel Givelber, "The Adversary System and Historical Accuracy: Can We Do Better?," pp. 253–268 in Westervelt and Humphrey.

CONTEMPORARY ISSUES

I njustice has been a constant throughout human history. In all places and at all times, it is possible to find individuals or groups who have been wronged, and it is possible to find individuals who have committed themselves to correcting injustices. Thus far, we have considered some key perspectives on justice and some formal legal systems established to promote justice. This section of the book will focus on a few contemporary issues related to justice.

It is not possible in a single book, or even in a library of books, to comprehensively address all of the forms that contemporary issues of justice might take. The discussion that follows considers four issues that concern justice and that are of global concern. The issues were also selected to represent a wide range of topics. Chapter 8, "Domestic Terrorism," focuses primarily on hate groups and anti-government groups in the United States, but the issue has far broader implications. Such groups are a problem in Europe, Canada, and nearly every developed nation. When such groups engage in violence, they believe that they are correcting injustices in society. Responding to these groups in a way that itself promotes justice is challenging.

Chapter 9, "Contemporary Slavery," debunks the myth that slavery is a thing of the past. Slavery is more widespread today than at any time in history. Although the number of slaves in the world has increased dramatically, the form in which slavery appears is very different today. The problem is compounded by rapid population growth, abject poverty, and a global economy that demands ever-cheaper labor. In many ways, contemporary slavery is more brutal and more insidious than slavery of the past—and more difficult to control.

Chapter 10 examines the issue of genocide. Like slavery, genocide appears more common than at any time in history. Advances in communications systems and in the technology of killing have made modern genocide substantially more efficient than genocides of the past. The promise of "Never Again," made by those who remember the Nazi Holocaust rings hollow in many parts of the world. The chapter considers the factors that lead to genocide and ways that nations may intervene to stop the killing.

Finally, Chapter 11, "The Environment," considers the link between the environment and justice. The poor, many of whom are minorities, generate less than their share of toxic wastes; yet, they often live in the communities most polluted by industrial waste and in which toxic waste is stored. Although there are many dimensions of the environment that could be considered in a discussion of the environment and justice, much of the chapter focuses on the availability and use of water. Some consider access to drinkable water a basic human right, but as the world's population grows, so does the number of people for whom clean water is not available.

The chapters in this section illustrate a wide range of issues concerning justice, and the complexity of responding to those issues to correct injustices. One purpose is to have readers begin to think of justice in broad terms and as an issue that touches on nearly every aspect of their lives.

DOMESTIC TERRORISM

When Americans think of terrorism, they probably first think of foreigners entering the country to set off bombs or to engage in other acts of mass destruction. In reality, most terrorist acts that occur in the United States are committed by Americans, many of whom would define themselves as patriotic. According to the Federal Bureau of Investigation (FBI), between 1980 and 2000, there were 335 incidents of terrorism in the United States, and of these, 247 (74%) were believed to have been committed by domestic terrorists, not by foreigners.[1] As Jenkins has observed, "Americans have never needed instruction from abroad in launching the organized mayhem we call terrorism."[2] What is domestic terrorism? According to the FBI,

> The FBI views domestic terrorism as the unlawful use, or threatened use, of force or violence by a group or individual based and operating entirely within the United States, Puerto Rico, or other U.S. territories without foreign direction committed against persons or property to intimidate or coerce a government, the civilian population, or any segment thereof in furtherance of political or social objectives.[3]

Domestic terrorism presents a particularly interesting issue in the study of justice. Many who engage in domestic terrorism believe they are pursuing justice and are answering to a higher call.[4] A democratic society is presented with the challenge of allowing free speech and free association while identifying dangerous groups within its borders and preventing major acts of violence by them—and doing so in a manner that is itself just.

TYPES OF DOMESTIC TERRORISM

We can categorize domestic terrorism in many ways. This discussion will focus on three types: anti-government, religion-based, and race-based. As is true of any such categorization, there is much overlap among these categories. For example, some groups may have equal contempt for Jews, blacks, and the federal government. The historical roots of the three categories are presented here separately to simplify the discussion. Examples of each in U.S. history will be presented, and then the focus will shift to their role in contemporary domestic terrorism, where more attention will be focused on how these categories overlap.

Anti-Government Terrorism

Anti-government sentiments and anti-government violence run through much of U.S. history. Before 1760, that is, before the revolutionary war, there were between 75 and 100 riots in America, with as many as 40 of them being efforts to overthrow regional governments.[5] The revolutionary war itself was a fight against a strong centralized British government. The nation that emerged was designed to have a weak federal government, keeping most power in the hands of state and local governments. Even this decentralized form of government was not enough for many early Americans. Between 1750 and 1850, there were at least 20 uprisings by colonists who "emptied jails, burned public buildings, closed court systems, and organized their own government institutions."[6] In 1786, almost 9,000 took part in an uprising, known as Shays's rebellion, against government-approved lending practices. This rebellion eventually became an effort to overthrow the government of Massachusetts.[7] Other rebellions occurred throughout the rest of the 1700s and through the 1800s, often arising in rural areas and spreading across the country.

Anti-government violence continued through the early 1900s. In 1920, anarchists set off a series of bombs in eight U.S. cities, including one at the doorstep of U.S. Attorney General A. Mitchell Palmer. An additional 34 package bombs addressed to prominent Americans were discovered by an alert New York postal clerk.[8] Jenkins vividly describes one anti-government group, called the Christian Front, whose plot was uncovered in 1940:

> The FBI smashes a dead-serious plot to overthrow the federal government and reveals that for more than a year the right-wing militias involved were undergoing army-style training, fired up by inflammatory talk radio. They planned to use their bombs, rifles, and machine guns to wage guerrilla warfare on American cities, and they claimed friends and allies in government and the military. They aimed, in one reporter's words, to "bomb selected buildings, seize public utilities, blast bridges, terrorize Jews, appropriate Federal Reserve gold, assassinate fourteen Congressmen, and set up a dictatorship." The goal: to remove all liberal and anti-Christian forces from government, not the least the liberal President and his activist wife.[9]

In the late 1960s and early 1970s, a left-wing radical group, the Weather Underground advocated the violent overthrow of the government and was engaged in both militant protests and scattered incidents of bombing, including a bomb that exploded in the U.S. Capitol building.[10] In the 1980s, a right-wing group, known as The Order, underwent military-style training and engaged in armored truck robberies and counterfeiting in the hopes of raising money to stage a violent revolution.[11]

Perhaps the best example of how anti-government sentiments have run through U.S. history is the case of Timothy McVeigh. On April 19, 1995, a fertilizer bomb exploded outside of the Alfred P. Murrah Federal Building in Oklahoma City, destroying much of the building, killing 168 and wounding countless others. When he was arrested for his role in the bombing, McVeigh was wearing a t-shirt with a quote from Thomas Jefferson, who thought that to preserve democracy it might be necessary to have a violent revolution every 20 years. The quote, which was Jefferson's response to Shays's rebellion, read, "The tree of liberty must be refreshed from time to time with the blood of patriots and tyrants."[12]

Religion-Based Domestic Terrorism

From the time of the earliest settlers, America has had a history of religion-based hatred. The earliest hatreds targeted Catholics, later Mormons, and still later Jews. Coates makes the following comment about the Catholic religion in early America:

> Throughout colonial times Catholics were a tiny minority in the Americas . . . And their fellow colonists wanted to keep it that way. In 1704 the Maryland legislature enacted an "Act to Prevent the Growth of Popery," which imposed a heavy fine for attending Catholic religious services. In 1750 Harvard College offered lectures "for detecting and convicting and exposing of the idolatry of the Romish church, their tyranny, usurpations, damnable heresies, fatal errors, abominable superstitions and other crying wickedness in her high places." After the American Revolution, New Jersey incorporated in its state constitution a clause stipulating that Catholics might not hold state offices. Similar measures were included in the constitutions of North Carolina and Georgia in 1776. The 1777 Vermont constitution required all holders of state offices to swear they were Protestants.[13]

Public schools taught children about the evils of Catholicism and "Pope Night" festivals were held in which Catholics were depicted as in league with the Devil. A popular game at these festivals was "Break the Pope's Kneck."[14]

In the early 1800s, anti-Catholic rallies were held and rumors were spread that guns were hidden under the altars of Catholic churches, to be used against Protestants. A series of popular novels described the secrets of life in a convent, which included the rape of young girls by priests, torture, starvation, and sexual sadism. The children born of these illicit affairs were said to have been killed and their bones bleached and collected in piles.[15] Nuns and priests were attacked, and in 1834, a mob burned the largest convent in Boston to the ground. For several decades, Catholic churches were vandalized, burned, and bombed. Some Protestant ministers saw the immigration of Catholics as a sign that Armageddon was near and gave sermons linking the pope to the devil.[16]

The inventor of the telegraph, Samuel F. Morse, published editorial letters in a New York newspaper warning about the pope's conspiracy to take over the United States, using immigrant Catholics as foot soldiers.[17] "When the pope sent a block of Leonardo da Vinci's marble as a Vatican contribution to the Washington Monument, a nativist mob stole it from a shed and tossed it into the nearby Potomac River."[18]

A political party, the Know-Nothings, had a platform that was explicitly anti-immigrant, including a provision that no Catholic could hold any public office. At the height of their influence, "the Know-Nothings sent seventy-five members to Washington to serve in Congress and controlled several state legislatures,"[19] including the entire state government of Massachusetts. Through their political arm, the American Party, the Know-Nothings nominated former president Millard Fillmore as their presidential candidate in the 1856 election. Although he lost the election, coming in a distant third, he did receive 22 percent of the popular vote.[20]

By the early 1900s, large numbers of Jews were immigrating from Europe and were quickly added to the list of hated groups. During the 1920s, Henry Ford used the newspaper he owned in Detroit to print a series of essays, "The Protocols of the Elders of Zion," The series itself was a modified version of a Russian manuscript, and though some believed Ford himself may have written it,[21] it was more likely the work of the newspaper's editor William J. Cameron.[22] These essays were then compiled in the book *The International Jew*, which claimed to describe a secret plan by Jewish leaders to take over America by manipulating the banking system and the media. Ford published additional copies to be distributed at each Ford dealership.[23]

Race-Based Domestic Terrorism

The third dimension of domestic terrorism that has run through the history of the United States is that based on race. The discussion here separates race-based domestic terrorism from the other two categories. That distinction is artificial but useful for organizing the discussion. Many of the groups that engaged in acts against religious groups also engaged in acts against racial minorities.

From the very beginning, colonial settlers made numerous attempts to wipe out Native Americans, killing them, offering to pay one tribe to wipe out another—and then killing the first rather than paying—and even giving Indians blankets infested with smallpox.[24] Native Americans also had their share of extremists committed to wiping out the foreigners who came to their land uninvited, and the violence of these extremists often matched that by the early settlers.[25] These attempts at mutual destruction continued until Native American tribes were either wiped out or segregated and brought under control on reservations. Both Native Americans and colonists were slaughtered, but over the long term, the advantage fell to the colonists whose casualties were quickly replaced by new waves of immigrants. In the end, violent colonists simply out-numbered violent Native Americans.

From the arrival of the first slaves, there were instances of behavior that clearly fit the definition of domestic terrorism. Domestic terrorist acts against blacks took a more organized form with the formation of the Ku Klux Klan in 1865 by a group of confederate soldiers in Pulaski, Tennessee. In 1867, Confederate General Nathan Bedford Forrest took charge of the Klan and gave it the organization it had lacked. The Klan arose to defend the Southern lifestyle opposed by the North—including clear ideas about the role of blacks in society. During its brief early history, the Klan acted as a vigilante force, intimidating blacks to keep them from voting, engaging in cross burnings, and conducting lynchings. Although Forrest attempted to control local units and coordinate their activities, his efforts failed, and the Ku Klux Klan became increasingly violent. Forrest officially disbanded the organization in 1869, but many of its activities did not end until 1871 when President Ulysses S. Grant ordered troops to help control Klan violence in South Carolina, resulting in the arrest of many Klan activists.[26] The sentiments that gave rise to the Klan did not disappear when the organization was disbanded, and some 30 years later, the Klan re-emerged.

The rebirth of the Klan in the early 1900s has been linked to two men. The first was Thomas Dixon, Jr., who had dabbled in southern politics, having been elected to the North Carolina legislature while he was still too young to vote. He eventually left politics and became a Baptist minister, and then a public speaker. In 1902, he wrote *The Leopard's Spots*, a book about efforts to protect North Carolina from a movement to free blacks and grant them equality. That was followed in 1905 by his most famous work, *The Clansman, an Historic Romance of the Ku Klux Klan*. The book, romanticizing the activities of the Ku Klux Klan and depicting blacks as little better than savages, was a hit and was eventually turned into a stage production, with Dixon himself playing a key character. More important, a young film director, D. W. Griffith, embellished on the basic story in the book to create the first full-length motion picture, an epic called *The Birth of a Nation*. The film was a lavish production, scored by a 30-piece orchestra and including panoramic battle scenes.[27]

It would be difficult to overstate the impact of *The Birth of a Nation*. As Coates observed,

> In 1915, when a nickel bought dinner, a penny bought a daily newspaper and two cents covered a passable breakfast, *The Birth of a Nation* premiered in theaters that charged two dollars for a ticket. It grossed $18 million and was seen by an estimated 50 million people.[28]

President Woodrow Wilson was said to have been touched by the film. The Chief Justice of the U.S. Supreme Court, Edward White, also gave his stamp of approval after making it known that he had at one time been a loyal Klansman himself.[29]

Two weeks before the film opened, William Simmons held a rally in Atlanta to celebrate the revival of the Klan, even burning a cross within sight of the theater. The film gave a great boost to Simmons' efforts, and Klan membership grew rapidly in both Georgia and Alabama. Then, in 1920, Simmons hired two publicists to take the organization national.[30] These publicists suggested that to make the Klan appealing to a wider audience, it should expand the list of groups it hated to include Catholics and Jews. Both Catholics and Jews were immigrating to the U.S. in large numbers and including them would make the Klan appealing to Know-Nothings and other groups opposed to "aliens" of all sorts.

By the 1920s, the Klan had as many as 4 million members—electing governors in Oklahoma and Oregon, and dominating Indiana politics.[31] The organization made an effort to reach out to fundamentalist ministers, with as many as 40,000 joining the ranks of the Klan, many of them serving as local leaders.[32] Klan members in full regalia would recruit members during church services, after which they would contribute to the church.

The success of the Klan in the mid 1920s also gave it visibility that led to news coverage of the violence supported by the Klan. Major groups began publicly denouncing the Klan. The position of the Klan further deteriorated when one of the most powerful Klan leaders in the nation, David Curtis Stephenson, was convicted for murdering a young white girl. By the end of the 1920s, membership had dropped to as low as 40,000.[33] In 1944, a substantially weakened Klan was dealt another blow when "its charter was revoked, the Internal Revenue Service placed a $685,000 tax lien on its assets, and the organization disbanded."[34]

From the late 1940s through the 1950s, the Klan was engaged in periodic acts of violence, but seemed to have a new energy in the 1960s, perhaps as a reaction to civil rights efforts. During the 1960s, black churches were bombed and civil rights workers killed.[35] In 1966, a Congressional investigation led to the convictions of the leaders of seven major Klan organizations and a report detailing the use of legitimate groups as fronts for Klan activity. Membership again declined, to as few as 5,000 by 1973, perhaps because of an FBI program targeting Klan organizations.[36]

From its low point in 1973, Klan membership gradually increased, and such leaders as David Duke began bringing young people into the Klan by recruiting on college campuses. Duke also welcomed women into the organization as equal members, and he welcomed Catholics.[37] By the 1980s, membership was again on the decline and the organization faced lawsuits that threatened its existence.

The Ku Klux Klan remains one of the more visible examples of a group engaged in domestic violence with a focus on race. Although membership in the Klan has waxed and waned throughout the organization's history, it has shown a remarkable resilience and is likely to be a force to be reckoned with for some time.

This discussion has included only a sampling of the more prominent cases, but the examples show that domestic terrorism has a long history in the United

States. Indeed, it would be difficult to find any period in U.S. history when one or more of these three categories of domestic terrorism was not an issue. Our attention now turns to describing the contemporary face of domestic terrorism.

CHRISTIAN IDENTITY AS A UNIFYING THEME

Among domestic terrorist groups, there has always been some overlap in the targets of their hatred. Even though there continue to be groups whose main focus is on the government, religion, or race, some believe that contemporary hate groups are more likely than those in the past to cooperate with other groups whose particular target for hate is unlike their own. The precise reasons for this are unclear, but one factor that may help unify these groups is an ideology known as Christian Identity. The Christian Identity movement has spawned Identity churches, but the power of the ideology is in its internal logic, which blends anti-government sentiments with racism and religion-based hatred. Many of the ideas central to Christian Identity are familiar and comfortable to people representing a wide variety of hate groups. Further, even if individuals do not buy into the entire package of Christian Identity ideas, elements of Christian Identity can be found in the beliefs of many of the most prominent domestic terrorists groups. And, as Coates observed,

> Because it is a religion with all the traditional trappings, preached by Bible-quoting pastors from pulpits in churches very much like those most Americans grow up in, Identity allows its born-again men and women to practice with suddenly clear consciences the bigotry, hatred and even criminal violence that they had been taught from childhood were sinful.[38]

The Christian Identity movement has been traced to a belief system known as British Israelism. British Israelism began in the 1600s and was characterized by the belief that the British were descendants of the ten lost tribes of Israel. In its original form, British Israelism was neither anti-Semitic nor racist. When British Israelism moved to the United States in the 1930s, it began to take on its current form, which includes both extreme racism and extreme anti-Semitism.[39]

Christian Identity is fundamentalist in that followers believe the Bible is literally true and that their beliefs have a Biblical basis. Thus, to challenge their beliefs is to challenge God, making it difficult to persuade them they are wrong. They focus particular attention on the first and last books of the Bible, Genesis and Revelation. Genesis explains how things came to be as they are today, and Revelation shows what lies ahead.

Their interpretation of the Bible sets Identity members apart from other fundamentalists. According to Christian Identity, our current "problems" began with the creation. God created Adam and Eve in his image, and they had two sons, Cain and Abel. Abel was the fruit of a union between Adam and Eve and thus was created by God. All direct descendants of Abel are descendants of God's creation. Cain, on the other hand, was the product of a union between Eve and the devil, in the form of the serpent in the Garden of Eden. Consequently, Cain and his descendants are the products of the devil. Much of the world's history has been a battle between the "good" descendants of Abel and the "evil" descendants of Cain. The descendants of Abel eventually came to populate northern Europe, and the descendants of Cain are the people we today know as Jews. When Identity members complain about the Jewish media, the Jewish control of banks, or the influence of Jews in politics, they are expressing a deep concern about the devil taking control of major social institutions.

This interpretation of the Bible explains their hatred for Jews, but what about people of color? For followers of Christian Identity, people of color are not really people but are little more than animals. Some claim that people of color, who they refer to as "mud people," represent a first (and failed) attempt by God to create man. Because people of color are not really human, race mixing between "good" whites and people of color is akin to mixing species. Similarly, because Jews are the embodiment of evil, intermingling of Jews with "good" white Christians is also an abomination.

Identity followers also look to the book of Revelation for a view of things to come. Their interpretation of Revelation leads them to believe the end will come through a great race war or through a war produced by economic collapse. The true children of God will survive and ascend into heaven, if they are prepared to fight the forces of evil to the death—hence, the appeal of Identity to some survivalists.

Drawing from the thinking of British Israelism, Identity followers believe that America's founding fathers were part of the true lost tribe of Israel, and God guided them to this country. Consequently, Identity followers believe the Declaration of Independence and the Bill of Rights are sacred documents, written under the direction of God. Amendments to the Constitution added after the first ten are the product of a government that had already been infiltrated by agents of the devil. Their term for this corrupted government is Zionist Occupied Government (ZOG). As proof that the government has been corrupted, they point to the number of Jews in policy-making positions in government, from the legislature to the president's cabinet. They also point to such things as legalizing abortion. They believe that abortion is an attempt to breed the white race out of existence, arguing that Christian white women most often practice it while people of color continue to proliferate. Identity's belief that Jews have taken over major institutions, including banks, is also palatable to conservatives living in the farm belt, who believe that the lending practices of banks are designed to destroy the small farmer.[40]

Identity churches compose only a small portion of the hate groups in America. A report by the Southern Poverty Law Center suggests that of the 676 hate groups in 2001, only 31 were specifically identified as Christian Identity churches.[41] Beyond these relatively formal organizations, however, ideas from Christian Identity have made their way into the philosophies of many contemporary hate groups. What makes the ideology of Identity so powerful is that elements of it are appealing to members of many groups with widely differing orientations, particularly to groups that emphasize anti-government sentiments, to those emphasizing racism, and to those teaching anti-Semitism. These unifying themes may help explain why groups that at one time were at odds are increasingly working together. As Coates observed,

> Under Identity, common ground is established for the first time between such normally antagonistic segments of the far right as the violently anarchist Posse Comitatus, which is out to end all governments, and the neo-Nazis, with their complex formulae for an extremely intrusive new government. Espousing Identity, Posse members and Nazis can join forces to oppose the ZOG establishment that each hates so thoroughly.[42]

Thus, the influence of the Identity movement is likely many times greater than might be expected based only on the number of groups that define themselves primarily as Identity churches.

EMERGING TRENDS

Since 1981, the Southern Poverty Law Center has routinely monitored trends and has issued reports concerning domestic terrorism. These reports suggest that domestic terrorist groups have been slowly changing over time. For example, the influence of the Christian Identity religion persists but showed some decline in the early 2000s, being replaced by a range of other religions, many of them nature-based neo-pagan. There is also evidence of a growing sensitivity to environmental issues and globalization—issues traditionally associated with the political left. In his 1951 book, *The True Believer,* Eric Hoffer argued that the extreme left and the extreme right are closer to each other than either is to the political center—that it is easier to shift from one extreme to the other than to shift from an extreme to a moderate position. Trends identified by the Southern Poverty Law Center reinforce Hoffer's argument, suggesting that domestic terrorists are no longer drawing followers strictly from the political right.[43]

Another trend is the growth of the neo-Nazi movement. In 2001, there were more neo-Nazi groups than any other type of domestic terrorist organization in America, nearly double the number of the next largest group, the Ku Klux Klan. Unlike such groups as the KKK, these neo-Nazi groups are "militantly anti-American" and were quick to celebrate the September 11, 2001, attack on the World Trade Center in New York and the Pentagon in Washington, D.C. There have also been efforts by neo-Nazis in America to network with neofascists in Europe, and although they have expressed a hatred for Muslims, neo-Nazis have also shown a willingness to work with Muslim extremists to destroy the American system of government[44]—as it is sometimes said, "My enemy's enemy is my friend."

In addition to the rise of neo-Nazi groups, the new century also saw the rise of neo-Confederate groups. As might be expected, neo-Confederate groups predominate in the South and rely heavily on symbols of the pre–Civil War confederacy. Most neo-Confederate groups follow white supremacist ideologies and have a particular contempt for nonwhite immigration, affirmative action, school bussing, and interracial marriage.[45] Neo-Confederates have actively sought leadership positions in southern churches, espousing a theology that has much in common with Christian Identity.[46] Equally disturbing is the support these groups receive from elected officials. The Council of Conservative Citizens (CCC), for example, routinely publishes racist material and has members with links to such racist groups as the KKK and the National Alliance (a neo-Nazi group). The CCC also has a long list of national and state-level politicians who are either members or have spoken before the group, including 34 members of the Mississippi state legislature.[47]

In recent years, hate groups have also used technology extensively to spread their ideology and recruit new members. In 2001, the Southern Poverty Law Center identified more than 400 hate-based Web sites. Hate groups have also used short-wave radio, broadcasting as many as 1,100 hours of hate each month.[48] Finally, in an effort to attract youth to the movement there is now a substantial business in hate-based music. Resistance Records, a label specializing in youth-oriented hate-based music, sells more than 50,000 music CDs each year.[49]

Domestic terrorist groups have traditionally been dominated by males, with women serving as support and occasionally forming auxiliary units. This, too, has been changing. Although men still hold most leadership roles, women are increasingly moving into these positions, and they are playing a more direct role in these organizations.

Over time, particular organizations may come and go, and the particular targets of hate may shift. Still, domestic terrorism has proven difficult to control and perhaps impossible to permanently eradicate.

JUSTICE AND DOMESTIC TERRORISM

How should society respond to domestic terrorism in a way that appropriately punishes offenders and deters acts of violence, while respecting freedom of speech and the right to peaceably assemble? Several strategies have been tried. Beginning in 1964, the FBI undertook a program to

. . . disrupt and neutralize the KKK. This strategy involved infiltrating the Klan and included not only the use of informers and theft of Klan records, but also all manner of planted newspaper stories, rumors, and anonymous letters and postcards revealing Klan membership and accusing Klan leaders of everything from drunkenness, adultery, and misuse of funds to being informers for the FBI itself. By the 1970s, the Bureau claimed that one out of every six Klansmen worked for the FBI. This included at least one state leader, and there was talk of attempting to depose the United Klan's Imperial Wizard Robert Shelton and replacing him with an FBI informant.[50]

Although the FBI's program was effective in the short run, it eventually became known to the public and hurt the agency's credibility when it was revealed that this program was also used against civil rights leaders. Further, the FBI's efforts may have set the stage for an organizational strategy that came to be known as "leaderless resistance," in which domestic terrorist groups work in small decentralized units of a dozen or fewer members. To protect themselves from police investigations, these units plan operations independently, keeping their plans secret from anyone not part of their small working unit. In his novel *The Turner Diaries,* William Pierce advocated this strategy, which some believe was a guide for Timothy McVeigh when he bombed the federal building in Oklahoma City.

One way to limit the spread of hate groups might be to penalize those who publish materials or make public statements advocating hate or questioning the legitimacy of the government. In many countries, such speech is prohibited. In Germany, for example, it is a crime to display the swastika or other symbols of organizations that are banned by law.[51] Similarly, in Canada, it is a crime to make public statements that promote the hatred of any group.[52] Although this approach may sound appealing, there are several problems with it. First, in the United States such restrictions have been ruled to be in conflict with the constitutional protection of free speech. Probably no nation has stronger protections than does the United States for speech that most may find offensive.[53] Support for freedom of speech is deep and includes people from across the political spectrum, making it unlikely that banning hate speech will be considered constitutional in the near future. A second problem with banning hate speech is the lack of empirical evidence that it has much affect on the spread of hatred. Germany, for example, prohibits hate speech but continues to have an enormous problem with race-based hatred. We should not abandon our commitment to free speech without some evidence of what we will gain in return. Third, even if it is reasonable to ban speech that targets minorities or immigrant groups, it is another matter to ban speech critical of the government. As was seen in the Oklahoma City bombing, anti-government sentiments are an important element of domestic terrorism. Repressive dictatorships often arrest or kill people who question the authority or integrity of the government, but it is difficult to reconcile such a response with the principles of a democratic society. Finally, there is the issue of deciding what constitutes hate speech and what groups are to be included. For example, would it include blacks who make derogatory remarks about whites, or Jews who make such remarks about Christians? Would making jokes about blonde women constitute hate speech?

Limiting hate speech may be appealing in that such limits make a moral statement about how society views such speech. However, the practical difficulties that arise from such an approach probably outweigh the benefits from making a clear moral statement.

Another response to domestic terrorism, particularly that aimed at minorities and protected groups, is the passage of hate crime legislation. These laws provide for additional penalties if a crime was motivated, at least in part, by prejudice against a race, religion, or sexual orientation. In the United States, such laws did not exist before the mid-1980s, but since then they have proliferated.[54] In 1990, Congress passed the Hate Crimes Statistics Act, intended to keep a running count of the number of hate crimes each year. Unfortunately, neither hate crime laws nor efforts to track hate crime numbers have proven very successful.

One of the biggest problems with prosecuting hate crime cases is that it is necessary to know not simply what someone has done, but why it was done. Proving that an act was motivated by prejudice can be difficult, requiring the judge or jury to guess what was in the perpetrator's head at the time. Further, hate crime legislation seems to suggest that some victims are more valuable than others. For example, it suggests that killing someone during a robbery is less serious if the killer doesn't use racial epithets during the killing.

Hate crime laws are assumed to protect minorities, but this legislation has also been used against minorities. As many as 20 percent of hate crimes involve minority perpetrators and white victims.[55]

Deciding what offenses should be included is another complication of hate crime legislation. Is painting racist or anti-Semitic graffiti a hate crime? In some jurisdictions, it is treated as a hate crime, but in others it is not.[56] Although police agencies are encouraged to report hate crime statistics to the federal government, as many as one-third of the agencies do not report, and the consistency with which hate-based acts are reported appears to vary wildly from one police agency to the next.[57] The Southern Poverty Law Center concludes, "The system, already hobbled by the voluntary nature of reporting, is riddled with errors, failures to pass along information, misunderstanding of what constitutes a hate crime and even outright falsification of data."[58]

A final tool for responding to hate-based crime is to use the civil courts to sue organizations that promote race-based criminal acts (see also Chapter 13). The Southern Poverty Law Center was formed in 1971 as a small civil rights firm. In May 1979, it undertook the novel strategy for combating hate groups of taking the Ku Klux Klan to civil court and suing for monetary damages for the victims of their violence. This strategy has proven relatively effective against large organizations:

> Center civil suits would eventually result in judgments against 46 individuals and nine major white supremacist organizations for their roles in hate crimes. Multimillion-dollar judgments against the United Klans of America and the neo-Nazi Aryan nations effectively put those organizations out of business. Other suits halted harassment of Vietnamese fishermen in Texas by the Knights of the KKK and paramilitary training by the White Patriot Party in North Carolina.[59]

The strategy of taking hate groups to civil court holds promise and can be a useful tool for weakening their financial base. It is less useful, however, against small cells of domestic terrorists or against individuals acting on their own.

There is no magic formula for ending domestic terrorism. If efforts to stop domestic terrorism include infringing on basic legal rights, then the cure may be as offensive as the behavior it seeks to correct. Still, some of the strategies described here can play a role in chipping away at the base from which domestic terrorism arises.

CONCLUSION

Domestic terrorism is a part of the fabric of American culture. Hate-inspired acts against the government, racial groups, and religious groups can be traced back to before our country was formally founded. To say that it is ingrained in our culture is not to say it should be accepted and tolerated. It is easier, however, to label such acts injustice than to identify effective ways of responding that are consistent with democratic principles.

One irony of domestic terrorism is that government efforts to control such groups sometimes fuel the very behavior the government is trying to eliminate. Although the government has a duty to respond to illegal activity, the nature of that response is crucial. Heavy-handed actions by the government may fuel further paranoia and extremism, and those who die in a conflict with the government may easily become martyrs.[60] For example, it has been argued that Timothy McVeigh set off the bomb at the federal building in Oklahoma City in response to the federal government's assault on the Branch Davidian compound in Waco, Texas—two years to the day earlier.[61] Four agents for the Bureau of Alcohol, Tobacco and Firearms (ATF) had been killed and 20 more wounded trying to execute a search warrant on David Koresh, leader of the Branch Davidians, for failing to register firearms. Six Davidians were killed and 5 were wounded, including David Koresh. A 51-day standoff followed. Then, on April 19, 1993, agents of the ATF and FBI stormed the wooden compound, arguing they could wait no longer because children were placed in danger within the compound and had to be rescued. A fire broke out and when the smoke cleared, 76 Branch Davidians had been killed, including 25 children.[62] The government tactics used in the operation were questioned, and some thought government agents should be held directly accountable for the deaths. Such sentiments were particularly strong among those who, like Timothy McVeigh, already had a strong contempt for the government. For these individuals, the incident at Waco dramatically demonstrated a government out of control. Bombing the federal building in Oklahoma City would not only put the government on notice, but would serve as a wake-up call to all citizens. This scenario, of the government's response fuelling further acts of defiance, has been replayed on a number of occasions[63] and illustrates an irony. In responding to acts of injustice, the government may unwittingly sow the seeds for further violence.

Although the discussion in this chapter focuses on domestic terrorism, the implications for international terrorism are clear. The government's response to terrorism must be perceived as just. If it is not, the government's response will only fuel more terrorism.

Discussion Questions

1. How do you respond to someone who looks back through history and concludes that hate groups are a natural part of American society?
2. How has technology facilitated the spread of hate groups?
3. What are some of the problems with trying to make hate speech a crime?

Endnotes

1. Dale L. Watson, *The Terrorist Threat Confronting the United States*, testimony before the Senate Select Committee on Intelligence, Washington, D.C., 6 February 2002 (accessed online at www.fbi.gov/congress/congress02/watson020602.htm on 23 April 2002).
2. Philip Jenkins, "Home-Grown Terror," *American Heritage* 46(5), September 1995, p. 40.
3. Louis J. Freeh, *Threat of Terrorism in the United States*, testimony before the U.S. Senate Committees on Appropriates, Armed Services, and Select Committee on Intelligence, 10 May 2001 (accessed online at www.fbi.gov/congress/congress01/freeh051001.htm on 12 September 2003).
4. Lane Crothers, *Rage on the Right: The American Militia Movement from Ruby Ridge to Homeland Security.* (Lanham, Md.: Rowman & Littlefield, 2003).
5. Catherine McNicol Stock, *Rural Radicals: Righteous Rage in the American Grain.* (Ithaca, N.Y.: Cornell University Press, 1996).
6. Ibid., p. 18.
7. Ibid. Also see Samuel Eliot Morison, *The Oxford History of the American People* (New York: Oxford University Press, 1965).
8. Samuel Walker, *In Defense of American Liberties: A History of the ACLU* (New York: Oxford University Press, 1990).
9. Jenkins, pp. 38–39.

10. For an excellent history of this movement, see Ron Jacobs, *The Way the Wind Blew: A History of the Weather Underground* (New York: Verso, 1997).
11. A thorough account of this group is in Kevin Flynn and Gary Gerhardt, *The Silent Brotherhood: Inside America's Racist Underground* (New York: Free Press, 1989).
12. Cited in Garry Wills, *A Necessary Evil: A History of American Distrust of Government* (New York: Simon & Schuster, 1999), p. 205.
13. James Coates, *Armed and Dangerous: The Rise of the Survivalist Right* (New York: Noonday, 1987), p. 22.
14. A good overview of the evolution of hate in America is David Bennett, *The Party of Fear: The American Far Right from Nativism to the Militia Movement* (revised and updated edition) (New York: Vintage Books, 1995).
15. Ibid.
16. Coates.
17. Ibid.
18. Ibid., p. 24.
19. Ibid., p. 28.
20. Bennett.
21. Morison.
22. An excellent review of this topic is in Michael Barkun, *Religion and the Racist Right: The Origins of the Christian Identity Movement* (Chapel Hill: University of North Carolina Press, 1994).
23. Coates.
24. Francis E. Flavin, "A Pox on Amherst: Small Pox, Sir Jeffrey, and a Town Named Amherst," *Historical Journal of Massachusetts* 30, 2002, pp. 1–29.
25. John George and Laird Wilcox, *American Extremists: Militias, Supremacists, Klansmen, Communists, & Others* (Amherst, N.Y.: Prometheus, 1996).
26. David M. Chalmers, *Hooded Americanism: The History of the Ku Klux Klan* (New York: New Viewpoints, 1981); James Ridgeway, *Blood in the Face: The Ku Klux Klan, Aryan Nations, Nazi Skinheads, and the Rise of a New White Culture* (New York: Thunder's Mouth, 1990).
27. Chalmers.
28. Coates, p. 31.
29. Chalmers.
30. Coates.
31. Morison.
32. Ridgeway.
33. Ibid.
34. George and Wilcox.
35. Ibid.
36. Ibid.
37. Ibid.
38. Coates, p. 81.
39. Barkun.
40. For troublesome predictions for the future, see Joel Dyer, *Harvest of Rage: Why Oklahoma City Is Only the Beginning* (Boulder, Colo.: Westview, 1997).
41. "Active Hate Groups in the United States in the Year 2001," *Southern Poverty Law Center's Intelligence Report* no. 105 (Spring 2002), pp. 32–37.
42. Coates, p. 80.
43. "The Year in Hate," *Southern Poverty Law Center's Intelligence Report* no. 97 (Spring 2000), pp. 6–7; "Neither Left Nor Right," *Southern Poverty Law Center's Intelligence Report* no. 97 (Winter 2000), pp. 40–46.

44. "The Year in Hate."

45. "Rebels with a Cause."

46. "Confederates in the Pulpit," *Southern Poverty Law Center's Intelligence Report* no. 101 (Spring 2000), pp. 51–55.

47. "Sharks in the Mainstream," *Southern Poverty Law Center's Intelligence Report* no. 93 (Winter 1999), pp. 21–26.

48. "The Year in Hate."

49. "Money, Music and the Doctor," *Southern Poverty Law Center's Intelligence Report* no. 96 (Fall 1999), pp. 33–36.

50. Chalmers, pp. 398–399.

51. Alexis A. Aronowitz, "Germany's Xenophobic Violence: Criminal Justice and Social Responses," in *Hate Crime: International Perspectives on Causes and Control,* Mark Hamm (ed.) (Cincinnati, Ohio: Anderson, 1994), pp. 37–69.

52. Jeffrey Ian Ross, "Hate Crimes in Canada: Growing Pains with New Legislation," in *Hate Crime: International Perspectives on Causes and Control,* Mark Hamm (ed.) (Cincinnati, Ohio: Anderson, 1994), pp. 151–172.

53. Samuel Walker, *Hate Speech: The History of an American Controversy* (Lincoln: University of Nebraska Press, 1994).

54. James B. Jacobs and Kimberly Potter, *Hate Crimes: Criminal Law & Identity Politics* (New York: Oxford University Press, 1998).

55. Ibid.

56. "Discounting Hate," *Southern Poverty Law Center's Intelligence Report* no. 104 (Winter 2001), pp. 6–15.

57. Ibid.

58. Ibid., p. 7.

59. The Southern Poverty Law Center, *Seeking Justice: A Brief History of the Southern Poverty Law Center* (accessed online at www.splcenter.org/centerinfo/ci-index.html on 17 June 2002).

60. See Stuart A. Wright (ed.), *Armageddon in Waco: Critical Perspectives on the Branch Davidian Conflict* (Chicago: University of Chicago Press, 1995).

61. For a good discussion of this case, see Mark Hamm, *Apocalypse in Oklahoma: Waco and Ruby Ridge Revenged* (Boston: Northeastern University Press, 1997); and Peter Kraska, *Militarizing the American Criminal Justice System* (Boston: Northeastern University Press, 2001).

62. Hamm, pp. 103–145.

63. For other examples, see Daniel Levitas, *The Terrorist Next Door: The Militia Movement and the Radical Right* (New York: Thomas Dunne, 2002).

CONTEMPORARY SLAVERY

T he ending of the American Civil War in 1865 supposedly extinguished one relic of barbarism: slavery.[1] This "peculiar institution" had existed for centuries.[2] Some scholars believe that, historically, slavery began as civilization grew, beginning in the three ancient centers of Mesopotamia, Egypt, and India, and that slavery started as ancient humans shifted from hunter-wanderer cultures to agricultural-based economies. Labor was needed to help farm crops, build pyramids, fight wars, and serve the ruling elites. Enslaved peoples were seen as the spoils of war, necessities in building an economy, supporting the colonial systems throughout the world, validating racial hatreds, and upholding and supporting certain classes of individuals.[3] These theorists, however, probably underestimate the beginnings of slavery. Most likely, it had existed for thousands of years before the dawn of civilization. Surely, the spoils of prehistoric wars must have included enslaving the vanquished. No matter the origins, the ending of slavery in the nineteenth century was considered a major step in the march toward civilization.

Today, however, there are more enslaved people in the world than ever— an estimated 27 million people are currently enslaved.[4] There are more slaves now than all of the people stolen from Africa before the Civil War in America. The slave population of the world now is greater than that of the entire population of Canada and six times larger than that of Israel.[5]

This new slavery touches most people of the world. For example, those who enjoy eating candy do not realize that slavery is behind most chocolate production. In 1998, the International Labor Organization (ILO), a UN agency, found an emergence of child slavery in the cocoa fields of the Ivory Coast, where 43 percent of the world's cocoa comes from. Companies like Hershey's and M&M Mars were charged with complicity. These child slaves came from Mali, Burkina Faso, and Togo, nations even more destitute than the Ivory Coast. Parents in these countries sold their children in hopes that good jobs awaited them.[6]

In the Sudan, black Christians and animists resisted Khartoum from imposing an Arabic Moslem state and religion. Civil war resulted, with the Sudanese army being encouraged to turn captives and their families into slaves. In 1998, one automatic weapon could be traded for six or seven child slaves. In 1989, a woman or child from the Dinka tribe—a tall, proud people living along the Nile—could be bought for $90. The next year, as raids increased and flooded the market with captives, the market price slid to $15. Frequently, these slaves were forced to convert to Islam; those refusing had their Achilles tendons cut. Slaves caught trying to escape were castrated or branded like cattle.[7]

In March 2001, an explosion in a rural primary school in Jiangxi Province, China, killed 42 people, mostly 10- and 11-year-old children. Apparently, a money-strapped school system had set up an enterprise, this one making firecrackers, and forced children to work during and after school. Most of the money had gone into the pockets of corrupt school officials.[8]

The next month, a suspected child slave ship eluded arrest off the coast of Africa. The ship, called *Etireno,* had made regular trips from Benin to Gabon for the previous five years filled with human cargo, mostly young boys, to work in cotton and cocoa plantations; girls on board were destined to be domestics and prostitutes.[9]

Even in America, we have examples of slavery. Christi Elangwe, from the Cameroons, was a slave in Germantown, Maryland, for five years. Protection Project, a Johns Hopkins University program, estimates that there are one million undocumented immigrants trapped in slavery in America.[10] Asian slaves are used in the sex industry. Latin American slaves work in the fields. Those from the Middle East and Africa become domestics. President Bill Clinton's Inter-Agency Council on Women declared it "the fast-growing criminal enterprise, behind guns and drugs, in this country."[11] In 2003, the U.S. attorney general announced at a conference on human rights, "Each year, tens of thousands of people—predominantly women and children—are trafficked into the United States." During the previous two years, the Justice Department successfully convicted 36 defendants in sex trafficking cases, but this number hardly scratches the surface of the problem. The Justice Department estimates that as many as 50,000 victims of slavery end up in the United States each year.[12]

This "new slavery" has grown for several reasons. First, there has been a dramatic increase in population since the end of World War II. Second, this population growth has occurred at the same time as rapid social and economical changes. Third, the greed and chaos caused by the political and economic instability has allowed slavery to grow unnoticed. Fourth, slavery has become very profitable. Not because slave holders make expensive things, but because the modern slave is so cheap. One student of this problem has called them the "disposable people."[13] Fifth, the international community, perhaps complacent following the victories of the abolition movement of the nineteenth century, has not noticed the presence of the new slavery.[14]

TABLE 9.1 COMPARISON OF OLD AND NEW FORMS OF SLAVERY	
Old Slavery	**New Slavery**
Legal ownership asserted	Legal ownership avoided
High purchase cost	Very low purchase cost
Low profits	Very high profits
Shortage of potential slaves	Surplus of potential slaves
Long-term relationship	Short- term relationship
Slaves maintained	Slaves disposable
Ethnic differences important	Ethnic differences not important

It is important to distinguish between the old and new slavery. Under the old slavery, legal ownership was asserted, but under the new slavery, such ownership is avoided. Slaves were expensive under the old slave system; today the purchase price is very cheap. Profits from slavery in past times were low, but today high profits await the slaver. Historically, there was a shortage of slaves, but today they are abundant. Under the old slavery system, the relationship between slaver and slave was long-term and patriarchal; today, the relationship is short and more uncaring. Under the old system, slaves were maintained; under the new, they become disposable. Finally, under the old system, racial and ethnic differences were important in upholding and justifying the slave system. Today, such ethnic differences are not as important. Table 9.1 summarizes the differences.[15]

New slavery also has taken different forms from that of the old. Three types exist today that could mask the presence of slavery. First, *chattel slavery* is the oldest and closest to the old slave systems. Under this form a person is captured in war, or is born, or is sold into permanent slavery. This occurs most often in northern and western Africa and represents the smallest proportion of slavery. Mauritania is often used as an example of this slavery. Second, *debt bondage* is the most common form of modern-day slavery. Under this system, a person pledges or sells himself or herself into slavery as a surety against a loan, sometimes a loan as small as $25. However, with high interest and all kinds of hidden costs, the debt is never reduced, and the person becomes trapped in slavery. Even though ownership of the person is never asserted, complete control of the person is maintained. This form is most common in India and Pakistan. Third is *contract slavery*. A phoney contract for work is drawn up, and the workers are taken to a labor site far removed from their homes and isolated from their families. There, they are enslaved. This is most common in Southeast Asia, Brazil, and some Arab states. Brazil and Thailand offer examples of this type of modern slavery. Against those broad observations, let us turn to some specific examples.[16]

CHATTEL SLAVERY IN AFRICA: MAURITANIA

Mauritaria, a military dictatorship in northwest Africa and buffer between Arab north and black Africa to the south, is characterized by its chattel slavery. The size of California and Texas combined, Mauritania has only 2.2 million people, making it a country with the lowest population density on earth. It is practically all desert, located at the western end of the Sahara. More than one-third of the country, the eastern region that borders Mali, is barren and is called the "empty zone." This zone, about the size of Great Britain, has no roads, no towns, and almost no people. In the more populous regions, generally around the capital of Nouakchott, there is ongoing tension between the people from the black south and those from the Arab north.[17]

This former French colony probably contains the world's largest concentration of chattel slaves. In 1993, the U.S. State Department determined that as many as 90,000 blacks lived as the property of North African Arabs (known as Beydanes or White Moors). Other sources add 300,000 part-time and ex-slaves, known as Haratins, many of whom continue to serve their owners because of fear or need. The slaves are chattel. Most often, they are used for house and farm labor, for sex, and for breeding. They may be exchanged for camels, trucks, guns, or money. Their children are property of the master and are born, live, and die as slaves.

TABLE 9.2   MAURITANIA COMPARED WITH OLD AND NEW SLAVERY

Old Slavery	Mauritania	New Slavery
Legal ownership asserted	Ownership illegal but upheld by courts	Legal ownership avoided
High purchase cost	Relatively high purchase cost	Very low purchase cost
Low profits	Relatively high profits	Very high profits
Shortage of potential slaves	Shortage of potential slaves	Glut of potential slaves
Long-term relationship	Long-term relationship	Short-term relationship
Slaves maintained	Slaves maintained	Slaves disposable
Ethnic differences	Important ethnic differences accented	Ethnic differences not important

Africans in Mauritania converted to Islam more than a century ago. Though the *Qur'an* forbids the enslavement of fellow Muslims, racism outranks religious ideals. In fact, black Muslim Mauritanians are forbidden the basic rights of other Muslims.[18] In 1990, Human Rights Watch/Africa reported routine tortures and punishments of black Africans for the slightest fault. Beatings, denial of food, prolonged exposure to the sun with hands and feet tied together were common. For serious reprimands, the notorious "insect treatment" was used. Tiny ants would be stuffed into the ears of the slave, which are then sealed with stones and bound with a scarf. The slave's hands and feet are tied, and the errant slave is left in the hot sun for days. The presence of the insects can drive a person crazy. Such treatment guarantees future compliance. In some respects, Mauritania is just a stone's throw away from the Stone Age.[19]

A comparison of the old and new slavery with Mauritania as a component is illustrative (see Table 9.2).[20]

DEBT BONDAGE: PAKISTAN AND INDIA

Pakistan

Despite some modern trappings of capitalism, Pakistan remains a feudal country.[21] Partitioned after India's independence movement in the late 1940s, Pakistan became a refuge for those Muslims living in the subcontinent who were displaced by the tumultuous end of British colonialism. This modern-day feudalism is characterized by a strict caste system. Relationships and interdependencies characterize the social structure. Power is the most important attribute of Pakistan. Those who have it can do just about anything because power trumps any rule of law. The peshgi system, or debt slavery, is the underpinnings of Pakistan. It is estimated that one-third of all the land is owned by 0.5 percent of the population. Thus, there are about 15 million landless peasants available to work the kilns that produce bricks for building.[22]

Those highest in the caste system lay claim to a direct lineage to Muhammad. Strongmen or warlords come next in the power structure. At the bottom of the list are the Muslim Sheikhis, late converts to Islam and derogatorily referred to as Musselis. Even below the Musselis are the Christians. These two groups most often get caught up in debt bondage.[23]

Pakistan truly puts the *feud* in *feudalism*. Family fights going back generations go on unrelentingly. It is said in Pakistan that it is essential to have many sons because so many will die in feuds.[24] Armed gangs roam the countryside with modern weapons; murder, rape, and extortion are common occurrences. Even the government, the institution that should stabilize society, is involved in feud. Political leaders are constantly being assassinated. Pakistan is an Islamic republic, and rival sects are at constant verbal and violent war. It is estimated that an average number of 400 people a year are killed because of sectarian fighting. Of course, nonbelievers—such as Hindus and Christians—will be the first targeted and most severely treated. Part of the problem has to do with the law. Pakistan has two sets of law: state law (civil and criminal law) and Islamic law. Both are legal, but they are often contradictory. In power struggles, Islamic law will frequently displace the state law. For example, slavery is against the state law. But it is not against Islamic law as long as the slave is a nonbeliever. Bowing to the popular will and fundamentalist Islam, government officials break the law themselves. For example, the police—thoroughly corrupt—aid, perpetuate, and profit from the institution of debt slavery.[25]

Pakistan, particularly the Punjab region closest to India, is remarkably fertile. Advances in health care and greater agricultural productivity have made Pakistan's birth rate even greater than that of India's. Half the country's population is younger than 17.[26] Brick making has become a major industry. Brick structures are everywhere. Each family is allotted one eight foot by eight foot room in a brick complex of living spaces. There is a common toilet and shared water well. The water is not potable.

The soil of the region is particularly conducive to brick making and large kilns dot the landscape. There are at least 7000 kilns in the country, not counting the small backyard operations. The kilns are large operations, some of them the size of football fields with 15 to 35 families doing piece-rate work. Once the furnaces are started, they will burn continuously for four to five months. There are two seasonal closings, one in January and February when it is too wet, and another in July and August when it is too hot. The brick kiln villages are filled with families working off a debt owed to the owner of the kiln. Children make up a large proportion of the work force. They work along with their parents but they may be used as hostages to keep families from leaving the kilns. Because the real opportunity to work off the debt is unlikely, these children will probably spend their lives working as slaves.[27] As one authority has observed, "the first generation of brick workers was drawn almost entirely from the ranks of the displaced farm workers. Today their children and grandchildren inherit both the job and, often, the debt that holds them in it."[28]

The piece rate is so low that it is difficult to escape the debt. For example, on the average, a family is paid the equivalent of $2.00 per one thousand bricks made. If brick damage and rain is at a minimum, a family can earn about $14 to $16 per week, about the amount a family needs for a subsistence diet. Even if some catastrophic event such as illness or injury does not throw things out of kilter, the family still cannot earn enough to pay its way out of debt.[29]

Then there are the munshi or kiln managers. Many of these managers are honest enough; they just let the dynamics of low income take care of the matter of perpetual debt. Unlike many countries that sustain their slavery with high interest rates, Pakistan is Muslim and the *Qur'an* is quite clear about the sinfulness of usury. Deprived of high accumulative interest, the managers resort to other means to enslave their workers. A significant number of these managers become corrupt. They miscount the weekly average brick production or overstate the amount of damaged bricks. They use intimidation to force the workers to stay at the kilns. They threaten to sell off the promissory note, and hence the family and its indebtedness, to other managers. If the head of the family dies or runs off, the manager can literally sell the family and its debts to other slave managers. Finally, managers sexually exploit female members of the family.[30]

Unlike so much of the new slavery, the debt bondage system of Pakistan does not have a very high profit margin. Kiln owners, with all of their dishonest manipulations, barely make a profit of 10 to 15 percent.[31] Mechanization of the process could increase production but the old peshgi system persists. Worldwide criticism has increased in the last decade, however, and some labor organizers have tried to reform the system by using the courts. Still, the system continues. The large number of people begging for work sustains the slavery system. These are willing slaves. Slavery and bare subsistence seem better than the alternatives for some. As one authority puts it,

> A brick kiln owner will be approached by a family that is looking for work. Perhaps they have lost the right to land where they were traditionally peasant farmers or were turned off the land when the landlord mechanized, replacing peasant cultivators with tractors. They might even be refugees, driven from their home by the fighting in Afghanistan or the Kashmir. Whatever the reason, the family will be desperate, willing to accept even the hard and hot work in a brick kiln.[32]

Then there is the issue of honor. When the slaves first sign up with a kiln owner—largely of their own free will—they incur debt. This is in the form of money for food and fuel. Sometimes workers borrow additional money to meet a problem of impending marriage of children, or medical expenses or funeral costs. Therefore, debt quickly accumulates. In this region of the world, honor is of prime importance. These slaves do have the opportunity to escape. They are free during the off-season to leave the kilns and travel the region. To do so, the worker (and only the man of the family can leave) must obtain from the owner a slip of paper with the worker's name and amount of indebtedness. The workers can go to other kiln owners and negotiate to have their indebtedness purchased. The old kiln owner would not care—these are disposable people with a constant supply ready to take their place—because if they do leave, the old owner gets the money for the debt. The previous slave manager either keeps his slaves or receives hard cash that has been grossly and dishonestly inflated. The worker and his family simply move on, carrying with them past debt and future enslavement.[33] The slaves refuse to run away or seek other means of redress because they feel honor bound to pay off their debt, even though it is quickly seen that is impossible.[34]

Furthermore, despite window-dressing protestations by political leaders, the system seems to have the support of the authorities. The peshgi system has a long historic tradition in this region of the world. The police in particular have been a major supporter of the kiln owners and an obstacle to any meaningful reform. Across the country, the police are for hire. Although laws were passed in 1988 abolishing bonded labor, it continues unabated. Pakistan does not seem to have the will to end debt bondage.

India

Debt bondage has existed in India for thousands of years.[35] It is ancient and it remains vast. Reliable figures are hard to find, but it is estimated that the numbers are in the millions.[36] Slavery takes several forms. For example, in the practice of devadasi, a young woman is married off to a god. A poor family, in hopes of winning the favor of the gods, sells its daughter to a temple. She becomes a servant to that temple. In addition, she may be made a prostitute for that temple because many temples double as brothels.[37] Children are commonly put into debt slavery. Parents are given money, and the children are required to pay it off. For example in the state of Tamil Nadu, more than 45,000 children (between 4 and 15 years old) are gathered up each day in school buses and taken to match and fireworks factories. There they labor for 12 hours a day for 5 days per week (7 when an important holiday celebration is near).[38] In agriculture-bonded slavery, the family loses all freedoms and receives no wages. After taking on the debt and becoming slaves, the family gets two things: a daily bag of grain and access to a small plot of land on which to grow other food. The state of Uttar Pradesh is famous for its bondage. Behind the debt bondage here is the need to borrow money by poor illiterate people. These debts arise from urgent crises—such as illness, injury, or famine—or the need to pay for death rites or marriage celebrations. In one cruel irony, some men borrow heavily to get married only to eventually sell their wives into prostitution to pay off the original debt.[39]

The ancient caste system supports slavery. The upper classes own most of the land. The lower castes and untouchables are the impoverished ones who borrow money and become enslaved. Unlike Pakistan, where Islam forbids usury, Indian landlords charge interest in excess of 60 percent. Working at subsistence levels, fighting an ever-mounting debt because of interest, a family may be enslaved for generations. If a man runs away or dies, the debts of the father are assumed by the oldest son. One bonded servant declared, "I've always lived here, so did my father and grandfather. We've always been here and we've always worked for the same master. When my father died I had to take over his debt; that was almost thirty years ago." When asked if he had ever been out of debt, he responded, "No, never; neither were my father or grandfather." There is some evidence of a family enslaved for nearly 300 years.[40]

There have been some attempts to rid India of debt bondage. Several factors stymie such reforms. First, there is history and the caste system. Although some reforms since independence have bettered the position of the untouchables, the caste system and the prejudice that sustains it remains fixed and an obstacle to change. As one landlord said in defense of keeping slaves, "After all, they are from the Kohl caste; that's what they do, work for Vasyas like me."[41] Second, government officials are corrupt and wink at the practice. There is an attitude that the system is actually good for the slave. Again, one landlord justified his owning of slaves this way: "They benefit from the system and so do I; even if agriculture is completely mechanized I'll still keep my bonded laborers. You see, the way we do it I am like a father to these workers. It is a father-son relationship: I protect them and guide them. Sometimes I have to discipline them as well, just as a father would."[42] Third, there are profit issues. Landlords can expect profits of more than 50 percent with bonded laborers. If they paid the daily local rate for workers, their profit would sink to 36 percent. If they paid the national minimum rate for workers, the profit would sink to 1 percent.[43]

Perhaps the most promising attempts to "rehabilitate" those in debt bondage have occurred in India. An investigative reporter exposed the existence of bonded slavery in Tamil Nadu. Officials swept in, released 321 bonded laborers, and gave them each 500 rupees to go home. A law had been passed setting up vigilance committees to spot bonded laborers, register them, cancel their debts, protect them from their former masters, and send them to their original homes with a small amount of money. Half the costs were carried by the central government and the other half by the state government. As one student of the system noted, "It is the modern Indian equivalent of the forty acres and a mule that American slaves were praying for (but never received) at the end of the U.S. Civil War."[44] Some states even went further in this "rehabilitation" program. In Bihar, the grant money was doubled. Also, this state focused on children bonded in the carpet industry. In Karnataka, the freed slave was allowed to keep the land the master had originally bestowed for the slave's personal use. In Uttar Pradesh, vigilance committees tracked down brothels to release girls held as sex slaves. In Orissa, low-level government jobs were set aside for freed laborers. In just one state, Uttar Pradesh, 26,000 bonded laborers were rehabilitated between 1979 and 1989.[45]

However, much corruption has grown up around the rehabilitation programs. Officials keep larger parts of the money grants. Land allotted to the freed laborer was often unusable. Former masters took chunks of the land the government had set aside for the freed laborer. Fraudulent contractors supplied sick (or even in one case a dead one) cows to the freed slaves. There is no record of a former master or contractors being prosecuted for keeping or defrauding slaves. Little preparation for freedom was given. It has been noted that bonded slavery is like prolonged stays in a prison, one needs to be prepared for the "real world" or is likely to fail. People were given equipment to start a small business—for example, a bicycle repair shop—but no training on how to repair bicycles. Despite its failings, however, India remains the only example of a country trying to deal with the problem of modern slavery.[46]

CONTRACT SLAVERY: BRAZIL AND THAILAND

Brazil

Portuguese colonizers introduced slavery early in Brazil's history.[47] From the beginning in the sixteenth century to the nineteenth, millions of slaves were shipped from Africa to Brazil.[48] In fact, their numbers were far greater than those sent to the United States, but the death rates were so high that their total number never became as great as in America. The slave traffic ended in the nineteenth century, but slavery in the country continued. In 1888, Brazil emancipated its slaves, the old slavery, becoming the last country in the Americas to abolish legal slavery.[49] In the 1960s and 1970s, Brazil underwent an economic boom. Infant mortality declined, city populations grew, industry expanded and pockets of poverty grew. Enormous slums sprung up in the cities. Today, Brazil has some of the greatest economic disparities in the Western hemisphere. Fifty-thousand Brazilians, out of 165 million, own nearly everything. Millions own little if anything and the unemployment rate is staggering.[50]

The governments of Brazil have been largely corrupt, selling off large lots of federal land at low prices to the elite classes. Some big companies—Nestlé and Volkswagen are examples—cut down the forests and use local contractors to make charcoal. Making charcoal is a skilled activity. As the forests in their home states are depleted, these charcoal workers congregate in small town ghettoes eager to find any means to feed their families. When recruiters, called gatos or cats, arrive, there are hundreds of workers to choose from. The gatos take these workers deep into the interior with promises of transportation home, money loans to provide for their families, and good food and lodging at the work site. The state identity papers and labor cards of each of the workers is taken by the gato. Without these papers, the workers are trapped. When they get to the charcoal-making workplace, however, they find a concentration camp with armed guards and threats to their freedom. Theoretically free to go, in reality these workers now are enslaved. The gato and his thugs are in complete control and can use violence at any time. The workers are not enslaved for life; the period is from 2 months to 2 years. In fact, the gatos do not want to own the workers but just want to exploit workers until they are broken and then dispose of them.[51]

The work sites, called batterias, are isolated. Far from towns and villages, they are surrounded by desolation, with tree-stripped and blackened terrain. In each camp, numerous furnaces burn the wood. More than 40 workers might be huddled in together in this wilderness. No matter how hard they work to pay off their debts, they constantly slip into more indebtedness. As one worker put it, "I haven't had anything, absolutely nothing. See, with this gato my debt is always running ahead of my earnings."[52] People are enslaved and the environment is ruined. Eucalyptus is burned using a minimum of oxygen so the wood won't be consumed. The wood oils, intense heat, and lack of air soon make the workers ill. If they survive, most will suffer from black lung disease. Unfortunately, the charcoal burners in the back woods are only one example of slavery in Brazil. Slaves are also used to cut down the Amazon rain forest. They harvest sugar cane, mine gold, and act as prostitutes. The rubber industry and cattle and timber industries rely on contract slave workers as well. Brazil has one of the largest populations of slaves in the Western hemisphere.

Sex Slavery in Thailand

Thailand provides one of the best examples of the new contract slavery. This slavery is connected to the sex industry. Modern-day Thailand has become notorious for its sex slaves. It has been estimated that there are one-half to one million prostitutes in Thailand, one-fifth of them are enslaved. The annual profit to the Thai economy from prostitution is estimated to be $1.85 billion. Thailand's reputation as a sexual playground has grown to such an extent that "sex tours" from other areas of Asia regularly come to Bangkok.[53]

There are several reasons for the pervasiveness of sex slavery in Thailand. First are geographical reasons. Southern Thailand is rich and fertile and has industrialized rapidly. The north, however, has remained poor. Many of the mountain tribes are destitute.[54] The bustling metropolitan areas are magnets to the impoverished rural people.

Second, the economic boom that hit Thailand in the 1990s was confined to the cities. The rich carried on a historic tradition of going to brothels, and during the economically prosperous times, many working-class men could afford to do so as well. The rural areas, however, remained poor. But these areas were exposed to the goods enjoyed by the rich. Televisions, VCRs, and other consumer items were seen as desirable even though they were outside the paltry budgets of the rural poor. Some families were willing to sell their daughters to get these appliances.[55]

Third, there has been a tradition of men visiting prostitutes. Between 10 and 40 percent of married men visit prostitutes regularly; 50 percent of single men do. For most Thai men, it is a legitimate form of entertainment done with friends after an evening of dining and drinking. In business circles, an interlude with a prostitute might be part of closing a business deal. In addition, there is a great desire for virgins. Some Asians think that sex with a youthful virgin will restore their youth and put off the aging process. Furthermore, as the HIV and AIDS epidemic hit Asia, many men felt that they were safer having sex with virgins. Many wives grudgingly support prostitution as better than their husbands having mistresses, which could be a greater threat to their marriages.[56]

Fourth was the historic Buddhism. Basic to Thai Buddhism is the belief that things in this life are the result of activities of the past lives; in a cosmic way, the pain and frustrations of this life are just compensations for past sins. Furthermore, tradition has it that Buddha himself sanctioned prostitution. Sex was not a sin; it was merely one of many attachments humans had to this worldly existence and therefore should be accepted. Impersonal sex—sex without romance and love—was acceptable as normal. Furthermore, popular Buddhism was anti-female. On the ladder of existence, females were lowly placed. In addition, all children owed their parents a large debt. From their earliest years, children are expected to contribute to their family's income.[57]

Agents come to the poverty stricken rural areas where the average income is $100 to $180 per month. These agents will give the family $88 to $2000 per girl based on the girl's physical beauty. The agents promise to bring back the girl once the "loan" has been paid. Most of the young women and girls are ignorant about what prostitution is; many think it is merely sitting around in a restaurant. When they arrive in a major city like Bangkok, the girls are put into brothels. These are usually nondescript places with signs saying "restaurant." The average number of girls per brothel is 20. The sex workers are rarely older than 30; most are younger than 18. Expenses are constantly added to the loan so it becomes impossible for the girl to ever pay it off and return home; they become locked into the sex industry.[58]

These sex slaves have two major threats. First, violence is a constant problem. Customers sometimes exert their will violently. Pimps use random and arbitrary violence to keep the prostitute compliant. Police chase down and round up runaways and often rape them. One young prostitute was murdered; her pimp and the police later were found to have killed her. Then there is the psychological violence toward these young imprisoned women. In time, they come to believe that they are unfit for anything else. They become dependent on the pimp and madam.[59]

Second is the threat of disease. Thailand has one of the highest rates of HIV infection in the world. Culturally, it is difficult to get men to use condoms, and recently, the wives of men who visit prostitutes have become a large number of the victims of sexually transmitted disease. Forced contraception by needle by the pimp has increased the spread of disease among the girls.[60]

Everyone except the sex slave prospers from this industry. The parents of the girl receive some money or consumer goods. One girl who had to have an operation was pressured by her own mother to return to the brothel and fulfill her obligation to the madam and to the family. The procuring agent receives a profit for the girls brought to the brothel. The brothel receives an enormous profit. It has been estimated that the average monthly expenses for a single brothel are around $10,000. The average monthly income, however, is nearly $90,000. The girls are so cheap and plentiful that they become disposable. Very little money is spent on their care. The police receive bribes of money and sexual services for tolerating prostitution. Finally, the entire Thai economy is bolstered by the sex slave industry.[61]

Sex slavery is not limited to Thailand. In Laos and Cambodia, where the average annual income is $300, a 12- to 16-year-old girl can be bought easily. As a virgin in a Tokyo brothel, that girl would fetch $3000 to $5000 for her first encounter. In other countries such as Bangladesh, Pakistan, Nigeria, and some Caribbean or Central American countries, where standards of living are low and unemployment high, the lure to leave and take up prostitution is great. After a U.S. government report determined that 50,000 women were illegally trafficked into America for sex exploitation, the Victims of Trafficking and Violence Prevention Act of 2000 was passed. a governmental office was set up to study and combat this problem. In December 2000, the United Nations adopted an international convention against organized crime and a Protocol to Prevent, Suppress and Punish Trafficking in Persons, Especially Women and Children. Only 4 out of 40 nations needed to ratify the protocol have done so.[62]

CONCLUSION

New slavery is alive and thriving in the world today. The existence and pervasiveness of modern-day slavery comes as a surprise to most. In our modern world of globalization, it is virtually impossible to avoid using products whose production processes have had modern slavery connections. One important question is that why, 150 years since the Emancipation Proclamation, does this institution still exist?

First is the drag of history and tradition. So much of the new slavery discussed in this chapter exists in countries still experiencing feudalistic tendencies. Mauritania is a modern example of the existence of the old slavery in modern times. India and Pakistan have a mix of the old and new elements of slavery. Those countries are very feudalistic. Class lines are sharply drawn, and the expectations and advantages of the lower classes are marginalized. Furthermore, an intellectual rationalization has grown up that sounds strangely reminiscent of the pro-slave advocates in America before the Civil War. This notion that the bonded person is childlike and better off under the patriarchal rule of the owner is common throughout those places that retain the new slavery.[63]

Second, perhaps, is the conceptualization of the new slavery itself. The world community tends to think of slavery along historical archetypes. Ownership has been a key part of any definition of slavery, but that is not part of the new slavery. In reality, two other words are essential: control and violence.

Thus, an important part of modern-day slavery is the violent control of a person. Our image of an antebellum American slave on a plantation crowds out our idea of sex slaves and debt bondage. On the face of it, people working off a debt do not seem to be real slaves. Only when you see the impossibility of getting out of debt, the force used to keep people in slavery, and the lack of regard for these "disposable people" does the magnitude and cruelty come to our attention.

Third, a population explosion, particularly in poverty stricken countries, provides enormous numbers of "disposable people." When these people who already are living on the borders of starvation meet an additional economic crisis, they are likely to fall into slavery.[64]

Fourth, globalization of business has provided opportunity for slavery to flourish, and made all consumers complicitous. In the last generation, economic changes have pushed corporations into poor countries looking for the cheapest labor. Business people look for the best deals possible and do not worry about politics of the host country. Multiple layers distance the corporate headquarters and Wall Street from the grime and crime of Third World new slavery. Haitian men, women, and children are enslaved in the sugar fields of the Dominican Republic; that sugar is earmarked for export to the United States. Only on occasion do companies like Nike and Gap have their complicity with modern slavery and sweat shops exposed. Then the dicey issues of corporate guilt and consumer responsibility mingle.[65]

Fifth, despite some protests by international organizations such as the United Nations, the international community has been quiet and acquiescent regarding the problems of the new slavery. The League of Nations drew up a Slave Convention in 1926, the first attempt to address the issue in the twentieth century. The United Nations adopted the Slave Convention in 1953, and by 1990, 86 nations ratified it and set out to prevent and suppress the slave trade and abolish slavery in all of its forms. The UN set up a Working Group on Contemporary Forms of Slavery in 1975. Every year it evaluates the state of slavery in the world. It has been particularly interested in the problem of children as sex slaves. The ILO has adopted two conventions that require ratifying states to suppress any form of forced labor. The World Health Organization (WHO) has conducted hearings on sex exploitation, debt bondage, and the sale of children.[66]

Other international organizations have been slow, unenthusiastic, or too poor to confront the problem of modern slavery. The main international group concerned with slavery is Anti-Slavery International (ASI). Founded in 1839, it has worked diligently against the old slavery. But today it has only 6000 members, a very small number compared with those in Greenpeace and Amnesty International. Some other groups address slavery as part of their larger mission. For example, the Catholic Agency for Overseas Development (CAFOD), Oxfam, Human Rights Watch, and United Nations International Children's Emergency Fund (UNICEF) have taken up the issue. But these groups work independently and there is no uniform strategy. Even the United Nations has been particularly timid in labeling countries as slave nations.[67]

Sixth, the lack of democracy seems to be a problem. New slavery flourishes best in those societies that have no voting opportunity for the slaves and do not have media institutions to publicize and outrage the public about the existence of slavery. In addition to the lack of a voice for the people is the problem of governmental corruption. Slavery exists best in countries with dishonest officials. Even if there are laws against slavery, as there are in most of the countries described in this chapter, implementing them is another matter. The police in Thailand, Pakistan, and Brazil are slave catchers. To hold and keep their slaves, the slave holders must use violence, and the police must allow it to exist. Judicial and legislative officials in most of the countries with bonded labor are easily bribed. Very few slaveholders are ever punished. Without the rule of law, the rule of men prevails, and, frequently, men in these countries are greedy and corrupt.[68]

Seventh, local anti-slavery groups do not get the public support they need. Each country used as an example in this chapter does have groups trying to eliminate bonded labor; for example, the Pastoral Land Commission in Brazil, SOS Slaves and El Hor in Mauritania, the Human Rights Commission in Pakistan, and South Asian Coalition on Child Servitude in India. Members of these small but vocal organizations are in constant danger of bodily harm or arrest.[69] Some countries, such as India with its official Rugmark program that identifies carpets made by freed laborers, have moved ahead of others, but across the board, progress has been very slow. Lately, even the Rugmark program has been exposed as having corrupt carpet inspectors.[70]

Finally, there is a feeling among the nations of the world that this nineteenth century issue was laid to rest long ago. Perhaps a sense of moral superiority over our ancestors is in place. To acknowledge that we as apathetic consumers of the global economy live in a world of slavery, with as many slaves as in any other era, is too difficult and painful to acknowledge. This relic of barbarism will remain until contemporary society takes on the moral strength and courage of the abolitionists of the nineteenth century.

Discussion Questions

1. Why are most people ignorant about contemporary slavery?
2. If a person willingly enters into the new slavery, is it still slavery?
3. How does the slavery of "disposable people" relate to issues of economic justice?

Endnotes

1. See Eugene Genovese, *Roll, Jordan, Roll: The World the Slaves Made* (New York: Vintage, 1976), pp. 410–420.

2. Melton Meltzer, *Slavery: A World History* (New York: DeCapo Press, 1993), pp. 5–6. Also see Robin Blackburn, *The Making of New World Slavery: From the Baroque to the Modern, 1492–1800* (London: Verso, 1997), pp. 31–95.

3. For discussions of these principles, see David Brion Davis, *The Problem of Slavery in Western Culture* (Ithaca, N.Y.: Cornell University Press, 1966), pp. 62–125. Also helpful is Roger L. Ransom, *Conflict and Compromise: The Political Economy of Slavery, Emancipation, and the American Civil War* (Cambridge: Cambridge University Press, 1989).

4. Kevin Bales, *Disposable People: New Slavery in the Global Economy* (Berkeley: University of California Press, 1999), p. 8

5. Ibid., p. 9.

6. Mark Memmott, "Slavery, Related Abuses Growing Worldwide, Report Says," *USA Today*, 25 May 2001, p. 13A; and Alexandra Zavis, "Children Toil in African Fields," *Chicago Tribune*, 6 May 2001, p. 6.

7. "Paying for slavery," *Chicago Tribune*, 17 May 1999, pp. 1, 8.

8. "Forced Child Labor Turns Deadly in China's Needy School System, *Los Angeles Times*, 9 March 2001.

9. *Christian Science Monitor*, "Wandering Ship Highlights African-Child Slave Trade," 16 April 2001.

10. David France, "Slavery's New Face," *Newsweek*, 18 December 2000, pp. 61–65; and Emma Dorothy Reinhardt and Charles Jacobs, "A Secret Slave Trade Survives in US," *Boston Globe*, 22 November 2000.

11. France.

12. "A Crackdown on the Traffic in Humans," *New York Times*, 26 February 2003.

13. Bales, p. 8.

14. Ibid., pp. 12–13.

15. Ibid., p. 15.

16. Ibid., pp. 19–20.

17. Murray Gordon, *Slavery in the Arab World* (New York: New Amsterdam, 1989), pp. 18–47. See also U.S. Senate Committee on Foreign Relations, *Slavery Throughout the World: Hearing Before the Committee on Foreign Relations,* 106th Congress, 1st sess., 28 September 2002. Also helpful is U.S. Senate Committee on Foreign Relations, *International Trafficking in Women and Children: Hearing Before the Committee on Foreign Relations*, 106th Congress, 2nd sess., 22 February 2000 and 4 April 2000.

18. Robert Segal, *Islam's Black Slaves: The Other Black Diaspora* (New York: Farrar, Straus, Giroux, 2001), pp. 183–187. Also see Humphrey J. Fisher, *Slavery in the History of Muslim Black Africa* (New York: New York University Press, 2001), pp. 63, 69, 93.

19. Bales, p. 118.

20. Ibid.

21. See a series by Cassandra Balchin in *The Nation* in September 1988 (vol. 247) on the problem of slavery in Pakistan.

22. Bales, p. 154.

23. Ibid., p. 173.

24. Ibid., p. 175.

25. Ibid., pp. 179–183.

26. Ibid., p. 184.

27. Ibid., pp. 150–151.

28. Ibid., p. 155.

29. Ibid., p. 156.
30. Ibid., pp. 159, 167, 170.
31. Ibid., p. 193.
32. Ibid., p. 165.
33. Ibid., p. 170.
34. Ibid., p. 169.
35. Utsa Patnaik and Manjari Dingwanez (eds.), *Chains of Servitude: Bondage and Slavery in India* (Madras, India: Sangam Books, 1985), pp. 1–34.
36. Bales, p. 198.
37. Ibid., p. 199.
38. See Human Rights Watch, *The Small Hands of Slavery: Bonded Child Labour in India* (New York: Human Rights Watch, 1996), pp. 14–16.
39. Bales, p. 203.
40. Ibid., pp. 202, 210, 212.
41. Ibid., pp. 218–219.
42. Ibid., p. 219.
43. Ibid., p. 220.
44. Ibid., p. 224.
45. Ibid., pp. 225, 228.
46. Ibid., p. 229.
47. For an overview, see Alison Sutton, *Slavery in Brazil: A Link in the Chain of Modernisation* (London: Anti-Slavery International, 1994).
48. For an overview, see Robert Edgar Conrad, *Children of God's Fire: A Documentary History of Black Slavery in Brazil* (Princeton, N.J.: Princeton University Press, 1983).
49. Leslie Bethell, *The Abolition of the Brazilian Slave Trade: Britain, Brazil and the Slave Trade Question, 1807–1869* (Cambridge: Cambridge University Press, 1970), pp. 62–87. Also Robert Conrad, *The Destruction of Brazilian Slavery, 1850–1888* (Berkeley: University of California Press, 1972), pp. 3–19.
50. Bales, p. 229.
51. Ibid., pp. 128–129.
52. Ibid., p. 135.
53. Ibid., p. 43.
54. Ibid., p. 38.
55. Ibid., p. 40.
56. Ibid., pp. 46–48. See also Mark VanLandingham, Chanpen Saengtienchai, John Knobel, and Anthony Pramualratana, *Friends, Wives and Extramarital Sex in Thailand* (Bangkok: Institute of Population Studies, Chulalongkorn University, 1995), pp. 9–25.
57. I. B. Horner, *Women Under Primitive Buddhism* (London: Routledge, 1930), pp. 40–43.
58. Bales, pp. 41, 53–57.
59. Ibid., pp. 61–64.
60. Ibid., pp. 58–60.
61. Ibid., pp. 55, 57–59. See also Thanh-Dam Truong, *Sex, Morality and Money: Prostitution and Tourism in Southeast Asia* (London: Zed Books, 1990), pp. 175–179.
62. M. Cherif Bassiouni, "Sexual Slavery Crosses Moral and National Boundaries," *Chicago Tribune,* 17 February 2002, pp. 1, 5.
63. Bales, p. 233.
64. Ibid., p. 234.
65. Ibid., pp. 235–240.

66. United Nations High Commissioner for Human Rights, *Fact Sheet No. 14, Contemporary Forms of Slavery* (Geneva: United Nations, 1991), pp. 3–4, 6–7.
67. Bales, p. 260.
68. Ibid., p. 245.
69. Ibid., p. 247.
70. Ibid., p. 257.

GENOCIDE

Men must either be caressed or else annihilated; they will revenge themselves for small injuries, but cannot do so for great ones; the injury therefore that we do to a man must be such that we need not fear his vengeance.—Machiavelli[1]

G enerally speaking, genocide refers to a coordinated and planned effort to deliberately wipe out a racial, ethnic, or political group. Genocide has been practiced throughout history. There are several mentions of genocide in the Old Testament and, if one believes biblical accounts of the great flood, God may have practiced genocide.

In the modern era, advances in technology have greatly facilitated the commission of genocide. The development of modern communications systems has made it easier to coordinate efforts to eradicate groups, modern transportation has made it easier for killers to reach their victims, and advances in the machinery of death (e.g., automatic weapons, bombs, armored vehicles, armed aircraft, and chemical weapons) have made the process of killing more efficient.

Although the practice of genocide is ancient, the term is relatively new— Raphael Lemkin created it in 1944. Lemkin was a Polish scholar who studied Nazi efforts to wipe out Jews and Gypsies in Europe during World War II, after he lost his entire large family to the Holocaust.[2] The term *genocide* is the result of combining the Greek word *genos* (race, tribe) and the Latin *cide* (killing).[3] The term was created because of a need to describe the carnage of the Holocaust, so there is a tendency to equate *genocide* with the Holocaust. Although the Holocaust fits anyone's definition of genocide, examples of genocide can be found far back in history, and there have been many examples since the Holocaust. As Melson observed, "Since the Second World War many more people have been killed as victims of domestic massacres and partial or total genocides than by international war."[4] And, since Melson's 1992 statement, there have been hundreds of thousands, perhaps millions, of additional deaths from genocide. Genocide is a contemporary international issue, of which the Holocaust is only one example.

DEFINING GENOCIDE

The term *genocide* has become part of our everyday vocabulary. Its popularity may be partly attributable to the powerful images it conveys. Describing killings as genocide makes them seem more sinister, calculated, and far reaching. Perhaps this is why it has been applied in a number of areas that some scholars of genocide would deem inappropriate, including family planning, race mixing, drug distribution, cocaine addiction, abortion, bisexuality, medical research, dieting, language regulation in the schools, and establishing Indian reservations.[5]

Although most people seem to "know" what is meant by *genocide,* it has been surprisingly difficult to define in precise terms, and academics have argued about what should be included in the definition. In his original statement on the issue, Lemkin defined genocide as "a coordinated plan of different actions aiming at the destruction of essential foundations of the life of the national groups, with the aim of annihilating the groups themselves."[6] His definition referred to actions carried out by people working under the authority of the state and included such nonlethal actions against the group as efforts to destroy a group's "culture, language, national feelings, religion, and the economic existence . . . and the destruction of the personal security, liberty, health, [and] dignity."[7]

Lemkin worked hard to gain recognition of the term *genocide* and to encourage nations to work together to prevent future acts of genocide. In 1948, the United Nations adopted the Genocide Convention, including in its definition of genocide many of the elements found in Lemkin's definition (see Box 10.1).[8]

The United Nations thus created a law that, for the first time, recognized genocide as an international crime. Although this action by the United Nations "has undoubted symbolic value, it has never had any practical effect."[9] Although passed in 1948, the United Nations has been slow to charge member nations with genocide or to act against those engaged in genocide.

The definition of genocide offered in the UN's Genocide Convention has been frequently criticized. Ironically, though, many of those same critics then use the UN definition in their own work. This is because the UN definition is among the only internationally recognized definitions of genocide and because in the future the Genocide Convention is likely to serve as the basis for international actions against genocide. Discussing the criticisms of the UN definition is a useful exercise because it can clarify why the United Nations has sometimes

10.1   *United Nations' Definition of Genocide*

Article II
In the present Convention, genocide means any of the following acts committed with intent to destroy, in whole or in part, a national, ethnical, racial or religious group, as such:
  (a) Killing members of the group;
  (b) Causing serious bodily or mental harm to members of the group;
  (c) Deliberately inflicting on the group conditions of life calculated to bring about its physical destruction in whole or in part;
  (d) Imposing measures intended to prevent births within the group;
  (e) Forcibly transferring children of the group to another.

been slow to act in situations where genocide has been alleged and because the discussion can highlight some of the difficulties in defining genocide.

One problem with the UN definition is that it omits the mass killing of political and social groups, thus excluding a substantial number of contemporary genocides.[10] Thus, as Heidenrich observes, the UN definition excludes the case of Cambodia:

> In Cambodia in 1975–79, the Khmer Rouge, followers of Communist leader Pol Pot, murdered people for "political" reasons as inane as for simply wearing eyeglasses. The Khmer Rouge, being Communists, wanted to eliminate all bourgeois intellectuals—and they assumed that any Cambodian who wore eyeglasses must be one. In their effort to socially re-engineer Cambodian society using terror and killing, later dramatized in the motion picture *The Killing Fields*, the Khmer Rouge murdered an estimated 1.7 million Cambodians out of an original population of only 7 million. In per capita terms, the Cambodian nation suffered the worst mass murder ever inflicted upon a population by its own government. Yet according to the international legal definition of genocide, the great majority of those victims were not victims of "genocide" because they were killed according to a purely political, not a racial, criteria.[11]

A second problem with the UN definition is that it is unclear how many people must die for genocide to have taken place. It is obvious if the numbers are in the millions or even in the tens of thousands. What if 5,000 people are killed? What about 500? What about 5? Is it a proportion of the group's members, such as more than one-quarter or more than one-half? Similarly, what if there is an attempt to wipe out a group but the attempt fails, killing only 50 of the group's two million members? Even though only a small proportion of the group was killed, the intent may have been to wipe out everyone.

A third problem is that the UN definition requires there be intent. In other words, it is essential to know what was in the minds of the killers. In some cases, such as the killing of Jews and Gypsies by the Germans, there is abundant documentation to show intent. A more common circumstance is for the killers to deny that destroying the group was the intent. Instead, they will argue the killings were the result of police actions to restore order, or that the victims were the casualties of war, not of genocide. Unless there is evidence to the contrary, one may avoid being charged with genocide under international law by simply denying intent.

Most scholars make a distinction between acts of war and acts of genocide. War involves killings that result from battles between two or more groups, each of which is in a position to fight. In contrast, genocide involves victims who are unable to defend themselves or to otherwise engage in battle. However, neither the UN definition nor most other definitions of genocide facilitate making a relatively straightforward distinction between war and genocide. For example, on August 6 and 9, 1945, during World War II, the United States dropped atomic bombs on Japanese civilians in Hiroshima and Nagasaki, killing at least 140,000 men, women, and children. Another 130,000 civilians were killed in the firebombing of Tokyo. The bombings took place in time of war and were against a civilian population unable to defend itself. Some scholars argue that the bombing should be called an act of genocide,[12] others disagree,[13] and still others confess they have difficulty resolving the issue.[14]

No definition of genocide is universally accepted or can be easily applied across a range of specific situations. Leo Kuper, who wrote a great deal on the limitations of the UN definition, nevertheless resigned himself to working with that definition in his research.[15] Perhaps it is best to think of current definitions of genocide as orienting frameworks for thinking about the general issue, rather than as tools for making precise distinctions in real-world situations.

CONDITIONS LEADING TO GENOCIDE

Genocide is a crime so horrible it is hard to imagine. Thus, it has been difficult to understand why genocide might occur. A good theory or explanation of genocide would allow us to better predict, and perhaps prevent, future acts of genocide. Numerous explanations have been put forward, but none are completely satisfactory.

An important first step toward explaining genocide is to develop a typology. Putting genocides into categories forces us to consider things that are common to all genocides. Developing a typology also encourages us to think more systematically about what we mean by genocide, thus having the added benefit of furthering the work of developing a good definition of the term.

A number of typologies have emerged.[16] Some categorize genocides by the motivations of the perpetrators, others make distinctions among genocides based on characteristics of the victims, others focus on types of perpetrators, and still others focus on types of society. As an illustration, Chalk and Jonassohn's typology assumes there are four types of genocide based on motive: (1) eliminate a real or potential threat; (2) spread terror among real or potential enemies; (3) acquire economic wealth; or (4) implement a belief, a theory, or an ideology.[17] Organizing past examples of genocide by using a typology helps us describe what genocide looks like, but is not enough to explain genocide. Chalk and Jonassohn's typology, for example, does not suggest why a potential threat is responded to with genocide in one society but not another, or why a group may be seen as a threat for decades before a genocide is undertaken. And, just as no definition of genocide has been universally accepted, there has been no typology of genocide to which most researchers would subscribe.

But if the reasons for genocide are difficult to fathom, it has been easier to describe conditions under which such acts are more likely to occur. Some have suggested that the stage is often set for genocide in conditions of war, colonization, or decolonization.

Genocide and War

Most scholars distinguish between acts of genocide and acts of war. Although the two are not the same, periods of war may facilitate the surfacing of a society's genocidal tendencies. There are several reasons for this: First, in times of war, normal restrictions on government behavior are lifted and the state is granted the authority to take actions that might otherwise not be allowed. And, in times of war, citizens of the state are more likely to support this expanded authority. Second, the perceived threat to society posed by a group, such as the Jews in World War II Germany, may seem much greater in times of war, when people are quite naturally sensitive to any threats to their national security. Third, the leaders of a country at war may find that the presence of a hated group is a useful tool for mobilizing the masses. Finally, the horrors of genocide may be less immediately apparent to other countries, whose focus is on the war and who might well be initially fooled by claims that the killing is an act of war rather than of genocide. The result is that other countries are reluctant to intervene.

During World War II, the Japanese atrocities in Nanking, China, provide a good example of using war as an excuse for engaging in genocidal acts and using the climate of war as an excuse for other nations to do nothing. In 1937, after capturing several other key cities in China, the Japanese army attacked Nanking and killed as many as 300,000 in only seven weeks. The level of brutality is hard to imagine:

> Chinese men were used for bayonet practice and in decapitation contests. An estimated 20,000–80,000 Chinese women were raped. Many soldiers went beyond rape to disembowel women, slice off their breasts, nail them alive to walls. Fathers were forced to rape their daughters and sons their mothers, as other family members watched. Not only did burials, castration, the carving of organs, and the roasting of people become routine, but more diabolical tortures were practiced, such as hanging people by their tongues on iron hooks or burying people to their waists and watching them get torn apart by German shepherds. So sickening was the spectacle that even the Nazis in the city were horrified. . . . [18]

Just as disturbing was the failure of the rest of the world to act, even though news of the holocaust quickly spread to other countries. For many years after the event, Western countries remained silent, a silence that one author has described as the second rape of Nanking. Even today, although nearly every American schoolchild has heard of the Nazi holocaust against the Jews, few are told about the rape of Nanking.

Genocide and Colonization

Colonization may be associated with genocide when the colonizer views its own actions as morally right, and the area being colonized as unclaimed—or more properly as not being claimed by any legitimate group.[19] In America, for example, much of the land found by Columbus was considered unclaimed, and the "savages" inhabiting it were often seen as less than human. Their skin was a different color, they were not Christians, their language was different, and they used substantially more primitive technology. All of this made it easier for "good Christians" to purposely infect Native Americans with smallpox and to send in armies to kill as many of them as possible (see Chapter 8). Similarly, Spanish and Portugese are now the primary languages of South America because colonizing efforts successfully destroyed much of the existing culture throughout South America.

Genocide and Decolonization

The stage is often set for genocide when decolonization occurs. When a strong colonial power withdraws from a society, or when a strong unifying leader is replaced, existing ethnic tensions may rise to the surface and the consequence may be genocide. There are numerous examples of this throughout history, including efforts at "ethnic cleansing" that occurred in the 1990s in Yugoslavia in what is now known as Bosnia Herzegovina. Until his death in 1980, Marshal Tito tightly controlled Communist Yugoslavia and kept long-standing ethnic tensions under control. During the 1980s, Yugoslavia was led by a Serbian, Slobodan Milošević, who encouraged tension between Serbian Christians and Muslims. Then, in 1991, Slovenia and Croatia declared their independence from Yugoslavia and a civil war broke out. Although both the Muslims and the Croats were engaged in violence against the Serbs, the (Christian) Serbian response against Muslims was extreme, accounting for as much as 90 percent of the violence, with Croatians accounting for only 6 percent of the violence and Muslims only 4 percent.[20] Serbian atrocities included "killings, rapes, and other abuses against the Muslim civilian population. . . . [and] It appears unquestionably to be the case that the victims of killings were selected because they were Muslims, that in the overwhelming proportion of cases they were defenseless, and that the killing was intentional."[21] Milošević and others were eventually arrested and put on trial for the crime of genocide.

In addition to these three general conditions that set the stage for genocide, several authors have suggested other relevant conditions. Porter provides a list that includes many of these key elements. He suggests that the likelihood of genocide increases in nation-states where the following conditions exist:[22]

a. Minority groups have previously been and are presently defined outside the universe of moral obligation by the dominant group. Such victims have been labeled "outsiders," "scum," or other epithets in order to stigmatize and dehumanize them.
b. Pervasive racialistic ideologies and propaganda are found in the nation-state's society.
c. There is a strong dependence on military security.
d. Powerful, monolithic exclusionary political parties are present.
e. The leadership has strong territorial ambitions.
f. The power of the state has been reduced by defeat in war and/or internal strife.
g. The possibility of retaliation for genocidal acts by kin of the victims or of interference by neutral nations is at a minimum.

Thus, genocide is not a random occurrence but is likely to emerge when a variety of conditions are present simultaneously. The last item on Porter's list—the likelihood of interference from kin of the victims or from neutral nations—leads us to consider how genocide has been responded to in the past.

RESPONDING TO GENOCIDE

Complaints about the UN definition of genocide are not merely word games of only academic interest. Whether particular actions fit the legal definition of genocide under international law will determine whether there is legal authority to bring charges against offenders. The UN's Genocide Convention was purposely vague regarding how violators would be brought to justice and completely silent on appropriate punishments. Many countries were uncomfortable with developing an international court because it would mean giving up some of their own sovereignty. Such concerns may explain why the U.S. Congress did not ratify the UN Genocide Convention until 1986, nearly 40 years after the UN initially passed it.

As a compromise designed to gain the cooperation and signatures of as many countries as possible, the UN Genocide Convention called for signatory countries to pass their own laws against genocide and to determine their own penalties. Furthermore, Article VI of the Convention called for the trial of those charged with genocide to be held in the country in which the crime took place and to be conducted by a tribunal conducted by that government, or by an international tribunal that *might* be formed by other UN signatory nations. Because genocide is most often carried out with the blessings of the government in power, it seems absurd to have that same government reach a judgment about whether genocide occurred, to conduct a trial, and to then determine the proper penalty for it.

The second option, an international tribunal, has rarely been used. In August 2001, a UN war crimes tribunal in the Netherlands found a Bosnian Serb general guilty of genocide for killing as many as 8,000 Bosnian Muslims in 1995. This was the first genocide conviction since World War II. The general was sentenced to 46 years in prison.[23] In July 2001, the UN war crimes tribunal began actions against former Yugoslavian president Milošević. Whether these represent an emerging trend to bring charges of genocide before an international tribunal is still unclear. In the same year, the United States withheld its overdue payments to the United Nations because of objections to the UN's plan to establish a permanent International Court of Justice.[24]

For whatever reason, nations have been slow to respond to genocide and only rarely intervene to stop it. Further, when the genocidal actions of a nation become known, it is unlikely that nation will suffer consequences of any kind. Expressions of outrage by other nations are not unusual, but those expressions are seldom followed by meaningful action.

GENOCIDE IN THE PAST CENTURY

It would be nice to believe that humanity has progressed to the point that genocide is a thing of the past, a product of a simpler and less-developed period of the human race. However, little evidence supports such a belief. To the contrary, the twentieth century witnessed more deaths through genocide than any other century.[25] Some have argued that genocide is fostered by pluralistic societies in which people of very different cultures and backgrounds are brought together. If that is true, then the increased interaction between cultures that results from modern transportation, modern communication, and the development of global businesses may set the stage for future acts of genocide. At the very least, these facts of modern life facilitate the movement of refugees threatened by genocide, who in turn, may then attempt to retaliate.

It is not possible to describe all the known acts of genocide, or even to describe all that have been committed in the twentieth century. Charny, for example, suggests that a conservative estimate of the number of people killed as innocent victims of genocide, not including combatants in war, is 170,000,000 between 1900 and 1987 alone.[26] Obviously, any estimates of the casualties of genocide are just that, estimates. By any account, however, the numbers are staggering.

Given the large number of genocides that have occurred just in the past century and the need to provide some background on each as it is discussed, we will elaborate on only two instances to illustrate the concept of genocide with relatively concrete examples. Both are examples in which the nations of the world knew or should have known that genocide was happening but did little or nothing to stop it, although there were expressions of outrage after the fact. The Armenian genocide is among the first of this past century and the genocide in Rwanda is a more contemporary example.

The Armenian Genocide (1915–1918)

The Armenian people had lived in an area now known as Turkey for nearly 3,000 years and were among the first groups to adopt Christianity. For at least a thousand years before their genocide, the Armenians lived in an area dominated by Muslim Turks. At the time of the genocide, the area was under the control of the Ottoman Empire, which was in serious decline, having lost many of the lands it had controlled in earlier centuries. The Armenians were a non-Muslim minority and were treated "as second class citizens subject to legal restrictions that denied them normal safeguards. Neither their lives nor their properties were guaranteed security."[27] They were not allowed to take part in government, were required to pay special taxes, were not allowed to carry arms, and because they lived in a country guided by Islamic law, they could not testify in court against Muslim defendants.[28] Further, most citizens had been segregated into their own religious communities known as millets, and this segregation made it easier to later target Armenians for extermination.

In 1913, the Young Turk Party seized power, gaining control of the army and putting sympathizers in key positions in every major town and city.[29] The Young Turks were ultranationalists who believed in the formation of an exclusively Turkish state, while wanting to expand the boundaries of their country by attacking countries to the east, in an area controlled by the Russians. This area was also the historic homeland for the Armenians and is the location of present-day Armenia.

For the Young Turks, having an exclusively Turkish state meant adopting policies that would "purify" the country by removing the Armenian people. A string of defeats in their efforts to expand the boundaries of their country was blamed on the Armenians. By claiming that the Armenians had collaborated with the enemy and had therefore caused the military defeat of the Turkish army, the Young Turks could more easily gain popular support for purification policies. Purification began on a large scale in 1915, just one year after World War I had begun. The war provided a convenient cover for the genocide, allowing the Young Turks to claim that the dead were casualties of war, not of genocide. The war also distracted major world powers that might otherwise have intervened to stop the killing.[30]

The genocide itself began in 1915, although there were a series of lesser massacres before that. Three strategies were used to eliminate the Armenians: deportation, execution, and starvation. Armenian political, religious, educational, and intellectual leaders were separated from their communities and executed. To further reduce the likelihood of resistance, young able-bodied men were also executed, leaving women, children, and the elderly. By far the largest number of victims occurred among women and children as part of a deportation process. In towns throughout the country, hundreds of thousands of Armenians were given as little as three days notice to begin a journey on foot that covered hundreds of miles and lasted for weeks. The final destination was the Syrian desert to the south. However, most Armenians did not survive the journey, which was in actuality a death march. The government had made no provisions for food or water during the march and when marchers passed near rivers, they were often killed if they tried to stop for a drink. In addition, women and children were often stripped naked and abused. Along the way, they were attacked and killed by bands of criminals who had been released from prison by the government and sent out with instructions to butcher as many of the Armenians as possible, and to do so in the most violent manner possible. Citizens also attacked the marchers. "As columns of defenseless Armenians were marched through towns and villages they would be set upon again and again, sometimes by brigands but more often by Turkish or Kurdish villagers."[31] Young children who were not killed, or who did not die from exposure or starvation, were abducted and placed in Turkish and Muslim homes and were required to adopt the language and religion of their captors.[32] For those Armenians who survived the long march,

> The killing units completed their task at a place called Deir el-Zor. In this final carnage, children were smashed against rocks, women were torn apart with swords, men were mutilated, others thrown into flames alive. Every cruelty was inflicted on the remnants of the Armenian people.[33]

When all the killing was done, at least 1,500,000 Armenians had been slaughtered and a people who had been living in the area for 3,000 years had nearly vanished from the face of the earth. A relatively small number of Armenians managed to escape the carnage, but their culture and history did not. All art, literature, and other records of the history and culture of the Armenian people in Turkey were destroyed. Churches were destroyed, and even Armenian place names were changed.[34] Although symbols of Armenian culture were destroyed, throughout the four years of the genocide, there was relatively little destruction of Armenian property. Instead, as the Armenians were driven out Turks simply took their homes, land, and other property. In this way, everyday (non-Armenian) citizens of Turkey benefitted directly from the genocide. The Armenian genocide is among the most tragic in this century because it most completely succeeded in destroying a people and all traces of their culture.

Rwanda (1994)

Rwanda, located in west-central Africa, is slightly smaller than the state of Maryland, only about 125 miles at its widest point and only about 100 miles at its longest point.[35] At the time of the genocide, it was among the most densely populated countries on the African continent. Rwanda is among the poorest nations in the world, and in 1994, it was facing a drought in which "it was estimated that as many as 800,000 people would need food aid to survive."[36]

There are two major ethnic groups in Rwanda. The Hutus make up about 85 percent of the population, and most of the remaining people are Tutsi. These groups had lived in the region for more than two thousand years and during that time developed a shared language and culture. The Tutsi, although far fewer in number, had historically held positions of power in Rwanda, whereas Hutu were more generally commoners. Rwanda came to be ruled by Belgium after World War I, and in the 1920s, the Belgians ordered that only Tutsi, who already held most positions of leadership, should be officials in the Rwandan government. This required differentiating between Hutu and Tutsi, and beginning in the 1930s, Rwandans were required to register with the government and declare their ethnicity.[37] By the 1950s, tensions between Hutu and Tutsi had grown, and the Belgium government sought to bring peace by placing some Hutu in positions of power. In 1961, Rwandans voted to establish a republic in which citizens elected their own representatives. Because of their overwhelming numbers, these elections placed many Hutu in positions of power. At this time, Hutu began to attack Tutsi who had previously held power and drove as many as 10,000 from the country. The Hutu depicted the refugees as enemies of Rwanda and eliminated any powerful opponents within Rwanda. The Catholic Church, which had supported the Tutsi and had many Tutsi among its priests, shifted allegiance and threw its support behind the new Hutu leadership. Other Christian churches remained officially neutral but openly worked with Hutu officials.[38]

Tutsi refugees would periodically launch attacks against Hutu-led Rwanda. They also orchestrated the slaughter of Hutu in neighboring Burundi in 1972, killing as many as 200,000. By the late 1980s, the number of Tutsi exiles had grown to nearly 600,000 people.[39]

By the late 1980s, Rwanda was at war with the Rwandan Patriotic Front (RPF), an organization led by refugees from Rwanda, many of whom were Tutsi. The RPF invaded Rwanda on October 1, 1990, and between that date and the victory of the RPF over the Hutu government in July 1993, "the killings wiped out one-tenth of Rwanda's population of seven million."[40] Although Rwanda was in a state of war beginning in 1990, the killings on each side were limited until the spring of 1994.

On April 6, 1994, the Hutu president of Rwanda was killed when his plane was shot down. The genocide of Tutsi in Rwanda began in earnest with that event and lasted for 13 weeks, during which time as many as 800,000 people were killed. Although the primary target of the genocide was the Tutsi, Hutu who were sympathetic to the Tutsi or who refused to take part in the killing were also targeted. Throughout the genocide, the Hutu couched their actions as necessary for self-defense in their war against the RPF. Although the killing of Rwanda's president appeared to be the trigger for genocide, it has been argued that planning for the genocide began months earlier. It has also been suggested that Hutu extremists hoping to use the event to mobilize citizens against the RPF and stir them to genocide may have shot down the president's plane.[41]

Rwandan military personnel often began the killing, later to be joined by Hutu citizens. At first, they moved from house to house, but later they arranged to bring victims together in groups—in churches, schools, and other public sites—where they could be massacred on a larger scale.[42] The Hutu government also made extensive use of the media, including radio, television, newspapers, and magazines to stir up anti-Tutsi sentiments.[43] Before the genocide, at least 29 percent of Rwandan homes owned a radio. Immediately before and during the genocide, government officials handed out free radios to Hutus and used radio broadcasts to incite the public by reporting fabricated stories about massacres committed by the RPF. Radio broadcasts were also used to persuade Hutu citizens that killing Tutsi and Tutsi sympathizers was their patriotic duty.[44]

At the time of the genocide, poverty was extreme and a drought left many in Rwanda starving. The government responded by delivering food, drink, and clothing to those willing to kill. Killers operating in the countryside were often promised land, a scarce and valuable commodity. Hutu willing to take property and destroy the homes of Tutsi were sometimes threatened with punishment or even death if they did not also kill the inhabitants. The original slaughter, described to the outside world in the language of war, was focused on young males. Later the killing would be extended to women, children, and the elderly.[45]

The killing of Tutsi women was often accompanied by sexual and physical abuse. "Tutsi women were often raped, tortured, and mutilated before they were murdered,"[46] although some managed to escape with their lives by giving the killers sexual favors. Violence was particularly fierce against Tutsi women who had married Hutu men.[47] Such marriages were defined as race mixing, and it was believed that children produced from such a marriage would be part Tutsi and thus be racially impure.[48]

In preparation for their war with the RPF, the Hutu government had supplied both guns and machetes to civilian Hutu males and provided training for many. Although guns were more efficient killing tools, machetes were often used because of the terror they caused. Many victims were simply hacked to death, or beaten to death with hammers or clubs. Victims sometimes had both Achilles' tendons cut in their legs before they were killed, so they were unable to run away.

It is now clear that other world powers were not only aware of the genocide as it was happening, but knew about it in advance. In addition to a large number of early indicators that preparations were being made for genocide, the head of the United Nations Assistance Mission in Rwanda (UNAMIR) specifically warned the United Nations of a plan to annihilate all Tutsi.[49] This information was available to the United States, the French, and the Belgians, all of whom had peacekeeping troops in the country. The response was not to strengthen peacekeeping forces and protect Tutsi citizens, but to withdraw all forces, including diplomatic representatives.[50] The withdrawal included UN soldiers guarding refugee camps within Rwanda, camps that were raided and their inhabitants killed soon after the UN troops left. The United Nations and other countries did not fail to act because they were unaware of the genocide. They failed to act because Rwanda was not of critical economic or political importance to them. As Lemarchand observed, "That a carnage of this magnitude could have been going on day after day, week after week, without interference from the international community speaks volumes for the lack of resolve to deal with massive human rights violations."[51]

The genocide in Rwanda is striking because it was so thoroughly planned and executed, because the methods were extremely cruel and brutal, because it is among the first of the modern genocides in which a number of the killings were captured on videotape—making it easier for the outside world to directly see the horror of the killing—and because other nations failed to intervene when human decency dictated otherwise. Unlike the genocide of the Armenians, other countries could not claim the distracting influence of a world war. Actually, there were no credible excuses.

The Aftermath of Armenia and Rwanda

It is difficult to conceive of a just response to genocide. To date, most efforts at holding those responsible for genocide accountable have been less than spectacular. After the Armenian genocide, the Young Turks who coordinated the killings fled the country, and the world was finally ready to publicly acknowledge the extent of the killing. A Turkish military court tried and sentenced to death (in their absence) four organizers of the genocide. "No attempt was made to carry out the sentence, however, and thousands of other culprits were neither tried nor even removed from office. Within a few months the judicial proceedings were suspended, and even accused and imprisoned war criminals were freed and sent home."[52] Other nations agreed that Armenians should be returned to their homeland and compensated for their losses, but were unwilling to provide aid and did nothing to force the Turkish government to act. Instead, the Turkish government continued changing place names and destroying any cultural memory of the Armenians. The government tried to quiet any discussions of the Armenian genocide and even successfully pressured the U.S. State Department to stop the production of a Hollywood movie about the Armenians.[53] Turkish efforts were so successful that most people have never heard of the Armenian genocide, and most scholars describe it as the forgotten genocide.

In Rwanda, the genocide ended in July 1994, but the killing continued on a smaller scale. This time, however, scattered fragments of the Tutsi-led RPF were now doing the killing and Hutu were now fleeing the country for safety. In an ironic reversal of roles, some of the Hutu directly involved in the genocide of the Tutsi were refugees and became leaders organizing military forays into Rwanda in an effort to destabilize the government. The RPF, for its part, launched attacks against these refugee camps, driving hundreds of thousands of Hutu back into Rwanda and killing thousands in the process. Meanwhile, some of the Hutu who have returned to Rwanda have organized guerrilla groups to attack the government.[54] Although nothing as organized as, or on the scale of, the 1994 genocide has occurred, each side has engaged in smaller massacres, with little interference from other nations.

The international community has been slow to act but has brought criminal charges against some of those involved in the genocide. In June 2001, a Belgian court convicted four people of war crimes for their actions in Rwanda. One was a factory owner, one a college professor, and two were Catholic nuns. The nuns "were charged with helping Hutu extremists kill more than 5,000 people at their convent."[55] In February 2003, a doctor, a minister who headed the Seventh-Day Adventist Church in Rwanda, and his son were all convicted for aiding and abetting the genocide, and three Catholic priests were awaiting trial on the same charges.[56]

Preventing Genocide—What Can Be Done?

Although nearly 80 years passed between Armenia and Rwanda, and although there were numerous genocides in between, it appears the world community learned little about preventing genocide or responding to it in a timely manner. Preventing genocide requires work at two very different levels. First, it requires identifying early warning signs of genocide. Second, it is necessary to find a way to motivate powerful nations to act when they become aware of genocide.

For genocide to happen, several things must come together. First, there must be strong group feelings, with one group viewing itself as superior to another. Second, the political machinery must be in place to enable the killers to organize and carry out the genocide. Third, ambitious leaders within the political machinery must seek to enhance their power. They do this by bringing together their people around common themes that another group is a threat, is less than human, and can only be dealt with by extermination. Finally, these leaders must be able to act without interference from significant numbers of their own people or from other nations that might threaten economic sanctions or even direct intervention.

Although it might seem that the conditions that foster genocide would be apparent to the outside world well before the genocide begins, history suggests that either other countries are unaware of these conditions or they are aware but choose to ignore them. Our attention now turns to each of these circumstances.

Early Warning Signs

The failure of nation-states to recognize when genocides are likely to occur often cannot be attributed to a lack of information but, rather, to the absence of any system for organizing hundreds or even thousands of scattered pieces of information from a variety of sources. In many cases, the various pieces of the puzzle may be there, but not recognized until it is too late. One way to respond to this is to better educate a variety of people about genocide, including journalists, religious groups, foreign diplomats, politicians, and media news editors. An encouraging development in this regard is the rise of "Genocide Studies" programs at universities around the world. Another response, suggested by John G. Heidenrich,[57] is to develop early warning centers. Such centers can identify likely outbreaks of genocide and can bring these situations to the attention of political leaders and the public. In many ways, such a center would be similar in principle to the Southern Poverty Law Center (aka Klanwatch), which monitors hate groups in America and issues alerts when serious problems are foreseen (see Chapter 8).

Getting Powerful Nations to Act

Ironically, during the past century—when communications were at their most advanced state in history and when the skill of intelligence gathering had been finely honed—there were probably more deaths by genocide than at any time in the history of mankind. Making powerful nations aware of an impending genocide is not enough, and awareness may not be the greatest challenge to preventing genocide.

The challenge is to engage those nations lacking the political will to intervene. An important element of this task is improving public awareness of genocides as they occur. Too often, the public is unaware of the nature and extent of a genocide until well after the fact. The same system of modern communication that can make world leaders more aware of impending genocides can also be used to educate the public about instances as they arise. An informed public is more likely to demand actions from its leaders. Thus, some of the same mechanisms for making nation-states aware of emerging genocides can also prompt them to act.

CONCLUSION

Genocide is not only a problem of the past, but of the present and the future. Although it is tempting to think that humankind is becoming more civilized, genocide illustrates at least one aspect of humanity that has not improved. It is likely that genocide will always be a possibility somewhere in the world. It is possible, however, to stop genocides from actually being carried out. All that is required is knowledge that a genocide is occurring and the will to intervene.

Discussion Questions

1. Other than the Holocaust, most Americans know very little about the many genocides that have occurred during the past 100 years. Why might that be so?
2. Why is it important to develop a specific legal definition of genocide that would apply to all countries? Why not let each country have its own definition and its own system for dealing with genocide within that country?
3. More people have been killed in genocide during the past 100 years than at any time in history. Why might that be true, and what might be done to change things?

Endnotes

1. Niccolo Machiavelli, *The Prince* (New York: New American Library, 1952), p. 37.
2. Israel W. Charny, "The Dawning of a New Age of Opposition to Genocide," in *Encyclopedia of Genocide, Volume I,* Israel W. Charny (ed.) (Santa Barbara, CA: ABC-CLIO, 1999), pp. xi–xxiv.
3. Raphael Lemkin, "Genocide," *American Scholar* 15(2) 1946, pp. 227–230; see also Raphael Lemkin, *Axis Rule in Occupied Europe; Laws of Occupation, Analysis of Government, Proposals for Redress* (Washington, D.C.: Carnegie Endowment for International Peace, 1944).
4. Robert Melson, *Revolution and Genocide: On the Origins of the Armenian Genocide and Holocaust* (Chicago: University of Chicago Press, 1992), p. 285.
5. For an example, see Frank Chalk and Kurt Jonassohn (eds.), *The History and Sociology of Genocide: Analysis and Case Studies* (New Haven, Conn.: Yale University Press, 1990); Helen Fein, "Genocide, Terror, Life Integrity, and War Crimes," in *Genocide: Conceptual and Historical Dimensions,* George J. Andreopoulos (ed.) (Philadelphia: University of Pennsylvania Press, 1994), pp. 95–107.
6. Raphael Lemkin, *Axis Rule in Occupied Europe,* p. 79.
7. Ibid.
8. United Nations, *Convention on the Prevention and Punishment of the Crime of Genocide. Resolution 260 A (III)* (accessed online at www.unhchr.ch/html/menu3/b/p_genoci.htm on 27 August 2001).
9. Chalk and Jonassohn, p. 11.
10. Samuel Totten, William S. Parsons, and Israel W. Charny (eds.), *Century of Genocide: Eyewitness Accounts and Critical Views* (New York: Garland, 1997); Chalk and Jonassohn; Leo Kuper, *Genocide: Its Political Use in the Twentieth Century* (New Haven, Conn.: Yale University Press, 1981).
11. For a pragmatic approach, see John G. Heidenrich, *How to Prevent Genocide: A Guide for Policymakers, Scholars, and the Concerned Citizen* (Westport, Conn.: Praeger, 2001).
12. Kuper.
13. Fein.
14. To see the semantics of it all, see Israel W. Charny, "Toward a Generic Definition of Genocide," in *Genocide: Conceptual and Historical Dimensions,* George J. Andreopoulos (ed.) (Philadelphia: University of Pennsylvania Press, 1994).
15. Leo Kuper, *The Prevention of Genocide* (New Haven, Conn.: Yale University Press, 1985).
16. Peter duPreez, *Genocide: The Psychology of Mass Murder* (New York: Boyars/Bowerdean, 1994); Chalk and Jonassohn; Kuper, *Genocide;* Charny, "The Dawning of a New Age of Opposition to Genocide," pp. 3–7.
17. Chalk and Jonassohn.
18. Iris Chang, *The Rape of Nanking: The Forgotten Holocaust of World War II* (New York: Penguin, 1997), p. 6.
19. duPreez.
20. Florence Hartman, "Bosnia," in *Crimes of War: What the Public Should Know,* Roy Gutman and David Rieff (eds.) (New York: Norton, 1999), pp. 50–56.
21. Steven L. Burg, "Genocide in Bosnia-Herzegovina?" in *Century of Genocide: Eyewitness Accounts and Critical Views,* Samuel Totten, William S. Parsons, and Israel W. Charny (eds.) (New York: Garland, 1997), pp. 424–433.
22. Jack Porter, "Introduction," in *Genocide and Human Rights: A Global Anthology,* Jack Porter (ed.) (Washington, D.C.: University Press of America, 1982), pp. 17–18.

23. "Court Rules Genocide Was Committed at Srebrenica," *Los Angeles Times* (electronic edition) (accessed online at www.latimes.com on 2 August 2001).
24. Naftali Bendavid, "Republican Spat Over World Criminal Court Holds Up UN Dues," *Chicago Tribune,* 17 August 2001, pp. 1–2.
25. Heidenrich.
26. Israel W. Charny, "Democide: A New Inclusive Concept Proposed," in *Encyclopedia of Genocide, Volume I,* Israel W. Charny (ed.) (Santa Barbara, CA: ABC-CLIO, 1999), pp. 15–18.
27. Rouben P. Adalian, "The Armenian Genocide," in *Century of Genocide: Eyewitness Accounts and Critical Views,* Samuel Totten, William S. Parsons, and Israel W. Charny (eds.) (New York: Garland, 1997), pp. 41–77.
28. Richard G. Hovannisian, "The Armenians in Turkey," in *The History and Sociology of Genocide: Analysis and Case Studies* Frank Chalk and Kurt Jonassohn (eds.) (New Haven, Conn.: Yale University Press, 1990), pp. 249–266; Richard G. Hovannisian, "Etiology and Sequelae of the Armenian Genocide," in *Genocide: Conceptual and Historical Dimensions,* George J. Andreopoulos (ed.) (Philadelphia: University of Pennsylvania Press, 1994), pp. 111–140.
29. Adalian.
30. Ibid.
31. Melson, pp. 144–145.
32. Adalian.
33. Ibid., p. 45.
34. Melson.
35. Central Intelligence Agency, *The World Factbook: Rwanda* (accessed online at www.cia.gov on 26 September 2001).
36. Alison Des Forges, *Leave None to Tell the Story: Genocide in Rwanda* (New York: Human Rights Watch, 1999), p. 1. Also available at www.hrw.org/reports/1999/rwanda.
37. Ibid.
38. Ibid.
39. Ibid.
40. Rene Lemarchand, "The Rwanda Genocide," in *Century of Genocide: Eyewitness Accounts and Critical Views,* Samuel Totten, William S. Parsons, and Israel W. Charny (eds.) (New York: Garland, 1997), p. 408.
41. Rene Lemarchand, "Rwanda and Burundi, Genocide," in *Encyclopedia of Genocide, Volume II,* Israel W. Charny (ed.) (Santa Barbara, CA: ABC-CLIO, 1999).
42. Des Forges.
43. Christopher Taylor, *Sacrifice as Terror: The Rwandan Genocide of 1994* (Oxford, England: Berg, 1999).
44. Des Forges.
45. Ibid.
46. Ibid., p. 10.
47. Taylor.
48. Ibid.; see also Des Forges.
49. Des Forges.
50. Lemarchand, "Rwanda and Burundi, Genocide."
51. Ibid., p. 511.
52. Hovannisian, "Etiology and Sequelae of the Armenian Genocide," p. 126.
53. Ibid.
54. Taylor.

55. "Two Nuns Guilty in Genocide," *L.A. Times* (electronic edition) (accessed online at www.latimes.com on 8 June 2001).
56. Marlise Simons, "Rwanda Pastor and Son, a Doctor, Convicted of Genocide," *New York Times,* 20 February 2003 (accessed online at www.nytimes.com on 12 March 2003).
57. Heidenrich.

THE ENVIRONMENT

I t may seem peculiar to talk about the environment as an issue related to justice, and such a discussion would probably not have taken place as little as 50 years ago. We depend on natural resources, such as air and water, to survive, but until relatively recently, there has been little appreciation for injustices that might arise from humankind's relationship with the environment. We do not use or dispose of natural resources in a way that affects all people equally, and issues of justice surround the way in which the benefits and the costs are distributed throughout society and among nations.

Some use the term "environmental justice" to describe injustices in the way natural resources are used. Environmental justice concerns the way in which environmental damage is disproportionately suffered by the powerless—primarily the poor and minorities. In America, race and income are intertwined. Some view the problem as more rooted in race than in economics. These individuals prefer the term *environmental racism*. Our discussion will use the more general term *environmental justice* to encompass both race and income.

In America, concern with environmental justice is relatively new. In 1971, the Council on Environmental Quality issued a report that was among the first to mention the possible link between toxic risk and income. In 1978, public attention was drawn to the issue by front-page stories about the potential health consequences of buried toxic waste in the community of Love Canal, New York. Then, in 1982, a protest in Warren County, North Carolina, prompted the government to study the process by which sites were selected for storing hazardous waste.[1] The study found that three of the four hazardous waste facilities studied were in predominantly African American communities and the fourth was in a low-income community. In 1987, the United Church of Christ issued a report concluding that race was a major deciding factor in the selection of sites for hazardous waste. In the early 1990s, a series of studies found that across the nation, nonwhites were substantially more likely than were whites to live in the most polluted areas.[2]

By the early 1990s, the environmental justice movement had sufficient visibility that it could influence national policy. In 1994, President Clinton signed Executive Order #12898 requiring the U.S. Environmental Protection Agency to consider environmental justice in developing its policies and regulations.[3] The Department of Energy also drafted guidelines requiring environmental justice be considered when determining compliance with Department of Energy guidelines.[4]

Ironically, concern about the environment and the resulting efforts to clean contaminated land, water, and air may contribute to environmental injustice. Once removed from the soil, air, or water, dangerous contaminants must be placed somewhere—and that is too often in the poorest communities. As Faber has observed,

> The waste, now commodified, becomes mobile, crossing local, state and even national borders in search of "efficient" (i.e., low-cost and politically feasible) areas for treatment, incineration, and/or disposal. More often than not, the waste sites and facilities are themselves hazardous and located in poor working class neighborhoods and communities of color. . . .
>
> For instance, in Sierra Blanca, Texas, the local economy has collapsed. Underemployment is so pervasive that 40 percent of the population lives below the poverty line. Since 1992, New York City and a "biosolids" company called Merco have shipped roughly 200 tons of processed sewage *a day* to the small town. Due to concerns that the sludge is poisoned with heavy metals, petroleum, and pathogens, community residents see this practice as posing a significant health threat and therefore a form of environmental racism. There are more than 200 other such sewage sludge sites in Texas alone.[5]

The use and disposal of natural resources is a global problem and the United States is a key figure in the process. Although the United States has only about 6 percent of the world's population, it "consumes approximately 30 percent of all raw materials used by the human population in any given year."[6] However, there is almost no portion of the world that is not experiencing, or will soon experience, conflict and injustice related to the use of natural resources. Consumption practices in the United States contribute to the problem but are not the only cause. This is a problem of global proportions.

The discussion that follows will take a global perspective and will include more than the disposal of hazardous waste or environmental contaminants. Much of the discussion will concentrate on issues of justice as they are related to how resources are extracted and how the benefits of those resources are distributed.

Oil is the natural resource that comes to mind when we think about problems arising from shortages of natural resources and when we think about air pollution and other environmental contaminants. The Gulf War was fought over oil and oil provides nations that produce it with the money to buy advanced weapons. Money from oil production probably funded the terrorists who brought down the World Trade Center on September 11, 2001. However, oil is only one of many valuable resources that play a key role in modern society and over which injustices arise. Other resources include natural gas, coal, uranium, gold, diamonds, timber, copper, iron, and water.

The problems of the environment and justice have many dimensions. Klare has argued that two factors make it likely that conflicts and injustices relating to natural resources will be an increasingly serious problem.[7] These factors are the growing importance of some resources and a growing worldwide demand for those resources.

Some resources, such as oil, have become essential for maintaining our economy and way of life. Until the early 1900s, oil played a minor role in the U.S. economy. Its derivatives, including kerosene, were used for heating and for light, but it was not yet used to power vehicles or modern machinery. Today, the economy would collapse if the flow of oil into the United States were suddenly interrupted. Protecting oil resources was a primary consideration in our decision to enter the Gulf War in 1990 and in our continued military presence in the Middle East.

A growing and nearly insatiable demand for resources, combined with limited supplies, contribute to injustices related to the environment. Advanced industrial countries consume far more resources than do developing countries. In the United States, for example, advances in technology and an improved standard of living have meant that energy consumption increases every year. The problem is compounded by population growth, which is most rapid in developing countries—countries whose per capita energy consumption is relatively small but will increase dramatically as the country develops. Because supplies are limited, however, there will be increased competition, violence, and even war over resources. Further, increasing demand given limited supplies will mean that many basic resources will be available only to the wealthy.

It is not possible here to cover every resource and every respect in which resources could be tied to justice. To illustrate the many ways in which environmental concerns and justice are connected, however, we will focus on the implications for justice of one natural resource—water.

WATER

Most industrial societies require oil, coal, and natural gas to maintain their industries, generate electricity, and provide fuel for planes, trains, ships, and trucks. These resources are essential for maintaining a modern lifestyle, but they are not essential to life itself. There have been and still are societies that do not depend on fossil fuels. Water is quite another matter. Access to water is a matter of life and death, something important enough for which to kill. And, although substitutes are available for many resources (for example, for some applications, oil from soybeans can replace oil extracted from the ground, and plastic can replace wood in building construction), to date there are no substitutes for water. Some have begun to refer to water as "Blue Gold,"[8] and in Texas water has become more valuable than oil and is now called "Liquid Gold."[9]

The first civilizations arose in river valleys, and most major cities were built along waterways. Although it would appear that water is everywhere, it is a finite resource. "Available fresh water amounts to less than one-half of one percent of all the water on the Earth. The rest is sea water, or is frozen in the polar ice."[10] The supply of water is fixed, but demand continues to grow. As a result of population growth and industrialization, water usage is doubling about every 20 years.[11] As Klare has observed,

> Of the amount [of water] that is readily available . . . half is already being appropriated for human use. As in the case of oil, population growth and higher standards of living are constantly boosting the global demand for water. If this pattern persists, total human usage will approach 100 percent of the available supply by the mid-twenty-first century, producing severe shortages in some areas and intensified competition for access to important sources of supply.[12]

Much of the water that is consumed by people, either directly or through irrigation, comes from underground. On every continent, the water table, or level of underground water, is falling. The situation above ground is no better. Many rivers—including the Colorado River, which runs from Colorado to California, and the Rio Grande which runs along the border between Mexico and the United States—are now drained of their water before they reach the sea.[13] In China, the famous Yellow River, which is 3,400 miles long, failed to reach the ocean for the first time in history in 1972 and is considered by some a dying river. There are similar concerns that China's Yangtze will also run dry.[14]

> Eighty percent of China's rivers are so degraded they no longer support fish. China is facing the likelihood of severe grain shortages because of water depletion and the shift of water resources from agriculture to industry and cities. The resulting demand for grain in China soon could exceed the entire world's available exportable supply.[15]

Mexico's Lake Chapala was 50 miles wide and was once called Mexico's inland sea. Today, fish and wildlife are disappearing from a lake that was once an average of 36 feet deep but now averages only 4.5 feet deep. The lake is the main source of drinking water for the city of Guadalajara; the river that feeds the lake is a source of water for Mexico City and that same river provides water to irrigate crops. In addition, beginning in the early 1900s, portions of the lake were drained for farmland.[16] What was once a beautiful oasis is rapidly becoming a dry desert.

One response to a water shortage is to remove salt from seawater, a process known as desalination. Unfortunately, this process is not very efficient, requiring tremendous amounts of energy and labor. It is only affordable for a handful of the very wealthiest nations, and there are no signs that less expensive and more efficient purification systems will be developed soon.[17] Further, the high cost of transporting water long distances means that desalination is unlikely to ever supply large amounts of water to people living inland.

Water is a finite resource that is not evenly distributed throughout the world. Some have an abundance of water but others have little. For example, "the world's arid and semiarid regions—which together constitute approximately 40 percent of the earth's land mass and house perhaps one-fifth of its total population—receive only 2 percent of the global water runoff."[18] The consequences of this uneven distribution can be staggering:

> More than one billion people lack access to clean drinking water and two and a half billion do not have adequate sanitation services. Preventable water-related diseases kill an estimated 10,000 to 20,000 children every day, and the latest evidence suggests we are falling behind in efforts to solve these problems.[19]

It has been estimated that 80 percent of the disease in the Third World is caused by contaminated water and that as many as 10 million people each year die as a result. The situation is worst in Asia and Africa.[20]

Water is not just used for drinking, but is essential for growing food. Most fresh water consumed in the world today is used for agriculture.[21] Worldwide, about 40 percent of all crops are grown through irrigation, which "accounts for two-thirds of water use worldwide and as much as 90 percent in many developing countries."[22] Making the problem worse, most irrigation systems are inefficient, with as much as half of the water never reaching intended crops because of leakage in transit to the farmland or because of evaporation. Even the choice of foods we eat affects how much water is used. For example, producing meat requires much more water than does producing vegetables.

> Growing a pound of corn can take between 100 and 250 gallons of water, depending on soil and climate conditions and irrigation methods. But growing the grain to produce a pound of beef can require between 2,000 and 8,500 gallons. We can conserve water not only by altering how we choose to grow our food, but also by changing what we choose to eat.[23]

Further, it can no longer be assumed that the oceans will provide an unlimited supply of food. By 2002, three-quarters of the world's fisheries had been overfished.[24]

Much of this discussion focuses on water as a global problem, but the United States is also facing water shortages. Oregon farmers, fearing the loss of their crops, have damaged federally owned canals to release water for irrigation—water that was being saved to rescue an endangered species of fish.[25] In reality, there may not be enough water to save either the fish or the farms. In the southeastern United States, Georgia, Alabama, and Florida are in a legal battle over access to water from the Chattahoochee River.[26] Faced with growth outpacing the supply of water, the city council of Santa Fe, New Mexico, considered a ban on all commercial and residential construction.[27] In these rapidly growing states, the need for water is outstripping the supply and the situation is reaching a critical level. Along the border between Texas and Mexico, American farmers are going bankrupt because Mexico has drawn water from the Rio Grande at such a rate that none remains for irrigation by American farmers.[28]

As the world population continues to grow while the supply of water is relatively fixed, injustices related to the use of water will become more frequent. Our discussion now turns to some of the forms those injustices might take.

Privatization of Water

Where clean water is scarce, it quickly becomes an expensive commodity, a product to be sold to the highest bidder. Hundreds of companies deal in water as a commodity. The two largest are French companies that together have water-related annual revenues of more than $10 billion. "The World Bank estimates the global market for water to be worth $800 billion. . . . In the U.S. alone, where the vast majority of water services remains in public hands, private water corporations generate revenues of more than $80 billion (U.S.) a year—four times the annual sales of Microsoft."[29]

Price is of little concern to the very wealthy, but for the poor a lack of affordable water can have deadly consequences. A World Health Organization report "estimated that 25 percent of the population living in cities in developing countries bought water from vendors, typically spending 10 to 20 percent of household income."[30] In India, some households pay as much as 25 percent of their household incomes for water.[31] Although the wealthy can afford to pay more, in practice they often pay less, even receiving government subsidies for their water. "Poor residents of Lima, Peru, pay private vendors as much as $3 for a cubic meter for buckets of often-contaminated water while the more affluent pay 30 cents per cubic meter for treated municipal tap water."[32] "In Bamako, the capital of Mali, poor people pay as much as 45 times more per unit of water than do the rich, who get water piped into their homes, often at subsidized prices."[33]

The idea that water should be privatized has been promoted by the World Bank, which sometimes requires privatization as a condition for loans to developing countries. In January 2000, thousands of citizens in the Bolivian city of Cochabamba took part in strikes that shut the city down for four days.[34] In February, thousands of Bolivians attempted to march peacefully in the streets. Again in April, citizens shut down the city, leading the Bolivian government to declare martial law and to arrest peaceful demonstrators. People traveled as far as 70 miles on foot to join the demonstrations. Bolivians had taken to the streets to protest skyrocketing water rates that went into effect after the Bechtel Corporation took private possession of Cochabamba's water supply. As part of the agreement, Bechtel even took control of wells that private citizens had dug for themselves. Soon after Bechtel took over, families earning less than $100 per month were charged as much as $20 per month for water. On April 10, the government backed down, returning government control of the distribution of water. However, because the government itself did not have the resources to upgrade the water system, returning control of the water to the public sector did nothing to improve the broken-down supply system or to improve the prospects for a long-term solution to the city's water shortage.

Bolivia is not an isolated case. Around the world, there is a move to privatize water. Privatization of water has been slowly emerging within the United States and some arrangements are beginning to involve massive amounts of water. In Colorado, a senator is accused of trying to privatize a federal reservoir for his own benefit.[35] In Southern California, a private firm is scheduled to provide as much as 47 billion gallons of water per year.[36] In Texas, an entrepreneur is offering to sell tens of billions of gallons of water to the highest bidder. He is expecting to make as much as $1 billion. Under Texas law, he may pump as much water as he wishes from his land, even if that underground supply crosses into other property (which it does) and his business leaves the surrounding region without water.[37]

Most jurisdictions in the United States recognize what are known as "riparian rights." This refers to the right of landowners to use water that flows through or near their property. Whether the water is considered private (and thus something that can be sold) or public depends on a variety of things: Is the water in a small stream or is it part of a navigable river? Is the water being taken at the source of the river or near its end? Riparian rights consider these factors in making judgments about who may take water from the river and how much they may take. Riparian rights also regulate such things as the amount of water that property owners may remove from a river or stream so that other property owners downstream have fair access to the water. These rights also consider what happens if the course of the river or stream changes. If the river no longer runs through the property can the owner still use water from the river? Although riparian rights exist throughout the United States, they have been of particular concern in the American West, where water is most scarce. Unfortunately, riparian rights were designed to apply only to water that flows above ground. In many jurisdictions, there are no restrictions on landowners who tap underground water sources.

Privately supplied water is not automatically a bad thing for consumers, but the potential for injustice is substantial. Corporations exist to make as much money as possible, and the temptation will be to sell to the highest bidder, even if that means the poor are left without water. This will be particularly likely if the market becomes concentrated in the hands of a few companies so there is little competition and if the supply grows short—a situation that has been compared to that of the oil cartels in the Middle East.[38] In that case, the poor will likely be priced out of the water market. A member of Newfoundland's legislature has been quoted as saying, "Water is the commodity of the next century and those who possess it and control it could be in a position to control the world's economy."[39]

Water and War

Because it is essential for life, it should not be surprising that wars have been fought over access to water. This was true in the past, and today wars have erupted, or are likely to erupt, over the issue of water in many places.

Several factors seem to increase the likelihood of water-related conflicts. First, conflicts can be expected where different countries share common water sources. A single river might flow through several countries or an underground aquifer might cross national boundaries. As it happens, the sharing of water systems is a relatively common occurrence. Researchers who have drawn maps of the world's water systems have found that major river basins are often shared by more than one country:

> 261 such basins extend over two or more international boundaries. These basins cover approximately 45 percent of the earth's land area, excluding Antarctica. No less than 145 nations depend on shared river systems for at least some portion of their freshwater supply, and a good number of these are almost wholly dependent on such systems. Many important underground aquifers, such as the vital "Mountain aquifer" lying beneath Israel and the West Bank, are also shared in this manner.[40]

Some of the most volatile regions of the world include nations that must share water. For example,

> The major shared [river] systems of the Middle East and Southwest Asia—the Nile, the Jordan, the Tigris-Euphrates, and the Indus—have been the sites of conflict throughout human history; indeed, many of the earliest recorded wars occurred along their banks.[41]

Problems arising from shared water systems are exacerbated when the countries involved also have differences in religion, political systems, or customs.

A second factor likely to facilitate water-related conflict is a shortage of water. As discussed earlier, many parts of the world have serious water shortages. Several factors can lead to extreme shortages. Population growth can lead to a dramatic increase in the demand for water. Unfortunately, some of the countries suffering the greatest water shortages are also those having the most rapid population growth. Industrialization and economic growth can also result in substantial increases in demand for water. Total annual water consumption in industrialized nations averages more than 1,500 cubic meters of water per person whereas countries with low levels of economic development may use less than 100 cubic meters of water per person each year.[42]

Water can be the source of conflict between nations and a target for warring nations. For example, during the Persian Gulf War "the Iraqis intentionally destroyed the water desalination plants of Kuwait and in turn suffered from the destruction of their water supply system by the allied forces assembled to liberate Kuwait."[43] Within the United States, right-wing extremist groups have long discussed the strategic importance of contaminating urban water systems as a tool for bringing social and economic chaos.

Although there are many examples of water-related international conflicts,[44] we will summarize only the case of Israel and her neighbors, particularly Jordan, here to give readers a sense of the nature of the problem.

Israel and Jordan

Israel and Jordan are located in a region with some of the most severe water scarcity problems in the world. Nine of the fourteen Middle Eastern countries face serious water shortages.[45] Since its formation in 1948, Israel has competed with Jordan for fresh water and both countries face substantial shortages. Although 1,000 cubic meters of water per person is considered a healthy minimum, in 1990 Israel's renewable water supply was 467 cubic meters per person and Jordan's was only 224 cubic meters.[46] Both countries rely on the same two major sources of water—the Jordan River and underground aquifers.

The Jordan River is relatively small, having only about 1 percent of the water that flows through the Congo River and only about 2 percent of the amount that flows through the Nile.[47] The Jordan originates to the north of Israel, fed by rivers in Lebanon, Syria, and Jordan. Over the years, these countries have made several efforts to divert or capture water flowing through their lands and into Israel. In each case, Israel has responded that this would threaten Israel's security and would be tantamount to a declaration of war. In the Six Day War of 1967, Israel attacked sites where Syria was building dams to divert water from Israel. Because of superior military forces, Israel was able to occupy parts of Syrian land and gain further control over the region feeding water into the Jordan. In recent years, Israel has been in conflict with Palestinians living on the West Bank. Water is again a key element (though not the only one) in that conflict. Israel draws most of the West Bank's underground water supply for its own use and rations water to the Palestinians in a manner that is blatantly unequal—"with Jewish settlers receiving five to eight times more water per capita than the Palestinians."[48] This has added to Palestinian resentment of the Israelis and "helped fuel the Palestinian *intifada,* or uprising, that began in 1987 and lasted for several years."[49] Water has also been an issue of contention between Israel and citizens of the Gaza Strip, a small area to the southeast of Israel from which Israel has been drawing on underground water supplies at a rate per capita ten times that of the Palestinians who live there.[50]

TABLE 11.1	COUNTRIES IN WHICH WATER HAS BEEN USED AS A MILITARY WEAPON, MILITARY TARGET, OR POLITICAL TOOL, 1990–2000

• Iraq	• Singapore	• Syria
• Malaysia	• Turkey	• Tajikistan
• India	• Zambia	• Kuwait
• Bangladesh	• Czechoslovakia	• Kosovo
• Hungary	• Angola	• Bosnia
• East Timor	• Yugoslavia	• Nambia
• Ecuador	• South Africa	• Peru

Note: This is only a partial listing. Several countries on this list have had multiple problems during this 10-year period.

Source: Gleick, Peter H. 2000. *The World's Water: Water Conflict Chronology* (accessed online at www.worldwater.org/conflict.htm on 8 February 2002).

Israel and Jordan have been taking water from underground aquifers at a faster rate than it can be replaced:

> By the mid-1990s, Israel was overexploiting its water, drawing down its aquifers at beyond replenishment rates by about 15 percent a year. . . . Jordan was doing even worse: it was using 20 percent more water than it was receiving. The coastal aquifers in the region . . . were seriously overpumped, and seawater intrusions were becoming a major problem—and a major political problem given that Jews were allowed to drill their wells deeper than Arabs or Palestinians. The already potent Palestinian grievances were being ratcheted up by the brutal politics of water.[51]

Water isn't the only issue in dispute between Israel and its neighbors. Land, religion, and politics have often triggered violence in the region. However, the role of water in such disputes is likely to increase. Through the 1990s and into this century, there have been efforts to negotiate peace agreements in the region, with water often serving as a key negotiating point. In 1994, Israel and Jordan signed a peace treaty that included provisions for the distribution of water. How long the peace will last is unclear, but long-term peace in the region seems elusive. The supply of available water continues to decline while the population of the region continues to grow. It is estimated that between 1998 and 2025, the population of Israel will grow by one-third and that of Jordan will double. It is difficult to imagine a scenario in which all sides will be able to receive enough water to meet their needs.

The Middle East is only one of many parts of the globe where water has played a role in conflict. In most cases, water is not the sole reason for the conflict, but magnifies the problem. Table 11.1 shows a list of nations in which water has been used as a military tool, as a military target, or as a political tool—as when Malaysia, which supplies about half of Singapore's water, threatened to cut off that water in response to Singapore's criticism of government policy in Malaysia.[52] Although such conflicts have occurred in the past, the frequency of these conflicts appears to be increasing. For example, Glick[53] was able to identify just 6 such conflicts that began during the 1980s, but 24 that began in the 1990s. It can be expected that the number of incidents will increase even more rapidly in the decades to come.

Water and Other Natural Resources

Before we close our discussion of water and justice, it is worth noting that the rush to extract other natural resources often affects the availability and quality of water for consumption or for growing crops. For example, on a Pacific island called Bougainville, a company established the world's largest open-pit copper mine, a "gaping chasm three-quarters of a mile deep, two and a half miles wide, and three and a half miles long."[54] The refuse from this mine was dumped into the local river system, which killed the fish and contaminated the island's water system. The nearby island of Papua, New Guinea, claimed to possess the island of Bougainville and received royalties from the mines, but the residents of Bougainville received almost nothing, and the government at Papua showed no interest in helping them. Eventually the residents rebelled against Papua and asserted their independence. After several failed attempts by Papua to retake the island, tensions between the two groups continue.[55]

Bougainville is one good example of how the extraction or use of natural resources can lead to water-related conflict, but there are additional examples throughout the world. In some places, clear-cut logging results in such high levels of soil erosion that once-safe streams and rivers are turned into mud. In other places, underground water supplies are threatened by radioactive waste stored underground. And the list goes on. Water is a natural resource connected to many other resources, and it touches nearly every aspect of our lives. It is not surprising that some have called access to clean water a basic human right.[56]

EMERGING ISSUES

It is likely that the use and equitable distribution of water will increasingly become an issue leading to conflicts between and within nations. It is also likely that oil will play a larger role in international conflicts in the next few decades. America is anticipating such conflicts by providing aid to countries that provide the United States with oil. The region of greatest concern is the Middle East because it provides a substantial proportion of the oil the United States imports each year, because it holds about two-thirds of the known oil reserves in the world, and because it is an unstable region. Before the September 11, 2001, terrorist attacks, "As much as one-fourth of the U.S. defense budget—about $75 billion per year—is allocated to American forces in the Persian Gulf and to those units stationed elsewhere that are kept available for deployment to the Gulf."[57] Since the attacks, the size of that allocation has increased substantially.

Beyond the examples of water and oil, many resources will raise issues of justice and will lead to conflicts in the very near future. Timber, for example, is technically a renewable resource. However, timber is not being regrown as quickly as it is being consumed. Consequently, timber has become extremely valuable. For example, large knotlike growths called burls create beautiful patterns in wood and are therefore particularly valuable. "A raw burl [from a single walnut tree] can sell for $5,000 or more in California and as much as $30,000 in Italy on the rare woods market."[58] Similarly at the time of a 1997 study, a single cedar tree could bring as much as $20,000.[59] Much of the forest land in Indonesia has been stripped bare, and there are concerns that the forests will disappear altogether within the next decade. The market for timber is so lucrative in Indonesia that illegal loggers "are apparently evading arrest by getting their wives to strip naked and distract officials while they make a quick getaway with the valuable hardwood. . . . Authorities were too embarrassed to take action when confronted by the women."[60] As time passes, timber will only become more valuable.

In Africa, money from gold and diamonds has led to wars between nations and has benefited a few while leaving most Africans living in poverty. Also in Africa, as many as 15,000 children as young as 11 have been forced into slavery to harvest the cocoa required to make chocolate.[61] As discussed in Chapter 9, slavery continues to be a serious problem throughout the world, and the harvesting of natural resources is an important dimension of the contemporary slave trade.

As resources are becoming more scarce, they are also becoming more valuable and will fuel further injustices. It is now profitable for large corporations and nations to harvest natural resources from areas once considered remote. High profits also lead companies and nations to do things they might not do otherwise. Dictators use the wealth generated by the sale of natural resources to finance armies that crush political opposition. The Congo, for example, has some of the richest deposits of natural resources in the world—diamonds, gold, and timber, to name only a few. Although dictators and armies have become fabulously wealthy from the Congo's natural resources, its people are poor and are subject to random acts of violence.

Klare describes one of the most disturbing trends.[62] The profits from natural resources are now so enormous that small nations and corporations can afford to hire private armies—mercenaries—to forcibly take those resources from anyone unwilling to hand them over. In many cases, people who have lived on their land for many generations are driven away with no compensation—in some cases, they are killed outright. These private armies, funded by the sale of natural resources, have also been tools for suppressing opposition to dictators who control those resources. These mercenaries generally don't concern themselves with doing what is right and just. They will kill, torture, and rape for anyone willing to pay their price. In the Congo, for example, tens of thousands of women have been raped by soldiers who have no fear they will ever be held accountable for their actions.[63]

The distribution, use, and disposal of natural resources have often led to conflict and injustice. It may not be possible to eliminate such conflicts, but it is possible to minimize them. Klare suggests that in a global economy, conflicts over resources can only be prevented through global cooperation.[64] Violence can only be avoided if the nations of the world work together to conserve scarce commodities and to arrange for their harvest and distribution in a just manner. Klare suggests that for such cooperation to exist, it will be necessary to develop international institutions. These institutions would be expected to maintain "an accurate inventory of the world's supplies of critical commodities and to develop mechanisms for the global allocation of these materials in times of extreme scarcity or emergency."[65] These institutions could also pool the world's scientific knowledge about the use of resources and about the development of substitutes for scarce natural resources. To be effective, such institutions would need enforcement authority, which would require some form of international court or tribunal.

Although such an international body to monitor and regulate the use of natural resources is an appealing idea, it is unclear whether such a body would work in practice. One major roadblock is the United States. The United States is the largest consumer of natural resources in the world, so its cooperation is essential to the success of any international body to regulate natural resources. However, the United States also has a long history of opposing anything that would undermine its sovereignty. The United States has long been only lukewarm to the United Nations and has generally not supported international treaties to protect the environment. And, the United States has long opposed the creation of an international court of justice that might enforce such treaties. Perhaps the best hope is that the world, including the United States, will come to appreciate that the nations of the Earth are increasingly interdependent on a finite supply of natural resources.

CONCLUSION

There are many connections between the environment and justice. First, natural resources are, in general, most available to those with the greatest economic resources. The gap between rich and poor in access to resources grows in direct proportion to the scarcity of natural resources. As resources become more scarce, the poor eventually are priced out of the market. For some resources, such as water, the consequences can be fatal. The justice of such a market-driven system is open to serious question, and injustices that arise from this system might easily lead to violent responses.

Second, murder, rape, and war all become tools for getting valuable resources. This is true today for such precious commodities as gold, diamonds, and oil. For example, the United States entered the Persian Gulf War to protect its supply of inexpensive oil, and soldiers in Africa use murder, torture, mutilation, and rape to maintain their access to gold and diamonds. Bales[66] has documented a variety of ways in which contemporary slavery is a tool for acquiring valuable resources (see Chapter 9). Money from the sale of resources can also be used to fund violence and oppression. Thus, environmental resources can provide both the incentives and the finances to engage in other forms of injustice.

Third, efforts to protect the environment can themselves be unjust and even deadly. The United States has seen relatively little extreme activism for the environment. Even so, in 2002 Congress held hearings on "eco-terrorism" and was told that in the previous five years, environmental activists had committed more than 600 criminal acts resulting in more than $43 million in damages.[67] Such environmental activist groups as the Earth Liberation Front (ELF) have publicly announced they will no longer limit their work to nonviolent acts.[68] The number of these incidents appears to be increasing, and one member of Congress has warned that "It's just a matter of time before a human life is taken."[69]

Finally, there is the issue of using the environment as a terrorist tool. For example, sabotaging just two dams on the Colorado River (Glen Canyon Dam and Flaming Gorge Dam) would "cause major damage to the water supply systems of more than 25 million people in the lower Colorado River basin."[70] Similarly, America has 103 nuclear power plants and a successful attack, of the type mounted on the World Trade Center in 2001, on any one has the potential to kill tens of thousands of people, perhaps hundreds of thousands.[71]

Except where severe shortages have already been felt, there is at present little appreciation for the full range of ways in which the environment and justice are related. As demand for resources grows and as shortages become more frequent, there will be a renewed appreciation for environmental justice. At this point, the prospects are not bright for resolving large-scale injustices linked to the environment, and environment-related injustices can be expected to become more severe and more difficult to resolve. Of the justice issues discussed in this book, injustices related to the environment may be the most difficult to resolve

Discussion Questions

1. Why do some people use the terms "environmental justice" and "environmental racism" interchangeably?
2. What factors are related to a country's level of water consumption?
3. What are the advantages and disadvantages of privatizing water? Why are some people worried about privatization?

Endnotes

1. For this incident, see James P. Lester, David W. Allen, and Kelly M. Hill, *Environmental Justice in the United States: Myths and Realities* (Boulder, Colo.: Westview, 2001).
2. See Daniel Faber, "The Struggle for Ecological Democracy and Environmental Justice," in *The Struggle for Ecological Democracy: Environmental Justice Movements in the United States,* Daniel Farber (ed.) (New York: Guilford, 1998).
3. Environmental Protection Agency (EPA), *Index of Environmental Justice Publications* (accessed online at www.epa.gov/compliance/environmentaljustice/index.htm on 16 January 2002).
4. This is covered in Martin V. Melosi, *Effluent America: Cities, Industry, Energy, and the Environment* (Pittsburgh: University of Pittsburgh Press, 2001).
5. Daniel Farber, "The Political Economy of American Capitalism: New Challenges for the Environmental Justice Movement," in *The Struggle for Ecological Democracy: Environmental Justice Movements in the United States,* Daniel Farber (ed.) (New York: Guilford, 1998), p. 38.
6. Michael T. Klare, *Resource Wars: The New Landscape of Global Conflict* (New York: Metropolitan Books, 2000), p. 15.
7. Ibid.
8. Maude Barlow, *Blue Gold: The Global Water Crisis and the Commodification of the World's Water Supply.* Report to the International Forum on Globalization of Water 1999 (accessed online at www.ifg.org/analysis/reports/bgsummary.htm on 31 January 2002).
9. Jim Yardley, "For Texas Now, Water and Not Oil Is Liquid Gold," *New York Times* (electronic version, 16 April 2001) (accessed online at http://nytimes.com on 31 January 2002).
10. Barlow.
11. Ibid.
12. Klare.
13. John M. Swomley, "When Blue Becomes Gold," *Humanist* (September/October 2000), pp. 5–7; James F. Smith, "Testing the Waters of Cooperation," *L.A. Times* (electronic version, 29 May 2001) (accessed online at www.latimes.com on 29 May 2001).
14. Erling Hoh, "China's 'Mother River' Is Dying: Parched Yellow Portends Vast Ecological Doom," *Chicago Tribune,* 5 July 2001, p. 4.
15. Maude Barlow, "Water Incorporated," *Earth Island Journal* 17(1) 2002, pp. 30–31.
16. Marla Dickerson, "Once-Grand Mexican Lake Is Being Drained of Its Life," *L.A. Times* (electronic version, 18 April 2003) (accessed online at www.latimes.com on 18 April 2003).
17. Marvin Cetron and Owen Davis, *Probable Tomorrows: How Science and Technology Will Transform Our Lives in the Next Twenty Years* (New York: St. Martin's, 1997).
18. Klare.

19. Peter H. Gleick, "Making Every Drop Count," *Scientific American* (February 2001), pp. 40–45.

20. World Health Organization, *Global Water Supply and Sanitation Assessment 2000 Report* (accessed online at www.who.int/docstore/water_sanitation_health/ Globassessment/GlobalTOC.htm on 4 February 2002).

21. Gleick.

22. Sandra Postel, "Growing More Food with Less Water," *Scientific American* (February 2001), pp. 46–47, 50–51.

23. Gleick, p. 44.

24. Laurie Goering, "Earth Summit Clashes with World Realities," *Chicago Tribune,* 25 August 2002, pp. 1, 12.

25. Deborah Schoch, "Dreams Dry Up in Klamath Basin: Public Policy Allowed Too Many Water-Reliant Interests to Come into Being," *L.A. Times* (electronic edition, 23 July 2001) (accessed online at www.latimes.com on 23 July 2001).

26. Larry Copeland, "Water Wars Brew in Southeast: Resource Is Nearing a Critical Point Because of Regional Growth," *USA Today,* 18 July 2001, p. 3A.

27. Tom Gorman, "Water May Be a Wet Blanket to New Growth," *L.A. Times* (electronic edition, 8 July 2002) (accessed online at www.latimes.com on 8 July 2002).

28. Dan McGraw, "A Boiling Tex-Mex Water War," *U.S. News & World Report,* 1 May 2000, p. 24.

29. The Blue Planet Project, *Fact Sheet 1: Facts on the World's Top Ten Water Companies* (accessed online at www.blueplanetproject.net/cms_publications/factsheet_1.pdf on 31 January 2002).

30. World Water Day 2001, *Water for Health—Taking Charge* (accessed online at www.worldwaterday.org/report/index.html on 4 February 2002).

31. Barlow, *Blue Gold.*

32. Ibid.

33. World Water Day 2001.

34. Jim Schultz, "Water Fallout: Bolivians Battle Globalization," *In These Times,* 15 May 2000 (accessed online at www.inthesetimes.com/issue/24/12/shultz2412.html on 31 January 2002); William Finnegan, "Leasing the Rain: The World Is Running Out of Fresh Water, and the Fight to Control It Has Begun," *New Yorker,* 8 April 2002, pp. 43–47, 50–53.

35. John Elvin, "Activists Attack Campbell for Privatizing Water Rights," *Insight on the News,* 15 (24 May 1999) (accessed online at http://FirstSearch.oclc.org on 4 February 2002).

36. James Sterngold, "Private Sector May Sell Water to Southern California Agency," *New York Times* (electronic edition, 26 December 2000) (accessed online at www.nytimes.com on 31 January 2002).

37. Yardley.

38. Barlow, "Water Incorporated."

39. Quoted in Swomley, p. 6.

40. Klare.

41. Ibid., p. 147

42. Peter H. Gleick, *The World's Water, 1998–1999: The Biennial Report on Freshwater Resources* (Washington, D.C.: Island Press, 1998).

43. Ibid., p. 111.

44. Ibid.; Klare; Marq de Villers, *Water: The Fate of Our Most Precious Resource* (Boston: Houghton Mifflin, 2000); Thomas Homer-Dixon and Jessica Blitt (eds.), *Ecoviolence: Links Among Environment, Population and Security* (Landham, Md.: Rowman & Littlefield, 1998).

45. Kimberly Kelly and Thomas Homer-Dixon, "The Case of Gaza," in *Ecoviolence: Links Among Environment, Population, and Security,* Thomas Homer-Dixon and Jessica Blitt (eds.) (Landham, Md.: Rowman & Littlefield, 1998), pp. 67–107.

46. Klare.

47. Ibid.

48. Ibid., p. 171.

49. Ibid.

50. Kelly and Homer-Dixon.

51. de Villers, p. 189.

52. Gleick, *The World's Water, 1998–1999.*

53. Peter H. Gleick, *The World's Water: Water Conflict Chronology* (accessed online at www.worldwater.org/conflict.htm on 8 February 2002).

54. Klare, p. 196.

55. Ibid.

56. Barlow, "Water Incorporated."

57. Klare.

58. Associated Press, "Thieves Destroying Walnut Trees for Valuable Wood" (accessed online at http://sddt.com/files/librarywire/DN95_10_09/DN95_10_091.htm on 16 January 1997).

59. Michael R. Pendelton, "Looking the Other Way: The Institutional Accommodation of Tree Theft," *Qualitative Sociology* 20 (1997), pp. 325–340.

60. "The Ol' Naked Wife Diversion," *San Francisco Chronicle* (electronic edition, December 2001) (accessed online at www.sfgate.com on 15 February 2002).

61. "The Chocolate Industry: Slavery Lurking Behind the Sweetness," *Global Exchange Newsletter* (accessed online at www.globalexchange.org/campaigns/fairtrade/cocoa/gxWinter2002.htm on 11 February 2002).

62. Klare.

63. *ABC News Nightline,* "The Curse of Wealth, Still the Heart of Darkness," aired 25 January 2002.

64. Ibid.

65. Ibid., p. 223.

66. Kevin Bales, *Disposable People: New Slavery in the Global Economy* (Berkeley: University of California Press, 1999).

67. Brad Knickerbocker, "Eco-Terrorists, Too, May Soon Be on the Run," *Christian Science Monitor* (electronic edition, 15 February 2002) (accessed online at www.csmonitor.com on 15 February 2002).

68. Ed Hunt, "Ecoterrors Troubling Trend," *Christian Science Monitor* (electronic edition, 7 October 2002) (accessed online at www.csmonitor.com on 7 October 2002).

69. Ibid.

70. David Orr, "Floodgates of Terror," *Earth Island Journal* 17(1) 2002, p. 38.

71. Harvey Wasserman, "Nuclear Power and Terrorism," *Earth Island Journal* 17(1) 2002 p. 37; Simson Garfinkel, *Database Nation: The Death of Privacy in the 21st Century* (Cambridge, Mass.: O'Reilly, 2000).

STRATEGIES FOR ACHIEVING JUSTICE

Earlier sections of this book have considered the difficulty of defining justice, examined some of the key formal systems that pursue legal justice, and described a sampling of contemporary issues concerning justice. A discussion of justice is incomplete, however, without also considering how justice might be achieved—particularly when we move beyond traditional criminal justice to consider justice more generally. This section of the book examines how individuals and nongovernment organizations can pursue justice. We also consider the emerging issue of global justice, in which there is an increasing recognition of laws and rights that transcend any single national boundary.

Injustice is pervasive and the scale of injustice can, at times, seem overwhelming. It may appear that individuals are powerless to stop injustice, but history has proven that belief wrong. In many instances, a single individual has changed the course of history for the better. Chapter 12, "Individual Strategies for Achieving Justice," suggests some of the ways in which individuals have helped achieve justice, with a particular focus on the use of public education, civil disobedience, lawsuits, and guerilla tactics. The chapter provides examples of the successful use of each approach, as blueprints for action that may be used by others.

Although individuals can make a difference, there are also advantages to using organizations to achieve justice. Organizations, like individuals, may use public education and civil disobedience to achieve justice. Organizations have also made effective use of civil action in court and of violence to achieve their objectives. Chapter 13, "Organizations Seeking Justice," provides examples of organizations that have used each of these approaches to systematically and successfully work for justice.

The final chapter, "Global Justice" concentrates on international efforts to recognize human rights that should be accorded to everyone and to correct injustices that cross national boundaries. The chapter discusses rules of war, such as the Lieber Code, and the creation of war crime tribunals to judge those who violate those rules. This chapter also discusses the creation of the Universal Declaration of Human Rights and the subsequent creation of the European Court of Human Rights, temporary tribunals, and the Permanent International Criminal Court. This chapter highlights the ways in which justice has gradually come to be viewed as an issue of international concern meriting an international response.

The chapters in this section show that achieving justice is possible, but success often requires hard work, dedication, and patience. The battle for justice is never ending, but it is a battle that must be fought for the sake of our humanity.

CHAPTER 12

INDIVIDUAL STRATEGIES FOR ACHIEVING JUSTICE

History is full of people who have worked to bring about justice. Some have brought about advances in justice purely through the power of their personalities. Others have worked tirelessly in their local communities. Another strategy has been to take issues of injustice to court. Still others have been able to use positions of power to advance justice. All four types are to be applauded; however, in the larger scheme of things, each type has its own limitations. It may be difficult for charismatic reformers to duplicate their successes elsewhere, and when they are gone, it may be impossible to find someone who is similarly charismatic to replace them. Those who work tirelessly to change their local communities are to be admired for their efforts, but their work is often unnoticed outside their local communities. Victories in court can be hard to win. Finally, most people do not occupy positions of power from which justice might be advanced, and it is often those in power who stand to gain from injustice.

This chapter focuses on individual actions to achieve justice and includes a discussion of people who have made a difference in their pursuit of justice and who have left behind blueprints for action by others—either explicitly in their writings or by the power of their example. Any such list is by its nature arbitrary and will of necessity be incomplete. Our intention is to select a few strategies for achieving justice that have had a lasting impact. We also intend that the strategies chosen represent a range of approaches to achieving justice.

There are many general approaches to achieving justice that individuals might take. In this chapter, we have selected four approaches to advancing justice: (1) educating the public, (2) civil disobedience, (3) civil procedures, and (4) guerilla tactics. For purposes of our discussion, each will be discussed separately, but it should be clear that effective strategies for bringing about justice might combine these approaches. The discussion does not attempt to include every strategy an individual might use. For example, we do not include the use of violence as a tactic. It is difficult to find examples of individuals who have successfully used violence as a tactic for positive social change *and* who have articulated the principles of the strategy so that others may apply it to their own situations. Examples of individuals using violence for negative purposes abound (e.g., Hitler), and it is possible to find examples of violence engaged in by groups or nations that led to a positive social change (e.g., the American Revolution). However, this chapter focuses on articulated strategies that have been advanced by individuals.

EDUCATING THE PUBLIC

Sometimes injustices exist and continue because the public is uninformed about the nature and extent of the problem. Individuals can make a difference by bringing injustice to light, but several conditions must be met for this strategy to work effectively. First, the problem must be one with which the public can relate, an issue that touches their daily lives. It can be difficult to mobilize people to act against child labor, torture, and even genocide in other countries, particularly if those countries are far away, are inhabited by people with whom there are limited interactions and who have very different cultures and customs.

Second, the educator must have an effective medium for reaching the public. This means that the educational materials must be presented in a way that the public can understand—for example, by presenting complicated medical issues in everyday language. It also means there must be a mechanism for physically distributing the materials to the public. A powerful documentary about child prostitution in the United States will have little impact if the public never sees the film.

Third, the public must believe the problem is one for which there is a solution. If, for example, people believe that nothing they do will stop a nation's use of torture, it will be very difficult to mobilize them—no matter how they personally view the problem and no matter how well informed they are about the issue.

There are numerous examples of using education to bring about change. Harriet Beecher Stowe's 1852 book *Uncle Tom's Cabin*, the story of the brutality of life under slavery, is said by Abraham Lincoln himself to have played a key role in starting the Civil War. Upton Sinclair's 1906 book *The Jungle* exposed the horrendous sanitary and working conditions in meat packing plants and led directly to the passage of the Pure Food and Drug Act. Ralph Nader's 1965 book, *Unsafe at Any Speed,* disclosed the unwillingness of the automobile industry to incorporate even the simplest lifesaving safety measures into the construction of automobiles. The book had a major impact on the automotive industry, causing it to give an emphasis to building safety features into auto-mobiles, and in the process saving tens of thousands of lives.

Rachel Carson's Silent Spring

To illustrate the power of the educational approach, this discussion will focus on the work of Rachel Carson, whose 1962 book *Silent Spring* has been cred-ited with starting the modern environmental movement. She grew up with a love of nature, an inquiring scientific mind, and a yearning to be a writer. Her interests led her to study zoology and English at Johns Hopkins University. From there, she began writing materials for the U.S. Bureau of Fisheries. She eventually became editor-in-chief for the U.S. Fish and Wildlife Service. Throughout her time in government service, she continued to write articles and books. Her book *The Sea Around Us* was a critical and public success, staying on the *New York Times's* bestseller list for 81 weeks.[1] This led to the reprinting of an earlier book, *Under the Sea Wind,* which also became a bestseller. These books led to numerous honors and awards from both the scientific and the lit-erary community. Carson had the rare gift for understanding complex scientific issues and writing about them in a language that lay people could understand, and in a style that has been described as poetic.

Although her earlier materials were educational, even inspiring, *Silent Spring* started a revolution in the way we think about the environment. The idea for the book was triggered by a letter from a friend who had observed a mosquito control plane flying over her bird sanctuary spraying the insecticide DDT. Shortly after the spraying, Carson's friend found some of her songbirds dead.[2] Carson immediately began investigating the use of pesticides, which at the time were commonly sprayed from airplanes to kill insects on crops. On the ground, trucks drove through neighborhoods spraying a fog of DDT to kill mos-quitoes, leaving large clouds of the poison floating in the air. It was known that "just a few millionths of parts too much DDT could cause fish and birds to pro-duce eggs that wouldn't hatch, or to hatch offspring that couldn't live."[3] Much less was known about the impact of DDT on people. Most of the information about the safety of these chemicals for humans was provided by the chemical industry itself, which was making millions each year from the sale of their prod-ucts. To reassure the public that these chemicals were safe, films were distrib-uted, including one showing school children eating picnic lunches while being enveloped in a cloud of DDT.[4]

The title, *Silent Spring,* reflected Carson's image of a springtime in which there were no songbirds left to sing. She realized that the chemical industry would attack any criticism of their products and that they had the resources to investigate any claims she might make. She examined all the scientific re-search she could find concerning the effects of these chemicals. "Carson first demonstrates the pollution of our water system and soil, then damage to plants and wildlife, and finally the more obvious kills of birds and fish."[5] She also focused on the tendency of some chemicals to accumulate in the body and the effects of these chemicals on key organs, including the most current thinking on the connection between cancer and both radiation and industrial chemicals. Critics were quick to accuse her of trying to ban all toxic chemicals, but that was never her position. What Carson opposed was society's willingness to freely and perhaps excessively use these chemicals without extensive research on their long-term impact.

Her attack on the use of industrial chemicals was so detailed, so systematic, and so carefully researched, while being so accessible to the average reader, that the book became a bestseller within a few days of its release. Within just three months, the book sold more than 250,000 copies.[6] Parts of her book were read into the *Congressional Record*. Her work also led to Congressional hearings and the formation of a presidential committee to investigate the use of pesticides; she has been credited with changing the way Americans think about the toxic chemicals they use. Just as importantly, her book influenced important policy makers, including Interior Secretary Morris Udall and Al Gore, who eventually became vice president. Although the initial impact of her book was felt in America, *Silent Spring* also was published in Great Britain, France, Germany, Italy, Denmark, Sweden, Norway, Finland, Holland, Spain, Brazil, Japan, Iceland, Portugal, and Israel.[7]

Chemical manufacturers saw the book as a direct attack on their industry and launched an all-out attack on the book and on Carson herself. They tried unsuccessfully to stop publication of the book, and when that failed, they launched a media campaign to discredit it. To undermine the credibility of the book, the chemical industry enlisted the aid of agricultural journals and magazines, trade associations connected to the chemical industry, and universities conducting research funded by the chemical industry.[8] *Time* and *Reader's Digest* both drew on materials provided by the chemical industry to criticize *Silent Spring*, although each magazine would in later years change its view, pointing with pride to articles they had published warning of the dangers of pesticides.[9] One testament to the care with which she had done her work was the frequency with which critics would eventually come to accept most of the key points in her book.

Two years after the publication of *Silent Spring*, Carson died of breast cancer and heart disease at the age of 57. The problems to which she drew our attention in 1962 persist. Today, more chemicals are being used than ever, and they are still used with too little knowledge about their long-term consequences. However, because of Carson, they are used more carefully, and there is now awareness that long-term consequences cannot be ignored. Just as importantly, her book has provided a roadmap to guide our search for those consequences.

Contemporary Examples

Many contemporary examples show how social change is sought through educating the public. Books are still a common medium for public education. A sample of more recent books addressing injustice and social problems includes the following: Kevin Bales' book *Disposable People* (1999), which is a powerful description of contemporary slavery. Eric Schlosser's *Fast Food Nation* (2001) uncovers the practices of the fast food industry and, much like *The Jungle* (1906), provides an exposé of conditions in the meat packing industry. In *The American Way of Death* (1978), Jessica Mitford exposes the dark side of the funeral industry in the United States and has led a number of states to enact legislation protecting consumers. And, in *Nickel and Dimed* (2001), Barbara Ehrenreich gives readers a firsthand look at the world of the working poor and shows the difficulty of getting by on a minimum wage job.

Although books remain a powerful tool for educating the public about injustice, the contemporary activist has the ability to use resources not available in the past. Films, particularly documentary films, can affect public perceptions of an issue. For example, Michael Moore's film *Roger and Me* (1989) provided a glimpse into the personal devastation that accompanies the shutdown of large factories, and Errol Morris's film *Thin Blue Line* (1988) sensitized the public to the issue of wrongful convictions. Television news magazines, such as *60 Minutes*, have also served a powerful education function.

Activists also have discovered the Internet as a tool for disseminating information and for organizing activities. So far, the Internet has not produced materials with the impact of *Uncle Tom's Cabin* or *Silent Spring*, but as the Internet becomes more widely available, materials with comparable impact will undoubtedly appear.

CIVIL DISOBEDIENCE

Civil disobedience, the intentional and public refusal to obey a law with which one disagrees, has been a powerful tool for bringing about change throughout history. There are Biblical accounts of citizens refusing to follow the orders of their government, and civil disobedience played an important role in the founding of America. Although the idea has been around for some time, it was articulated as an explicit strategy in a speech given by the author Henry David Thoreau in 1848.[10] This speech, later published under the title "Resistance to Civil Government," recounts his experiences during a night in jail for refusing to pay a local tax he believed supported a government that condoned slavery and that was involved in a war with Mexico—a war he believed was morally wrong. Although he objected to the war with Mexico and to government support for slavery, the opening statement of his speech suggests that his contempt was for government more generally:

> I heartily accept the motto, "That goverment is best which governs least"; and I should like to see it acted upon more rapidly and systematically. Carried out, it finally amounts to this, which also I believe,—"That government is best which governs not at all"; and when men are prepared for it, that will be the kind of government which they will have.[11]

In practice, Thoreau did not sacrifice much for his beliefs. He spent only one night in jail protesting the tax. Someone else paid the tax for him that year and for several years after. His speech was important, however, because it outlined the justifications for refusing to cooperate with unjust laws and has inspired others to consider civil disobedience as a strategy for change. However, few of those who were inspired by him seem to share his belief that government should be done away with altogether.

Gandhi

Among those purportedly influenced by the writings of Thoreau was Gandhi, a man who almost single handedly led India to independence from Great Britain and provided the rest of the world with a model for using civil disobedience as a tactic for change. Other individuals had practiced civil disobedience before him, but Gandhi provided a living example of its use, and he left behind extensive writings about civil disobedience and nonviolence.

Mohandas Karamchand Gandhi was born in 1869 in India. He was a mediocre student who was so shy that he ran home from school to avoid talking with other students.[12] He was greatly influenced by both parents. His mother was deeply religious, and as a follower of Hinduism, she was also a vegetarian. His father was a local official who was known for his honesty and fairness.

When Gandhi was only 16 years old, his father died, leaving the family in poverty. It was decided that Gandhi would borrow money to study law in England as a way to eventually support the family.[13] He finished his law degree and returned to India. However, he was still quite shy and failed as a lawyer. In one court case, he "was literally too shy to open his mouth in court and gave the brief to a colleague."[14] A failure as an independent attorney, he began writing legal briefs and doing odd legal work for other attorneys.

Gandhi was soon invited to South Africa to handle legal cases involving business transactions between Indians living in South Africa and English-speaking residents. While in South Africa Gandhi first developed his method of nonviolent resistance or civil disobedience, a method he called *satyagraha*.[15] Some suggest the turning point was an incident in which Gandhi was traveling in the first-class section of a train and was thrown off because a fellow passenger thought he was black—and blacks were forbidden from riding in first class. The incident made Gandhi more fully realize the oppressive nature of British colonial rule and led to his efforts to improve the conditions of Indians in South Africa.

In 1907, 14 years after he arrived in South Africa, a law was passed there "requiring the registration and fingerprinting of all Indians and giving the police the power to enter their houses to ensure that the inhabitants were registered."[16] Gandhi helped organize "peaceful picketing of registration centres, burning registration cards, courting arrest, and gracefully accepting punishment and police harassment."[17] These efforts had only limited success, but a short time later, he organized women and miners against immigration regulations, indentured labor, a local tax, and the government's failure to recognize Indian marriages. This time his efforts were more successful, leading to the Indian Relief Act in 1914.[18] Gandhi also appreciated the power of the written word to change people, and he began a weekly newspaper devoted to airing the concerns of Indians in South Africa.

In 1915, having been in South Africa for more than 20 years, Gandhi returned to India. He had left for South Africa a shy and little-known failure but returned a hero for his work to advance Indian rights. Soon after his return to India, he came to be called "Mahatma," which means "great soul." Some in India even considered him a reincarnation of God.[19] Although wealthy Indians gave him parties and testimonials, he was strongly drawn to the plight of the poor. When he traveled, Gandhi walked, or traveled by third class on the train. He abandoned Western dress in favor of simple peasant clothing made from homespun cloth, took a vow of celibacy, rejected material goods, and restricted his diet.

For years, Gandhi worked to improve conditions in India and to undermine the authority of the British, but always remained true to his philosophy of nonviolence and passive resistance. Gandhi's belief in nonviolence should not be confused with cowardice. Rather, it demanded extraordinary bravery. His commitment to nonviolence included demanding that protesters willingly submit to the blows of police batons and not even raise their arms in self-defense. Gandhi himself said that if he had to choose between cowardice and violence, he would choose violence because cowardice takes away from a man's self-respect.[20]

His activities toward Indian independence are too numerous to mention here, but several events served as turning points in India's road to freedom and highlight Gandhi's strategy for bringing about change. The first event occurred in 1919, one year after World War I ended. During the war, the British had suspended many liberties of Indians. Thousands of Indians who spoke against the British and for an independent India were tried in secret tribunals and sent to prison. Similarly, Indian newspapers were censored.[21] Indians hoped that when the war ended, civil liberties would be restored. Instead, in 1919, the Rowlatt Act was passed, which extended the wartime restrictions.

Gandhi's response to the Rowlatt Act was to call for a hartal—a work stoppage that would close shops, shut down factories, and close banks. He also called for distributing banned political literature.[22] The strategy was initially a success, but soon violence among his followers broke out in several cities, much to Gandhi's dismay. In one city, Amritsar, a British schoolteacher was attacked and pushed around by a group of Indian youth. The government responded to the violence by calling in troops and banning public meetings. Defying the law, a crowd met in a courtyard to protest the Rowlatt Act. Soldiers arrived and without warning, fired into the crowd of men, women, and children. The soldiers were ordered to keep shooting until they ran out of ammunition. In all, 1,650 rounds were fired, 379 people were killed, and 1,137 wounded. The general in charge issued an order that none of the injured were to receive medical treatment for 72 hours, even those who faced death without treatment. He also ordered any Indians traveling on the lane in front of the schoolteacher's house to crawl on all fours or risk being beaten to death.[23]

Gandhi responded to the massacre at Amritsar by calling for a boycott of British goods, British schools, and British jobs.[24] He traveled the countryside encouraging Indians to burn imported clothing and to only wear fabric made in India. Thousands of his compatriots were imprisoned for political dissent, and Gandhi himself was soon arrested and sentenced to prison for publishing articles calling for a free India. Throughout these ordeals, Gandhi held firm to his belief in nonviolence. There were times when his followers seemed to lose faith in nonviolence and lashed out against the British. When his words were not enough to stop the violence by his people against the British, Gandhi fasted—sometimes to the point of near death. Gandhi insisted that fasts were only used to instruct his followers and would have been useless as a tool for reforming the British.[25] The possibility that their violent acts might lead to the death of their revered leader was enough to prevent many instances of violence by his followers.

The second turning point in Gandhi's quest for an independent India came in 1930 and is among the best-known examples of his use of civil disobedience. At that time, the world economy was in decline, and farmers in India were in economic trouble. Gandhi decided to use the British government's tax on salt to both defy the British government and to unite his followers. Salt was a commodity that all citizens needed, and for the poor a tax on salt was particularly oppressive. Although salt was easy to gather along the seashore, it was illegal to possess salt that was not obtained from the government.[26] Gandhi announced to the British that he was to began a 240-mile march on foot from his camp to the sea, where he would intentionally harvest salt without paying a tax. The march lasted 24 days, and along the way, Gandhi stopped each day at villages to give speeches urging civil disobedience and asking citizens to join his march. For the convenience of police, the names of the 79 original marchers were printed in the newspaper.

Gandhi's salt march attracted international attention. Reporters from around the world followed the march and reported on the large crowds that gathered to greet Gandhi in each village. Along the way, at Gandhi's urging, local Indian officials working for the British government resigned their jobs. By the time Gandhi reached the sea, the marchers numbered in the thousands. Arriving at the ocean, Gandhi walked along the sand until he found a spot where the salt was thick. He picked it up and gave a speech urging other Indians to ignore the law and gather salt. Thousands followed his example; within a week, police were arresting people selling salt on the street and beating those who refused to use government salt.[27] Despite his insistence on nonviolence, some anti-British acts of violence did occur, and Gandhi was arrested and jailed. While he was in jail, his followers marched on the saltworks, where government salt was produced. The crowd of 2,500 was met by 400 police. The unarmed marchers peacefully approached the saltworks in rows of 24 men. They were beaten by the police but refused to in any way defend themselves, not even raising their arms to deflect the blows of the batons. Within a few hours, more than 300 protesters were wounded and several had died. There were not enough stretchers to carry the injured away, but still the rows of protestors kept advancing. This continued for days, and Indians staged raids on other salt facilities throughout the country.[28] The salt protests showed the world and the British themselves the brutal nature of British rule in India and the determination of the Indian people to be free.

A free India was on the horizon, but internal strife between Muslims and Hindus meant continued unrest. One issue was whether there should be one India or whether land with large concentrations of Muslims should be broken off into a separate country, Pakistan. Gandhi believed there should be only one country but some extremists erroneously believed he had secretly agreed to a separate Pakistan. In January 1948, at the age of 79, an extremist shot and killed Gandhi as he was preparing to conduct prayer services. In the 33 years between his return from South Africa and his death, he engineered independence for India and provided the rest of the world with a model for using nonviolent means to bring about change.

Several points about Gandhi's approach are worth noting. First, his refusal to follow the law was always done with a purpose and was always done openly. Before engaging in a specific act of civil disobedience, Gandhi respectfully notified authorities of his intention. Throughout his life, he remained optimistic about the nature of human beings and was always hopeful that if told of his plans in advance, authorities might be willing to negotiate for change.

Second, Gandhi was always willing to pay for his civil disobedience by going to jail. In fact, on many occasions he expressed disappointment because he was not jailed or because he was released from jail early. Being jailed showed his followers his dedication to their cause, gave him a chance to rest and to plan further actions, and allowed him time to write. Throughout his lifetime, Gandhi spent 2,338 days in jail—6.4 years.

Third, Gandhi and his followers were willing to suffer beatings and other physical punishments without returning violence or treating the attackers with contempt or disrespect. Violence or any demeaning of others was, in Gandhi's view, something that diminished the person practicing it. Gandhi believed violence was morally reprehensible and, ultimately, is an ineffective strategy for change.

Fourth, Gandhi's faith in his approach gave him great patience. His work toward a free India lasted 32 years, during which time he never gave up peaceful civil disobedience as a strategy for change. Although an independent India was always the long-term goal, he was a patient man who was willing to negotiate for smaller short-term steps toward that goal. Finally, Gandhi appreciated the value of using every available medium to spread his ideas. He not only led his followers by direct example, but he also gave speeches and was a prolific writer. He was constantly writing letters, essays for newspapers, and even published his own newspapers. After his death, the government of India began collecting his writings. To date, there are 90 volumes of his work, each more than 500 pages long. Because he committed so many of his thoughts to writing, we have a clear guide to the principles underlying his approach to social change.

Contemporary Examples

There are many examples of civil disobedience as a strategy for change. During the 1950s and 1960s, the American civil rights movement used many of the strategies Gandhi developed, including peaceful marches, boycotts, and sit-in demonstrations. Dr. Martin Luther King, Jr., was among those in the civil rights movement who studied Gandhi's work. In the 1950s, the Reverend Leon Sullivan successfully led boycotts of 29 companies that had refused to hire blacks in Philadelphia. He also established training programs to prepare blacks for the jobs newly opened to them. Sullivan recognized, just as Gandhi had in India, that full equality for American blacks would depend ultimately on economic equality. By the 1970s, Sullivan's church had grown to more than 6,000 members, and he was nationally known for his civil rights work. Sullivan treated government and corporate leaders with respect while offering them workable strategies for improving the economic condition of blacks. In 1971, he became the first black on the board of directors at General Motors. He used his position to first improve the position of women and blacks at General Motors and then to attack racism in South Africa. He developed the "The Global Sullivan Principles"—a set of guidelines for South African companies that would break down the system of racial segregation known as apartheid. He was able to persuade major corporations to do business only with South African companies that agreed to follow the Sullivan Principles. In 1990, apartheid was revoked in South Africa, partly because of his efforts.[29]

Currently, the principles of civil disobedience are being applied to dozens of issues. In 2001, two elderly nuns (one 88, the other 68) were sentenced to federal prison for trespassing at the School of the Americas (renamed the West-ern Hemisphere Institute for Security Cooperation in January 2001). Through the School of the Americas in Georgia, the United States has trained a number of brutal South American dictators.[30] Also in 2001, protesters in Puerto Rico at the Navy training base on Viques Island were arrested trying to stop bombing exercises. Among those arrested were Robert F. Kennedy, Jr., the governor of Puerto Rico, and noted political activists.[31] Other protesters have disrupted meetings of the World Trade Organization, boycotted merchants selling prod-ucts made with slave labor, blocked access to abortion clinics, and perched in trees to prevent logging. There is now an organization, the Rukus Society, that runs camps training activists to protest without injuring others or being injured themselves.[32] Civil disobedience is a powerful tool that is still evolving. Pro-viding perhaps a glimpse into the future of this tactic, there has already been discussion of electronic civil disobedience.[33]

CIVIL PROCEDURES

Civil action represents an important way for individuals to pursue justice. Tech-nically, civil procedures include a wide array of issues, including family relations (divorce, child custody, adoption, and so on), inheritance, contracts, and dis-putes about property. This discussion focuses on one particular aspect of civil law, the law of *torts*. The word *tort* is derived from the Latin word *tortus,* which means wrong or twisted.[34] Those found blameworthy in civil court are called "tortfeasors."[35] Under tort law, an individual who has been injured sues another to compensate for that injury and uses the court as a neutral arbitrator between the two sides. Sometimes the courts are asked to order those accused to take a particular action or to stop a particular behavior, as when a shopkeeper sues a local gang to stop loitering on the sidewalk outside his shop. More commonly, people who sue under tort law are generally seeking money to compensate for their injuries, or to punish the wrong doer. The case of a customer who slips on the wet floor of a restaurant and then sues the restaurant owner for damages is one example of a tort.

Americans have a love-hate relationship with civil suits. On the one hand, they justifiably mock cases they consider absurd, such as the following:

- The man who sued the devil for causing evil in his community.[36]
- The overweight children who sued McDonald's for their own obesity.[37]
- The man who sued the American Dental Association for not warning con-sumers about the risk of "toothbrush-related injury."[38]
- The Texas cattle industry sued Oprah Winfrey for $12 million for dis-paraging beef.[39]

Civil suits, or even the threat of civil suits, add to the cost of medical care and have forced some doctors out of business.[40] Civil suits add to the cost of products we buy every day. Outrageous cases and the potential cost to innocent consumers are among the reasons why there are frequent calls for tort reform.

Despite the many justifiable criticisms of tort law, it can serve as an important tool for pursuing justice. For example, in the state of New York, women who are raped are encouraged to report the crime, cooperate with a criminal prosecution, and then bring a separate civil suit against their attacker.[41] Because civil and criminal procedures are considered separate legal systems, such actions are not considered double jeopardy under law. In many jurisdictions, shoplifters are not arrested and charged for their crime, but are sued by the store.[42] Residents of Los Angles brought lawsuits against street gang members, compelling them to limit their activities.[43] In Peoria, Illinois, residents of one neighborhood sued men who cruised their neighborhood looking for prostitutes.[44] To understand why someone might use civil justice instead of, or in addition to, criminal justice, it is necessary to understand the differences between the two systems of justice.

First, *under criminal law, crime is a public offense. Under civil law, the offense is a private matter.* Suppose Fred Smith is arrested for assaulting Jim Jones in California. The case will appear in court as the *State of California versus Fred Smith.* Technically, the state is the victim and the state is seeking justice. Jim Jones is almost incidental to the criminal proceedings, although his testimony may be important in gaining a conviction. If Jim Jones sues Fred Smith in civil court, the case will be titled *Jones versus Smith.* In civil court, the case is a matter of dispute between two individuals.

Second, *the criminal law punishes the guilty whereas the civil law repairs the damage done to the victim.* Thus, under criminal law, the primary question is what should be done *to* the offender. In civil law, the primary question is what should be done *for* the victim. The judgment handed down in a criminal case is called a sentence, whereas in a civil case it is called a remedy.

Third, *under criminal law, the state brings the wrong to the attention of the court. In civil law, the individual brings the wrong to the attention of the court.* This is an important distinction. If a prosecutor decides not to bring charges, there is little the victim can do. Similarly, if an abused woman decides she does not want charges brought, the prosecutor is free to ignore her wishes and go forward with criminal charges. In civil court, it is the individual victim's responsibility to bring the matter to court and the wishes of the injured person take priority.

Fourth, *the sentence or fine is paid to the court in a criminal case. In a civil case, the individual receives the fine or damage award.* Thus, someone convicted of shoplifting may be required to pay a fine to the court, but the store is likely to gain nothing but the return of its stolen merchandise. If the store, instead, sues the shoplifter, it will receive any financial penalty imposed on the offender—a penalty that can include all its legal costs for taking the case to court—and it may even be awarded extra money as punishment of the offender, something known as punitive damages.

Fifth, *the standard of proof is higher in criminal cases than in civil cases.* In criminal cases, one must be found guilty "beyond a reasonable doubt." In most civil cases, one need only be found accountable by the "preponderance of evidence." To convict in a criminal case, there must be no reasonable doubt that the person is guilty, but in a civil case, it is only necessary to show they are more likely to be responsible than to be not responsible—the judge or jury need be only 51 percent certain of guilt.[45] The O. J. Simpson case illustrates why this distinction makes a difference. After Simpson was acquitted in a criminal proceeding, the Goldman family, whose daughter was allegedly killed by Simpson, sued in civil court and won a substantial judgment against him. It might appear that the criminal and civil findings were contradictory, but given the very different standards for conviction, there may not be a contradiction at all.

Sixth, *someone accused of doing harm in civil court has fewer constitutional protections than does someone accused and facing justice in criminal court.* Many people are familiar with the constitutional protections provided the accused in criminal court. Defendants in criminal court have the right to an attorney, and if they cannot afford an attorney, one will be provided for them. All criminal defendants have the right to a speedy trial. The criminal court defendant has the right to remain silent and the right to face his or her accusers. These rights, as detailed in the Bill of Rights to the Constitution (see Chapter 4), were designed to protect the accused from the power of the government. However, in civil cases, the accuser is not the government but another individual. For this reason, many constitutional protections available to criminal defendants do not apply to defendants in civil court. For example, the accused in a civil proceeding is not provided with an attorney if he or she cannot afford one, and there is no right to a speedy trial. Someone facing civil charges does not have the right to remain silent. Should they refuse to testify, their silence can be considered in the decision about their case. Further, whatever they say in the civil proceeding can be used against them in any criminal action.[46] Witnesses who are some distance away do not have to appear in court, but may give a deposition—testimony under oath that is taken outside of the courtroom. And, although double jeopardy protections do apply in civil cases, double jeopardy does not apply across criminal and civil cases. In other words, someone found guilty of a crime in a criminal case can still be sued in civil court for the same behavior. This is not considered double jeopardy because the civil and criminal justice systems are considered separate systems.[47] Similarly, entering a guilty plea in criminal court may be used as evidence in a civil proceeding. When money is involved, the defendant in a civil suit has a right to a trial by jury. Juries in civil cases vary in size from 4 to 12 members. In some jurisdictions, the defense and prosecution can negotiate the size of the jury. Some jurisdictions require jury verdicts to be unanimous, but others require only a majority.[48]

Sometimes the perception is that civil suits are primarily about greed and money. Money can be an important part of justice—as when an innocent accident victim sues to have his medical bills paid by a reckless driver. It is also true that greed is sometimes a motivating factor. It would be a mistake, however, to focus on money and fail to see the other respects in which civil law can be used to achieve justice. Civil justice can give the injured a sense of having a voice in exacting justice. Civil procedures can help victims who feel the criminal justice system has failed them. Finally, civil procedures provide a mechanism for imposing punishments beyond those provided by the criminal justice system. Consider the example of O. J. Simpson, mentioned earlier. When the Goldman family sued O. J. Simpson for the death of their daughter, they were probably not motivated by money. Instead, they appear to have been motivated by a desire to exact justice. In Chapter 13, we will see how organizations have also recognized the value of civil justice as a tool for pursuing justice.

GUERILLA TACTICS

Education, civil disobedience, and civil suits can be powerful tools for bringing about social change. There are occasions, however, when none of these tools seem effective. When conventional tactics fail, it can be useful to turn to the unconventional, what we describe here as guerilla tactics. Guerilla tactics are very different from acts of terrorism. The tactics described here do not use violence and are usually, though not always, within the law. Where violations of the law occur, they are designed not to harm others. We would define unusual or outrageous approaches that use violence or harm others as acts of terrorism.

The use of guerilla tactics has been largely defined by the work of one man, Saul Alinsky. Alinsky died in 1972, but he left behind a rich legacy of examples of his approach, a rich set of written materials describing his philosophy, and an institute to train others to follow his example.

Much of his career was as a community organizer, working to help poor neighborhoods obtain basic city services and to help local residents get jobs. In his terms, he worked to help the Have-Nots take power away from the Haves. Alinsky grew up in one of the poorest slums of Chicago and that's where he began his work. By the time of his death, he was known throughout the world for using tactics that were outrageous but highly effective.

There were several key elements to Alinsky's work. We will first list these elements and then give an example of how he used them to better local communities.

First, Alinsky assumed that *people always act out of self-interest* and that one way to gain their cooperation was to appeal to their self-interest rather than to higher moral principles. He argued that the principle even applied to ministers and priests. For example, when he approached clergy for help, he found that appeals to justice and moral principles were far less effective than was emphasizing how a better standard of living would put parishioners in a better position to contribute to the church.

Second, Alinsky firmly believed that communities and groups could only produce long-term change if residents were committed to that change—*a desire for change must come from the local community itself.* As an outsider, he could mobilize them, but he would not impose on them his idea of what changes were needed.[49] Alinsky believed it was important to be seen as legitimate by local residents, and he accomplished this in several ways. He never spoke down to them or treated them with paternalism. He also found that being insulted or attacked by those in power made him more credible to the Have-Nots. Perhaps the most effective way to show his solidarity with them was to be arrested and jailed. Alinsky looked forward to being jailed because it gave him instant credibility with the Have-Nots and it gave him time to reflect on strategies and to write.

Third, Alinsky's tactics *centered around the idea of power.* Unlike Gandhi, Alinsky saw conflict as a positive force essential to a free society. He believed the challenge was always to find ways to pressure those in power to make concessions. He says, for example, that his book *Rules for Radicals* (1971) was written for people without power who wanted to take it away from people with power. While the Haves have access to the power that comes with money, the Have-Nots have power in their large numbers of people.

Fourth, Alinsky believed that *ethical standards of right and wrong must change to fit the times.* He noted that in war, the ends justify almost any means, and he viewed his efforts to help the poor as a battle against those in power. In his view, any effective means is automatically judged by the opposition to be unethical, and people who spend a great deal of time worrying about the ethics of the tactics used by the Have-Nots are really allies of the Haves.

Fifth, Alinsky *used humor as a weapon.* Gandhi often used gentle humor to endear himself to those with whom he was negotiating. Alinsky also used humor, but he relied more on ridicule and humor at the expense of the Haves as a tool to gain their cooperation. As we will see in the example that follows, humor was one of the most powerful tools he used.

Sixth, Alinsky knew that *for unconventional tactics to work they had to be unanticipated* by the Haves. This meant doing things that were completely outside of the normal experiences of the Haves. It also meant not using the same tactic repeatedly because the Haves would soon anticipate the tactic and act to neutralize it.

Finally, Alinsky always *organized communities with specific objectives in mind* and specific ways in which the Haves could meet those objectives. He would not, for example, focus on general unemployment in an impoverished community, but would target a specific company or group in the community and make clear to them how they would benefit from hiring local residents. If the Haves threw up their hands and said "What do you expect us to do?," Alinsky had a very specific answer for them.

Thus, Alinsky took many of Gandhi's essential elements and added a confrontational element to them. An example will illustrate why his approach has been called radical:

Rochester, New York, was a city whose economy depended heavily on Kodak, but at that time, Kodak was doing little to hire or promote blacks. After a race riot in the community, a group of liberal clergy invited Alinsky to organize the black community in Rochester. Alinsky responded that the churches did not speak for blacks in Rochester, and he would come only if local blacks invited him. At first, there was little interest among black residents. Then the local press, the mayor, and others in the community power structure began publicly attacking Alinsky as a troublemaker who had no business coming to Rochester. After a series of these public attacks, the black community came together and invited him to help them organize. As one black later told Alinsky, "I just wanted to see somebody who could freak those mothers out like that."[50] Alinsky began attacking Kodak immediately upon his arrival. When asked at the airport why he was meddling in the black community after all Kodak had done for it, he replied "Maybe I'm uninformed, but as far as I know the only thing Kodak has done on the race issue in America is to introduce color film."[51]

Realizing that a traditional local boycott of an international corporation would be unlikely to bring about change, Alinsky formed a plan. At the time, the Rochester Philharmonic was a symbol of cultural pride for Rochester and for Kodak. Alinsky suggested the minority citizens select a performance with quiet music. They would buy 100 seats for that performance and give them to blacks from the local community. Before the performance, the group would be given a large baked bean dinner, leading to a "fart-in" at the performance. Alinsky intended that the details of the plan be leaked to Kodak, in the hope they would make concessions before the plan was implemented. The plan was brilliant in that it would publicly embarrass Kodak while giving the company few options to save face. Arresting the blacks involved would only draw national ridicule to Kodak and raise questions about its hiring practices. As it happened, Alinsky decided not to employ this strategy, but it remains a classic example of his approach.

Today, there are few community organizers as outrageous as Saul Alinsky, but his name and tactics are well known among those who try to bring about positive social change. Those who directly involve the community in the development and implementation of strategies seldom use techniques as outrageous as those Alinsky conceived. Conversely, those who use outrageous techniques for drawing attention to problems—such as the Biotic Baking Brigade[52] that throws cream pies in the faces of important business and political leaders—

seldom seem to be involved in representing a grassroots constituency and often lack a pragmatic strategy for change.

Despite the fact that no single person has emerged as a successor to Alinsky, his work is largely regarded as a success. Alinsky succeeded in many of the individual projects he undertook, but he also succeeded on a much larger level in that he has challenged activists everywhere to think more creatively about the strategies they might adopt to bring about change.

CONCLUSION

Individuals can bring about positive social change and, as this chapter has shown, there are a variety of ways of doing this. The four approaches highlighted here—education, civil disobedience, civil procedures, and guerilla tactics—represent a continuum of approaches from the least to the most confrontational. Education is often the first tactic tried. When education fails, civil disobedience or civil suits may prove effective. Finally, guerilla tactics may be necessary when other strategies have failed. Whether through education, civil disobedience, civil suits, or guerilla tactics, the examples provided in this chapter are of people who not only worked for change, but also committed themselves fully to change.

Discussion Questions

1. What disadvantages are associated with each of the four approaches that individuals might use to achieve justice?
2. How might advances in technology shape the strategies that individuals might use to achieve justice?
3. What is the difference between Gandhi's form of civil disobedience and simple lawlessness? What is the difference between guerilla tactics and terrorism?

Endnotes

1. For one of the best biographies, see Philip Sterling, *Sea and Earth: The Life of Rachel Carson* (New York: Thomas Y. Crowell, 1970).
2. Ibid.
3. Ibid., p. 159.
4. Neil Goodwin (Producer), *Rachel Carson's* Silent Spring (Alexandria, Va.: PBS Video, 1993).
5. Carol B. Gartner, *Rachel Carson* (New York: Frederick Ungar, 1983), p. 89.
6. Sterling.
7. For the international impact, see Paul Brooks, *The House of Life: Rachel Carson at Work* (Boston: Houghton Mifflin, 1972).

8. Ibid.

9. Ibid.

10. William Rossi (ed.), *Henry David Thoreau: Walden and Resistance to Civil Government* (New York: Norton, 1992).

11. Ibid., p. 226.

12. Louis Fischer, *Gandhi: His Life and Message for the World* (New York: Mentor Books, 1982).

13. Yogesh Chadha, *Gandhi: A Life* (New York: Wiley, 1997).

14. Fischer, p. 20.

15. Bhikhu Parekh, *Gandhi* (New York: Oxford University Press, 1997).

16. Ibid., p. 3.

17. Ibid.

18. Ibid.

19. Fischer.

20. Ibid.

21. Ibid.

22. Ibid.

23. Indian Freedom Fighters, *Gandhi, Mohandas Karamchand* (accessed online at http://swaraj.net/iffw/profiles/gandhi_mk.htm on 13 April 2001); Fischer; Chadha.

24. Fischer.

25. Ibid.

26. Chadha.

27. Ibid.

28. Fischer.

29. Mike Sager, "A Tribute to the Reverend Leon Sullivan, 1922–2001," *Rolling Stone*, 5 July 2001, pp. 87–90, 92, 155; also see Leon Sullivan, *Moving Mountains: The Principles and Purposes of Leon Sullivan* (New York: Judson).

30. Evan Osnos, "Activist Nuns Cause Stir in Prison," *Chicago Tribune*, 8 August 2001, pp. 1, 14; Dahleen Glanton, "Protests Seek Close of Army Facility," *Chicago Tribune*, 22 November 1999, pp. 1, 16; Dahleen Glanton, "War Flares Anew over Army School," *Chicago Tribune*, 18 January 2001, p. 3.

31. "High Profile Trespassers Get No Mercy," *Chicago Tribune*, 7 July 2001, p. 9; "Defiant Sharpton Walks Out of Prison," *Chicago Tribune*, 18 August 2001, p. 10; Ivan Roman, "Court Sentences Gutierrez: Congressman Calls Charges an Effort to Ruin Reputation," *Chicago Tribune*, 30 August 2001, p. 13.

32. Dan Baum, "You Say You Want a Revolution?" *Rolling Stone*, 5 July 2001, pp. 82–83, 85.

33. Stefan Wray, *On Electronic Civil Disobedience*, paper presented to the 1998 Socialist Scholars Conference, New York (accessed online at www.thing.net/~rdom/ecd/oecd.html on 14 November 2001).

34. Bryan A. Garner, *A Dictionary of Modern Legal Usage*, 2nd ed. (New York: Oxford University Press, 1995).

35. James Calvi and Susan Coleman, *American Law and Legal Systems*, 4th ed. (Upper Saddle River, N.J.: Prentice-Hall, 2000).

36. Clarence Petersen, "Satan Gets a Lawyer in Arkansas," *Chicago Tribune*, 30 November 1986, Section 2, p. 1.

37. Amity Shales, "Lawyers Get Fat on McDonald's: New York Lawsuit Alleges Chain Is Responsible for Obesity," *Chicago Tribune*, 27 November 2002, p. 13.

38. Bruce Jaspen, "Toothbrush Injury Charges Have No Bite, Judge Decides," *Chicago Tribune*, 25 July 2000, Section 3, p. 3.

39. "Can You Libel an Emu?" *Chicago Tribune,* 20 January 1998, p. 12A.
40. Tom Gorman, "Physicians Fold Under Malpractice Fee Burden," *Los Angeles Times,* 4 March 2002 (accessed online at www.latimes.com on 4 March 2002).
41. Maureen Balleza, "Many Rape Victims Finding Justice Through Civil Courts," *New York Times,* 20 September 1991, pp. A1, B8.
42. Melissa Davis, Richard J. Lundman, and Ramiro Martinez, Jr., "Private Corporate Justice: Store Police, Shoplifters, and Civil Recovery," *Social Problems* 38(3) 1991, pp. 395–411.
43. David A. Price, "Got Gang Problems? Sue-Em," *USA Today,* 2 January 1997, p. 11A.
44. Douglas Fruehling, "Group Suing Man Convicted of Soliciting," *Peoria Journal Star,* 30 January 1995, pp. A1, A7.
45. For a good overview of civil law issues, see Howard Abadinsky, *Law and Justice: An Introduction to the American Legal System,* 5th ed. (Upper Saddle River, N.J.: Prentice-Hall, 2003).
46. Robert G. McCampbell, "Parallel Civil and Criminal Proceedings: Six Legal Pitfalls," *Criminal Law Bulletin* 31(6) 1995, pp. 483–501.
47. Ibid.
48. Carol J. DeFrances and Marika F.X. Litras, *Civil Trial Cases and Verdicts in Large Counties, 1996* (Bulletin Number NCJ 173426) (Washington, D.C.: Bureau of Justice Statistics, 1999).
49. For a readable and remarkable guide, see Saul Alinsky, *Reveille for Radicals* (Chicago: University of Chicago Press, 1946).
50. Eric Norden, "Saul Alinsky: A Candid Interview with the Feisty Radical Organizer," *Playboy* (March 1972), p. 173.
51. Ibid.
52. Biotic Baking Brigade (accessed online at http://bioticbakingbrigade.org on 17 December 2001)

CHAPTER 13

ORGANIZATIONS SEEKING JUSTICE

I n the previous chapter, we argued that individuals can make a difference, and much of the chapter was devoted to illustrating some ways individuals can pursue justice. This chapter continues the emphasis on pursuing justice, but focuses on the use of organizations as instruments of justice. Individuals can do much to correct injustices, but organizations have several advantages. Organizations can perpetuate themselves over time and continue a fight for justice long after their founders depart. Organizations often have a wider range of resources and staff and can simply do more than an individual can. For example, an organization dealing with environmental issues may have on it staff scientists, political lobbyists, and legal experts who together can provide a range of expertise not usually found in a single individual. And, these individuals can collectively put many more hours into addressing an injustice than would ever be possible for one person.

Many organizations deal with the issue of justice, and there are many approaches to addressing injustices. Our discussion will emphasize several important strategies, but cannot begin to cover every approach. Strategies included here are public education, the use of civil action in the courts, civil disobedience, and the use of violence or the threat of violence to achieve justice. Even though individuals may express frustration and a sense of injustice through violence, this is not the same as using it as a calculated strategy. Although not common, it is easier to identify groups that have used violence as a strategic tool for bringing about justice. This is not to condone the use of violence by organizations, nor to suggest that it is particularly effective. It can be difficult to correctly anticipate the response to violence. In some situations, violence may bring about change whereas in others the response to violence is a backlash that only makes change less likely.

We have selected the categories used to frame this presentation as tools for organizing the discussion. In reality, organizations don't always fit into simple categories. Many organizations use more than one strategy for dealing with a problem. An organization might, for example, publicize injustices as a method for educating the public while providing legal services to take perpetrators to court, and simultaneously lobbying members of Congress for new legislation. Organizations may also change the strategies they use to meet changing environments.

EDUCATING THE PUBLIC

One of the most common organizational approaches to achieving justice is to draw public attention to injustices. The hope is that those committing the injustices will be shamed into changing their behavior, or that the publicity will bring pressure to change. Numerous organizations use this approach. Two, Amnesty International and Human Rights Watch, will be described here to give the reader a sense of how these types of organizations work.

Amnesty International

In 1960, British lawyer Peter Benenson read a newspaper account of two Portuguese students who were dining in a restaurant. During their meal, they made remarks critical of Portugal's dictator and then raised their glasses in a toast to freedom. Their comments were overheard and reported to Portuguese authorities. The two were sent to prison for seven years for committing treason.[1] In the absence of any formal legal mechanism for freeing the prisoners, Benenson hoped that drawing the world's attention to the problem might help. He appealed for help from the public in a newspaper editorial describing the plight of eight people from different countries imprisoned for their religious or political beliefs.[2] Benenson described people imprisoned for expressing their religious or political views as "prisoners of conscience," and he urged readers to contact his office and write letters seeking the release of these prisoners. With the help of friends, Benenson soon expanded the focus of his work to include additional prisoners in other countries and soon his office was flooded with letters from people wanting to help.[3]

Benenson's initial success led him to believe it was worth launching a yearlong campaign to free religious and political prisoners around the world. He called the campaign "Appeal for Amnesty, 1961," The year 1961 seemed particularly fitting, because it was the 100th anniversary of the beginning of the Civil War and, thus, the end of slavery in the United States. It was also the 100th anniversary of the freeing of serfs in Russia.[4] As offers to help came in, Benenson adopted a practice of having small groups of volunteers "adopt" particular prisoners. The volunteers would contact the prisoner and the prisoner's family and would write letters to authorities on their behalf.

Benenson's organization grew quickly and came to be known as Amnesty International (AI). Eventually, the types of cases taken on by AI expanded, as did the alternatives for dealing with the cases. Missions were sent into countries where prisoners of conscience were being held to directly observe conditions and to gain facts firsthand. The key to the organization's success remains "the collection, organization, preparation and presentation of information."[5] When AI was founded, the idea of using public attention to end injustices was considered by some a ridiculous idea. The organization was dubbed "one of the larger lunacies of our time."[6] However, the strategy has proven its effectiveness. Even oppressive regimes sometimes change their behavior in the face of public scrutiny and condemnation. In 1977, AI was awarded the Nobel Peace Prize for its efforts.

Today, AI has more than 1 million members in more than 160 countries. There are more than 7,500 local chapters throughout the world as well as national-level sections in 56 countries. AI's home office remains in London, where its staff now numbers more than 350 people.[7]

Amnesty International's mandate includes freeing prisoners of conscience, making certain that political prisoners have fair and prompt trials, abolishing the death penalty, and putting an end to extrajudicial executions and "disappearances."[8] AI also works to end torture, detention without charges, and human rights abuses by armed opposition groups. Although AI lobbies and campaigns for international treaties to stop human rights abuses, its primary work is done by issuing reports detailing human rights violations. These reports are summarized in press releases, printed for distribution, and posted on their Web site, a site that now contains more than 10,000 files.[9] In 2000 alone, AI published nearly 3,000 documents. In addition, Amnesty International continues the tradition of sponsoring "adoption groups," citizens who volunteer to take on or adopt particular human rights cases. These citizens regularly write governments urging the release of individual political prisoners, and they maintain contact with the prisoners and their families.

Amnesty International is the story of how an organizational structure can give life to one motivated individual's ideas about correcting injustices. As an organization, AI has been able to address human rights issues on a scale far beyond what Peter Benenson might have hoped to accomplish by acting alone.

Human Rights Watch

The model established by Amnesty International has been adopted by other groups, most notably Human Rights Watch. Human Rights Watch has as its explicit objective:

> The embarrassment of governments to halt human rights violations. Publicity—pitiless, potent and persistent—has been the continuing and ultimate aim of the organization's numerous projects. And, at this specialty, HRW has developed an expertise unrivaled in the human rights business.[10]

Human Rights Watch began in 1978. It was originally formed as Helsinki Watch and was designed to "monitor the compliance of Soviet bloc countries with the human rights provisions of the landmark Helsinki Accords."[11] In the 1980s, Americas Watch was established to publicize human rights violations in South America, particularly those cases in which the violations were carried out by governments receiving support from the United States and in which the United States' government seemed willing to ignore those abuses.[12] In 1985, Asia Watch was created, followed by Africa Watch in 1988, and Middle-East Watch in 1989. Finally, these various committees were joined to form Human Rights Watch.[13]

Like Amnesty International, the focus of Human Rights Watch is on human rights violations by governments and organized political groups, rather than on individuals acting on their own. Both organizations report human rights abuses around the world and both organizations refuse to take money from any government, believing that government money might compromise their objectivity. Although both Amnesty International and Human Rights Watch use the United Nations' Universal Declaration of Human Rights (see the appendix) as the basis for their work, Human Rights Watch takes a somewhat broader approach, including such things as freedom of the press, academic freedom, the use of child soldiers, and the production and deployment of land mines. As an organization formed in the United States, Human Rights Watch devotes a considerable amount of energy to publicizing human rights violations in the United States, including conditions in U.S. prisons, the detention of immigrants, and racial disparities in the enforcement of drug laws. Human Rights Watch also places more emphasis than does Amnesty International on pressuring the U.S. government to use its clout to influence other nations to modify behaviors that violate human rights.[14]

At present, Human Rights Watch has a staff of 150 professionals and monitors human rights issues in more than 70 countries.[15] Although Human Rights Watch is significantly younger than Amnesty International and has a smaller staff, it has become a potent force. Some argue that its ability to publicize human rights violations and shame governments into taking corrective action now surpasses that of Amnesty International.[16]

It is a sad statement about the human condition that two organizations can together identify thousands of human rights violations each year around the world. A review of the projects identified by these two groups shows their concern is not with trivial or minor issues of justice, but with serious violations of human rights by governments and organized groups—rape, torture, slavery, and murder. Both Amnesty International and Human Rights Watch have proven very effective at publicizing human rights violations and using the attendant publicity to shame authorities into modifying their practices. As the technology for disseminating information improves, these organizations will be able to reach a wider audience and will be able to do so more quickly. Thus, the effectiveness of this strategy is likely only to improve over time.

Where existing laws do not allow for the punishment of governments that violate human rights, public shame may be among the only tools available to human rights groups. There are times, however, when injustices involve behaviors that are subject to existing laws. In these situations, more direct action may be necessary. Our focus now shifts to illustrating how this direct action might be carried out.

CIVIL SUITS

Education can be a powerful tool, but sometimes it is not enough. It may be necessary to work within the framework of existing laws and regulations to bring about change. This strategy requires, first, that the necessary laws and regulations be in place and, second, that some groups have the legal skills to fight the battle in court. Although it is possible to identify several organizations that have successfully used the law to bring about justice, one organization, the American Civil Liberties Union (ACLU), has been particularly effective at using this tactic.

From 1917 to 1920, America was engaged in the First World War. During that war, many basic civil rights, including freedom of speech, had little meaning. The 1918 Sedition Act made it a crime to criticize the government. For giving a speech critical of war, Socialist Party leader Eugene Debs was sentenced to 10 years in prison, and a filmmaker was prosecuted for making a film about the American Revolution that was critical of the British, who were our allies in World War I.[17] The U.S. Post Office refused to deliver magazines or other materials that in any way questioned the war. Conscientious objectors held in military prisons were often kept in solitary confinement on bread and water diets and subjected to brutality.[18]

Basic liberties were also restricted in response to a series of bombings by anarchists. In 1919, bombs went off in eight cities, including one on the doorstep of Attorney General A. Mitchell Palmer. In response, Congress passed new laws further restricting freedom. It became a crime to send anything written in German through the U.S. mail, or to fly a red flag—the Communists had just staged a successful revolution in Russia.[19] Foreigners were particular targets, and after the bombing, approximately 4,000 people in 33 cities were rounded up, beaten, and arrested without warrants in what were known as the Palmer Raids. Many of those arrested had no connection to radical movements, but appeared foreign. "Thousands were held without charges and were not permitted to see either counsel or family."[20]

Among those protesting the war was Roger Baldwin, who himself served a year in prison for his anti-war views. Baldwin was outraged that the "land of the free" allowed people to express only those views supportive of the government and that the government would so freely ignore basic principles outlined in the Constitution. In 1920, Baldwin formed the ACLU as a private voluntary organization whose only purpose was to defend the Bill of Rights to the Constitution. Baldwin and the ACLU provide an excellent example of the power of an individual to shape an organization, but also of the power of an organization to accomplish more than could be done by any single individual. As Walker observed,

> Without Baldwin, the ACLU would not have survived its early years, and as a consequence, the law of civil liberties probably would have developed differently. In his 30 years as director of the ACLU he created something that transcended his own efforts—both an organization that carried on long after he retired and, more important, an idea that inspired countless other people over the years. The defense of the rights of everyone, the downtrodden and even the advocates of the most hateful ideas, became the guiding principle of Baldwin's life and that of the ACLU.[21]

One of the continuing challenges facing the ACLU, and the nation, has been to determine just what is meant by the provisions granted in the Bill of Rights. Each freedom listed in the Bill of Rights is really freedom from the long arm of the government, but the Bill of Rights is a relatively short document that gives few clues to how its principles are to be applied to everyday situations. What words and behaviors are protected by "freedom of speech" and "freedom of religion?" What did it mean to be "free from unreasonable searches?" Even today, more than 80 years after the ACLU began its quest to defend these basic rights, society is still grappling with these issues. For example, is burning the flag in protest a form of free speech that is protected by the first amendment, or is it behavior that should be treated as criminal?

The ACLU was formed after the excesses of the Palmer Raids, and its immediate task was to decide which civil liberties issues to take on and how to best make a difference. Once the war was over, some of the most glaring violations of basic liberties were practiced against newly emerging labor unions. In many communities, it was against the law for workers to hold meetings to even talk about labor conditions and the possibility of organizing. Wealthy businessmen spent a great deal of money spreading propaganda that equated union membership with radicalism and un-American activity.[22] Any behavior that even suggested a protest might subject the actor to arrest. In Los Angeles, for example:

> When author Upton Sinclair and five friends marched up "Liberty Hill" to read the First Amendment, the police chief warned them to "cut out that Constitution stuff." Before they could finish they were arrested and charged with criminal syndicalism.[23]

The link between the ACLU and labor lasted until the 1930s, "when the Wagner Act established labor's right to organize."[24] By then, the ACLU had begun taking on other issues.

Within the ACLU, there were two differing opinions about how the organization could best improve civil liberties in America. Baldwin and several others thought that civil disobedience and other direct action was the best strategy. Others in the organization believed that the best long-term prospects for change would come from taking cases to court. Within the organization, each side followed it own approach. Those who worked through the courts did not achieve a victory until 1931, 11 years after the organization was founded.[25] Although their strategy was less dramatic and may have drawn fewer headlines, in the long term, it proved more successful. Eventually, it became the primary strategy used by the ACLU. Table 13.1 shows some of the more visible cases in which the ACLU has been involved, either directly, or in a supporting role.

Today the ACLU is supported by donations from its nearly 300,000 members and from private donors. It describes itself as the nation's largest public interest law firm. The ACLU has independent affiliate offices in all 50 states and handles about 6,000 cases each year. It has a staff that includes more than 60 ACLU staff attorneys and 2,000 attorneys who volunteer their time to the organization. It appears before the Supreme Court more often than any other organization, except the Justice Department.[26] As Walker observed,

> The ACLU can legitimately claim much of the credit—or be assigned the blame, if you prefer—for the growth of modern constitutional law. Consult a standard constitutional law textbook and note the cases deemed important enough to be listed in the table of contents—the proverbial "landmark" cases. The ACLU was involved in over 80 percent of them; in several critical cases the Supreme Court's opinion was drawn directly from the ACLU brief. As even its critics have charged, the ACLU has exerted "an influence out of all proportion to its size."[27]

There is a common perception that the ACLU is a "liberal" organization, but that is inaccurate. One might even argue that its commitment to limiting the power of government is quintessentially conservative. Politically, the organization strives to remain nonpartisan. It would be more accurate to describe the ACLU as "absolutist" because of its absolute commitment to the Bill of Rights, or as libertarian because of its belief that the government must be kept in check. This is why an organization that supports the rights of women to have access to abortions also goes to court to defend the rights of anti-abortion protestors. The ACLU will defend the right of American Nazis and members of the Ku Klux Klan to stage public demonstrations, but it also stands against racial profiling by the police. For the ACLU, the question is not whether the person represented has morally correct views, or is even likeable. The question is whether the government is unjustly restricting that person's rights. Because it is so absolutist in its defense of civil liberties, the ACLU has taken positions that sometimes outrage conservatives and liberals alike. The absolutist position means it is willing to defend people whose views ACLU members find offensive. As the organization puts it,

> We do not defend them because we agree with them; rather, we defend their right to free expression and free assembly. Historically, the people whose opinions are the most controversial or extreme are the people whose rights are most often

TABLE		
13.1	**THE ACLU GOES TO COURT**	

1925	Represented John Scopes who was accused of teaching evolution. Scopes was convicted, but the ACLU had its first experience as a legal advocate.
1933	Successfully fought a U.S. Customs Service ban on James Joyce's novel *Ulysses*.
1939	Successfully fought a ban on union organizing in Jersey City.
1942	Was one of the few groups to oppose the internment of American citizens of Japanese descent during World War II.
1950	Fought against the "loyalty oath" required of federal workers during the cold war period of the 1950s.
1954	Joined the legal battle against school desegregation in the case of *Brown v. Board of Education*.
1960	Supported the peaceful nonviolent tactics of the civil rights movement throughout the 1960s.
1973	Successfully supported a woman's right to an abortion in *Roe v. Wade*.
1981	Successfully challenged an Arkansas law requiring that the biblical story of creation be taught as a scientific alternative to the theory of evolution.
1989	Successfully overturned a Texas statute punishing flag desecration, which the ACLU argued was a form of political speech protected by the Constitution.
1996	Supreme Court recognized civil rights of lesbians and gay men by invalidating Colorado statute prohibiting gay rights laws.

Source: *Freedom Is Why We're Here* (accessed online at www.aclu.org/Files/OpenFile.cfm?id=10740 on 22 September 2003).

threatened. Once the government has the power to violate one person's rights, it can use that power against everyone.[28]

Proof that the ACLU is more libertarian than liberal can be seen in the announcement by two of the most conservative Republican members of Congress—Representative Dick Armey of Texas and Representative Bob Barr of Georgia—that when they stepped down from their seats in Congress in January 2003, they were accepting positions as lobbyists for the ACLU. They both expressed concerns that after the September 11, 2001, terrorist attacks, the U.S. government had gone too far in restricting the rights of American citizens. Barr also reported that he had been working with the ACLU since the Oklahoma City bombing in 1995 (see Chapter 8).[29]

The ACLU's primary efforts are in the courtroom, but it also engages in other activities to further civil liberties. The organization actively lobbies regarding legislation that may affect civil liberties, publishes books and other materials explaining basic rights, and takes public positions on issues related to civil liberties. However, the organization has had its greatest success in the courtroom. The ACLU is an excellent example of how much more can be done when an individual's vision for justice is pursued by an organization. It would be hard to find an organization that has been more successful at using the courts to achieve justice, has had that success over such a long period, and has done so in a way that will have a lasting impact.

Baldwin's belief that civil disobedience was the best way to bring about justice eventually lost out to the strategy of taking justice issues to court. For some organizations, however, civil disobedience remains an important strategy for change. We now turn our attention to a sampling of these groups.

Civil Disobedience

Civil disobedience is the intentional violation of the law, either because the law is seen as unjust, or to draw attention to a perceived injustice. In the previous chapter, it was suggested that Gandhi's work provided a model for the effective use of civil disobedience. Gandhi's approach involved more than simply breaking the law. His approach required that the lawbreaking take place as part of a strategy designed to achieve some higher purpose and that each act of civil disobedience had a very specific purpose. In response to the question "What do you hope to gain by this?," Gandhi was always able to provide a list of very specific things that realistically could be done by those in power. Gandhi's vision of civil disobedience also required that participants be willing to accept the legal consequences of their actions, and it required a commitment to nonviolence.

Many organizations and movements have experimented with civil disobedience, usually as only one of several strategies. Thus far, no organization has had such great success with civil disobedience that it is widely considered a model by others. No organizational counterpart to Gandhi has emerged thus far. No group has done for civil disobedience what Amnesty International has done for public education or what the ACLU has done for civil action. Yet, there are groups that make periodic forays into civil disobedience. During the civil rights movement, for example, several groups effectively used civil disobedience to challenge racial inequalities in the law.[30] However, the use of civil disobedience by those groups was relatively short-lived, and those organizations eventually moved on to other, less confrontational strategies. We now turn to some illustrative examples of the ways in which organizations have used civil disobedience to pursue their vision of justice.

Civil disobedience has become a tool used by organizations from both ends of the political spectrum. Anti-abortion demonstrators have been arrested for blocking clinic entrances, and environmental activists have engaged in sit-down demonstrations intended to disrupt international trade discussions. The use of civil disobedience by these groups can be illustrated with three brief examples.

Operation Rescue

In 1973, the U.S. Supreme Court, in the case of *Roe v. Wade,* ruled that women had a right to abortion. Although there had been opposition to abortion before *Roe v. Wade,* the decision mobilized many who opposed abortion. However, efforts were scattered and largely uncoordinated until 1986. That year, anti-abortion activist Randall Terry was serving a short jail sentence for blocking an abortion clinic when he developed the idea of organizing abortion foes around the country. He called his organization Operation Rescue (OR), and in 1987, he assembled more than 200 supporters to block the entrance to a New Jersey clinic.[31] Soon blockades were organized around the country and thousands were being arrested. Between May 1988 and August 1990, OR organized 683 "rescue operations," leading to more than 60,000 arrests and the jailing of nearly 41,000.[32] Despite OR's success in garnering public attention and in hampering the operation of clinics, the organization's strategy of civil disobedience fell into decline after the early 1990s. Lawler[33] attributes this decline to two factors: the failure of OR to develop a long-term commitment to civil disobedience in its followers, and the increased legal penalties facing both individual protestors and the organization itself. A visit to what was once the Web site for OR now directs browsers to a page for Operation Save America, an anti-abortion organization that appears to emphasize public education and awareness over civil disobedience.

Greenpeace

Greenpeace is an environmental organization that began in 1971 in a Vancouver Unitarian church. A group of concerned citizens wanted to stop the United States from testing nuclear weapons on the island of Amchitka, which is part of the Aleutian Islands off the coast of Alaska.[34] A small group boarded a boat with the intention of parking it at the test site. The group members didn't arrive in time to stop the testing, but they did gain substantial media attention. Over time, Greenpeace members honed their skills at both civil disobedience and at gaining publicity. As Wapner observed,

> Greenpeace chiefly wages its campaigns in world civic politics through "direct actions." These include positioning activists between harpooners and whales, plugging up industrial discharge pipes, parachuting from smokestacks and floating a hot-air balloon into a nuclear test site. None of these activities involves lobbying a government per se or calling for a particular policy change on the part of specific countries. Instead, the aim is to instill a sense of outrage among the largest audience possible.[35]

The work of Greenpeace is based on the Quaker notion of "bearing witness."[36] "Having observed a morally objectionable act, one cannot turn away in avoidance. One must either take action to prevent further injustice or stand by and attest to its occurrence."[37]

Today, Greenpeace has offices in 25 countries. It also has a fleet of eight ships, a helicopter, and a hot air balloon. It employs more than a thousand full-time staff members, hundreds of part-time staff members, and thousands of volunteers.[38] Although many people think of Greenpeace as an organization that focuses on saving the whales, its mandate is much broader, including saving ancient forests, ending global warming, stopping the dumping of toxic pollutants, controlling overfishing of the oceans, eliminating genetically engineered crops, and putting an end to all forms of nuclear production and use including nuclear power and nuclear weaponry.[39] The organization makes extensive use of modern technology to provide the press with video images of environmental harm.

Ruckus Society

Although the use of civil disobedience by organizations has not always met with long-term success, the strategy has great potential, and signs indicate that it may be maturing as a tool for change. In 1995, an organization called the Ruckus Society was formed with an approach to civil disobedience that made it unique. Although members of the Ruckus Society periodically engage in civil disobedience themselves, what makes the organization unique is the training it provides to others who wish to use civil disobedience to bring about social change. According to the Society, its mission is to provide "training in the skills of nonviolent civil disobedience to help environmental and human rights organizations achieve their goals."[40] The Society provides weeklong training programs across the country, in what are known as "Action Camps." Participants in these camps learn a variety of skills related to nonviolent civil disobedience, including instructions on using the media, advance planning and scouting out locations, climbing (trees, construction cranes, etc.), and the use of video cameras. Participants are also expected to stay for the duration of the camp, with the expectation that networks will form to be useful in future actions. The Ruckus Society is adamant in its emphasis on nonviolence. As its literature states, "Wherever the location, regardless of the subject, we condemn and do not train activists in any technique that will harm any being."[41]

As organizations go, the Ruckus Society is quite young. It is quite possible that people being trained by the Ruckus Society today will help some organization become a model for the use of nonviolent civil disobedience, a model as powerful as the example provided by Gandhi.

VIOLENCE

Vandalism and violence have long been tools of individuals who are extremists, who are mentally unstable, or who have been forced into violence by desperation. Individual radical environmentalists have engaged in arson, and individual radical anti-abortionists have bombed abortion clinics and killed doctors. However, the extent to which these actions are coordinated and directed by organizations is not always clear. Individual members of organizations like Earth First! may have voiced their approval of the $12 million arson fire that destroyed a Colorado ski resort, and members of the Army of God may believe that justice has been served when an abortion doctor is killed. However, expressing sympathy or approval of such actions is very different from directing or coordinating them. Even when organizations have a direct hand in violence, they are generally reluctant to publicly admit to their role, probably because they are unwilling to suffer the legal consequences of their actions. Admitting to violence can drive away moderate supporters and undermine the credibility of the organization and any claim it has to holding the moral high ground. Although disclaiming any involvement with violence is the general rule, there are highly visible exceptions. Two types of exceptions are worth noting here. First, there are groups for which violence is one component of a larger ideology of hate. The Klu Klux Klan, Aryan Nations, the American Nazi Party, and the Jewish Defense League are examples of groups purported to view violence as an acceptable strategy for achieving their vision of justice. The Klu Klux Klan, Aryan Nations, and neo-Nazi groups were discussed in Chapter 8. The discussion here will use the example of the Jewish Defense League (JDL). The JDL provides a good example, particularly given its willingness to openly express its belief in the necessity of violence.

The Jewish Defense League

Members of the Jewish Defense League have been particularly willing to publicly express their belief that violence is both justified and necessary. Founded in 1968, the JDL has viewed the Jewish people as under attack and has lashed out against minorities and other Jewish groups that take a more moderate stance. Violence is considered necessary in self-defense—to preserve the Jewish people.[42] One of the five principles on which the JDL was founded makes it clear that violence is considered a viable option:

> JDL upholds the principle of Barzel—iron—the need to both move to help Jews everywhere and to change the Jewish image through sacrifice and all necessary means—even strength, force and violence.[43]

In his book, *The Story of the Jewish Defense League,* JDL founder Meir Kahane devotes an entire chapter to justifying the use of violence. He concludes by arguing that "violence is never good but sometimes necessary and Jewish violence to protest Jewish interests is never bad."[44]

The issue of violence continues to swirl around the JDL. The Web site for the Anti-Defamation League, one of the moderate Jewish organizations often criticized by the JDL, provides an extensive listing of violent acts attributed to the JDL. In 1990, Meir Kahane was assassinated in New York City by an Arab extremist.[45] In December 2001, the JDL chairman and another member were arrested for plotting to bomb the offices of an Arab-American U.S. Representative and a Los Angeles-area mosque.[46]

For hate-based groups, violence can serve some useful functions. It can solidify members by having them engage in actions that reinforce their commitment to the organization. It can also use criticisms and attacks on its methods and ideas to further give members a sense that they are a noble embattled group. It is less clear, however, that the violence engaged in by these groups does much to advance their cause. To the contrary, their violence can do much to energize groups opposed to them. Further, when the leaders of organizations that use violence are unwilling to step forward and take responsibility for their actions, it raises questions about their true level of commitment and their genuine interest in achieving justice.

Aside from the violence of hate-based groups, our discussion will include a second category of organization that uses violence. These organizations are not driven by hate but by nationalism and the desire to create a new nation. Numerous examples can be found. The United States was formed using violence, as was the state of Israel. When these revolutionary groups begin their actions, they are often defined as terrorists, but if they succeed, they come to be viewed as visionaries. One example of a modern-day organization that uses violence with the aim of creating an independent nation is the Irish Republican Army (IRA).

The Irish Republican Army

Tensions between Ireland and England go far back in time, perhaps as much as 1,000 years before Columbus came to America,[47] and during much of that time, these tensions have led to violence. Over time, a number of Irish organizations have arisen to oppose the British. Today, one of the more visible of those organizations is the Irish Republican Army. The IRA first emerged in 1916 when seven men seized a government post office in Dublin and posted a signed proclamation, declaring themselves the "Provisional Government of the Irish Republic"[48] A number of organizations preceded the IRA and over time it split into a number of factions. Further, the influence of the IRA has waxed and waned over time.[49] Still, the impact of the IRA has been considerable, and it remains an important player in the effort to create an independent Ireland.

Throughout its history, the IRA has used violence to frustrate what it views as an occupying force. "Basically the IRA man felt that he was fighting for freedom, for an end to injustice, while his opponents sought superiority, so the end justified the means."[50] The IRA has used car bombs, radio-controlled bombs, bank robbery, and murder to further its cause. With financial support from Irish living in other countries, particularly the United States, the IRA also assembled an impressive assortment of weapons, including automatic weapons and rocket launchers. It has also been claimed that extremists in the IRA and their supporters have stolen enough weapons and munitions from the U.S. military to arm 8,000 men.[51]

In the latter part of the 1900s, the organization became more sophisticated in its operation. First, it abandoned its more traditional military structure in favor of small cells. These cells were usually made up of four people, with only the leader having contact with higher authority. Cell members were cautioned to keep their activities secret, even from family and friends. Thus, individual cell members had very limited knowledge of larger operations or of other people involved in the movement.[52] This protected the organization by making it difficult for informers to foil plans and by making captured operatives of little use to British authorities because those operatives knew little about larger plans for the organization. This approach has also been adopted by anti-government extremist organizations in the United States (see Chapter 8) and may have been an element in the 1995 bombing of the Alfred P. Murrah building in Oklahoma City.[53]

To educate members about the purpose and philosophy of the IRA without revealing their identity to other members, the IRA produced the *Green Book,* an explicit statement of the IRA's position on violence:

> Volunteers are expected to wage a military war of liberation against a numerically superior force. This involves the use of arms and explosives. Firstly the use of arms. When volunteers are trained in the use of arms they must fully understand that guns are dangerous, and their main purpose is to take human life, in other words to kill people, and volunteers are trained to kill people. . . . [The volunteer must have] convictions which are strong enough to give him confidence to kill someone without hesitation and without regret.[54]

After more than 1500 years and untold thousands of deaths, Ireland and Britain continue to fight over the issue of Irish independence. In the 1990s, there was talk of peace and agreements to end the violence (or at least that violence sponsored by organizations), but as of this writing, Ireland is still not an independent country and violence is still a feature of daily life in Ireland. Should independence come to Ireland, it is likely to have been facilitated by the use of violence and groups such as the IRA will probably then be defined by the world as patriots rather than as terrorists.

CONCLUSION

Organizations can work to bring about justice in many ways. This chapter has only scratched the surface in the methods that might be used and in its coverage of those methods. Constraints on space have precluded a discussion of the many organizations that work to organize local communities and neighborhoods,[55] or the vast network of organizations that promote peace,[56] to mention just two examples. The purpose of this chapter has not been to provide a comprehensive listing of organizations that work for justice, or to provide step-by-step instructions for building such organizations. Rather, our purpose has been to provide illustrative examples of organizational approaches that have been used with some success.

Having considered the power of individuals and organizations to make a difference, the next chapter addresses yet another concern in the pursuit of justice. What is to be done with nations or national leaders who grossly and intentionally violate human rights? When does the interest of the world community take precedence over the interests of a nation to govern itself—even if that process of governing involves unspeakable horrors?

Discussion Questions

1. How might the strategy an organization adopts be shaped by the particular problem it is addressing? That is, under what conditions would each of the four strategies described in this chapter be the most appropriate?
2. Think of organizations not described in this chapter that have had success at pursuing justice. What strategies do they use?
3. What are the circumstances under which violence might be a morally acceptable strategy for an organization seeking justice?

Endnotes

1. William Korey, *NGOs and the Universal Declaration of Human Rights* (New York: St. Martin's, 1998).
2. Ann Marie Clark, *Diplomacy of Conscience: Amnesty International and Changing Human Rights Norms* (Princeton, N.J.: Princeton University Press, 2001).
3. Ibid.
4. Korey.
5. Ibid., p. 166.
6. Jonathan Power, *Like Water on Stone: The Story of Amnesty International* (Boston: Northeastern University Press, 2001), p. xi.
7. Amnesty International, *Facts and Figures: The Work of Amnesty International* (accessed online at www.amnestyusa.org/about/facts.html on 22 September 2003). Also see Power.
8. Amnesty International.
9. Ibid.
10. Korey, p. 340.
11. Human Rights Watch, *Human Rights Watch: Who We Are* (accessed online at www.hrw.org/about/whoweare.html on 28 February 2002).
12. Ibid.; and Korey.
13. Korey.
14. Ibid.

15. Human Rights Watch.
16. Ibid.
17. Samuel Walker, *In Defense of American Liberties: A History of the ACLU* (New York: Oxford University Press, 1990).
18. Diane Garey, *Defending Everybody: A History of the American Civil Liberties Union* (New York: TV Books, 1998).
19. Ibid.
20. Ibid., p. 58.
21. Walker, p. 30.
22. Ibid.
23. Ibid., p. 54.
24. Ibid., p. 55.
25. Ibid.
26. American Civil Liberties Union, *Freedom Is Why We're Here* (accessed online at www.aclu.org/Files/OpenFile.cfm?id=10740 on 22 September 2003).
27. Walker, p. 4.
28. American Civil Liberties Union.
29. Jill Lawrence, "Conservative Favorites to Join ACLU," *USA Today*, 25 November 2002, p. 2A.
30. Peter Ackerman and Jack Duvall, *A Force More Powerful: A Century of Nonviolent Conflict* (New York: Palgrave, 2000).
31. Philip E. Lawler, *Operation Rescue: A Challenge to the Nation's Conscience* (Huntington, Ind.: Our Sunday Visitor, 1992).
32. Ibid.
33. Ibid.
34. Paul Wapner, "Environmental Activism and Global Civil Society," *Dissent* (summer 1994), pp. 389–393.
35. Ibid., p. 390.
36. Michael Brown and John May, *The Greenpeace Story* (New York: Dorling Kindersley, 1991).
37. Wapner, p. 391.
38. Ibid.
39. Greenpeace, *Inside Greenpeace: History and Mission* (accessed online at www.greenpeace.org/international_en/campaigns/intro?campaign_id=3940 on 11 March 2002).
40. The Ruckus Society, *About the Ruckus Society* (accessed online at http://ruckus.org/about/index.html on 7 March 2002).
41. Ibid.
42. Jewish Defense League, *The Five Principles of the Jewish Defense League* (accessed online at www.jdl.org on 13 March 2002).
43. Ibid.
44. Rabbi Meir Kahane, *The Story of the Jewish Defense League* (Radnor, Pa.: Chilton, 1975), p. 144, emphasis in the original.
45. Anti-Defamation League.
46. Vincent J. Schodolski, "2 Jewish Militants Jailed on Bomb Plot," *Chicago Tribune*, 13 March 2002 (accessed online at www.chicagotribune.com on 13 March 2002).
47. Tim Pat Coogan, *The Troubles: Ireland's Ordeal 1966–1996 and the Search for Peace* (Boulder, Colo.: Roberts Rinehart, 1996).
48. J. Bowyer Bell, *The Secret Army: The IRA*, 3rd ed. (New Brunswick, N.J.: Transaction, 1997).

49. Tim Pat Coogan, *The IRA*, 5th ed. (New York: St. Martin's, 2000).
50. Ibid., p. 381.
51. Ibid.
52. Ibid.; idem, *The Troubles*.
53. Mark Hamm, *Apocalypse in Oklahoma: Waco and Ruby Ridge Revenged* (Boston: Northeastern University Press, 1997).
54. Cited in Coogan, *IRA*, p. 547.
55. For a fuller discussion of these, see Robert Fisher, *Let the People Decide: Neighborhood Organizing in America* (New York: Twayne, 1994).
56. A nice overview of organizations that promote peace can be found in Elise Boulding, *Cultures of Peace: The Hidden Side of History* (Syracuse, N.Y.: Syracuse University Press, 2000).

GLOBAL JUSTICE

The preceding chapters have focused on a variety of ways in which individuals and organizations might pursue justice. Unlike the discussion of individuals and organizations, the concept of global justice is an emerging area in which a variety of fundamental issues have yet to be resolved. To date, there are no examples that illustrate this approach at its best. Despite this, global justice is of great importance. Improved transportation and communication have aided the movement of goods and ideas among nations, but it has also aided the spread of war crimes, genocides, slavery, and other serious human rights violations. As nations become increasingly interdependent, what happens in one country affects others. As a result, nations have struggled to find alternative ways to define acts of injustice that threaten the stability of other nations and to penalize violators.

This chapter focuses on international efforts to pursue justice, in which nations collectively respond to injustices committed either by other nations or by individuals in formal leadership positions within nations. The challenge is to identify acts that violate universal standards of justice while respecting the ability of nations to handle their own affairs and make their own judgments about what behaviors are acceptable.

The idea that universal standards of justice exist and that nations and national leaders can be held accountable for violating those standards is a relatively recent development. Even the notion of human rights is relatively new. Robertson argues that the first modern notion of human rights enforceable through the courts was the 1689 Bill of Rights in England.[1] By claiming these rights, the British formally ended the notion that the king ruled by divine right, and it became possible for Parliament to veto royal decisions. These rights, sounding much like the rights later enumerated in the Bill of Rights to the U.S. Constitution, included the right to have the lawfulness of imprisonment tested by the courts, also known as *habeas corpus*, and,

> The right of subjects to live under the law as approved by parliament without arbitrary royal interference; the right to due process in the selection of jurors; the right not to lose liberty through excessively high fixing of bail; and the right not to be inflicted with "cruel and unusual punishment."[2]

These rights were viewed as basic rights of British citizens and eventually became the justification for the American Revolution. However, the focus of the Bill of Rights in England was on rights *within* the British Empire. The notion of basic human rights that transcend national boundaries would come later.

The discussion of global justice begins with a discussion of war. Modern efforts at global justice have emerged because of wartime atrocities. Further, as was discussed in Chapter 10 on genocide, war is sometimes used to justify behaviors that would otherwise be indefensible.

WAR

There is little basis in reality for the popular saying "All's fair in love and war." Both courtship and war have recognized rules. As discussed in Chapter 2, St. Augustine delineated the criteria for a "just war." St. Augustine's rules focused on the circumstances under which it was morally justifiable to engage in war and on the treatment of civilians.[3] Written rules placing restrictions on the treatment of enemy combatants and the practice of war itself did not emerge until the mid-1800s during the American Civil War. President Abraham Lincoln recognized that the manner in which the Civil War was fought would have a lasting impact on the ability of the warring factions to peacefully coexist when the war was over. In 1863, he directed Dr. Francis Lieber to develop rules of war to guide the actions of Union soldiers.

Issued as General Orders Number 100 from the Adjutant General's Office in 1863, the Lieber Code is a remarkable document both in the range of issues it includes and in the succinctness of its writing. The Lieber Code is the source for modern military law and has been used as the basis for military codes in other countries. It has also been used to develop international law on war crimes.[4] The Lieber Code is divided into 10 sections with a total of 157 articles (major points) across those 10 sections, but is only about 25 pages long. To provide just a few examples, the Code includes a discussion of the following: what martial law is and when it applies to occupied territories; what occupying armies are forbidden from doing to property, civilians, and enemy soldiers; how deserters, traitors, spies, and prisoners of war are to be handled; flags of truce, prisoner exchanges, and the procedures for reaching a peace settlement.[5]

In St. Petersburg in 1868, at The Hague in 1899, and again at The Hague in 1907, nations reached a general agreement on the rules of war, including a ban on weapons that inflicted unnecessary suffering; attacks on undefended towns; attacks on hospitals, churches, universities, and historic buildings; and the use of poison or poison gas. There was also agreement that prisoners of war were to be treated humanely.[6] A series of additional international meetings expanded and clarified the rules of war. Most well known, perhaps were the rules for engagement, the treatment of prisoners, and the treatment of civilians outlined in the 1949 Geneva Conventions.[7]

In 1949, there were a series of conventions regarding the rules of war. These meetings, held in Switzerland, came to be known as the Geneva Conventions. The first convention provided guidelines for the treatment of sick and wounded combatants on land. The second convention focused on sick and wounded combatants at sea. The third convention provided guidelines for the handling of prisoners of war, and the fourth concerned the treatment of civilians in occupied territories.[8]

Starting in 2001, when the United States held Afghan fighters in Guantanamo Bay, Cuba, concerns were raised about whether these captives were treated according to the Geneva Conventions, but most Americans probably had little idea of what the Geneva Conventions required. According to the Conventions, prisoners of war cannot be tortured to extract information or be used for military labor. In addition,

> The prisoner must give his name, rank, regimental number and date of birth: on thus achieving POW status he is entitled to be "quartered under conditions as favorable as those for the forces of the detaining power" and to have nutritious food, warm clothing and bedding, and permission to pray and to smoke. POWs are to receive monthly pay . . . and must be allowed to receive food parcels and send and receive mail. They must be permitted to organize discipline in their own camps, and to make formal complaints about their treatment.[9]

Over time, each of these agreements, from the 1868 meeting in St. Petersburg to the 1949 Geneva Conventions, was more detailed than the last, but they all shared a failure to establish any enforcement mechanism. Without an enforcement mechanism, the prohibitions outlined in the various commissions and conventions had little meaning. During both World War I and World War II, the agreed-on rules of war were systematically violated by both sides.[10] Creating these rules of war was not sufficient to change the behavior of nations, but it was a necessary step toward creating an enforcement mechanism. Such a mechanism has still not fully evolved, but it is possible to identify early attempts. Perhaps the most important of these attempts was the series of trials at Nuremberg.

THE NUREMBERG TRIALS

At the end of World War I, there was a feeble attempt to hold the German leadership accountable for Germany's actions during the war. Articles 228 and 229 of the Versailles Treaty:

... provided that Germany should try its own war criminals: evidence against 901 of its nationals was handed over. ... 888 were acquitted, and of the thirteen convicted several were allowed to escape by prison officers who were publicly congratulated for assisting them.[11]

After World War II, there was again a call for tribunals by the victorious nations against the vanquished, but this time the process and the outcome were quite different. The victorious Allied nations—United States, England, France, and the Soviet Union—agreed on and produced the 1945 Charter of the Nuremberg Tribunal and established a Tokyo Tribunal to deal with Japanese war crimes. This charter provided relatively detailed rules of procedure under which leaders of the Nazi regime would be tried and punished.[12] The Nuremberg Trials were heavily stacked in favor of the prosecution:

> All prosecutors and judges were nationals of the Allied powers, and all defendants and, more regrettably, their lawyers were German. . . . The German defense lawyers, floundering in the alien Anglo-American environment of the adversary trial, were given limited facilities to prepare their cases and little notice of prosecution evidence.[13]

Some defense attorneys suffered reprisals from their local bar associations for having worked too aggressively in the defense of their clients. Even the location, the site where the German anti-Semitic laws were created, gave the prosecution a psychological advantage.[14] The German defendants, accused of wartime atrocities, were not allowed to present evidence of numerous Allied atrocities during the war, including the 30,000 people executed following what were transparently show trials in the Soviet Union between 1936 and 1938.[15] Charges at Nuremberg included "subverting the League of Nations," although the United States had never joined the League of Nations and the Soviet Union had been expelled from it.[16] Further, the trial was an ex post facto prosecution. That is, defendants were tried for behaviors they engaged in *before* those acts were defined as crimes.[17] This violated a fundamental principle of fairness recognized in most legal systems.

Perhaps the most unfortunate feature of the Nuremberg Trials was the manner in which justice was dispensed. As Robertson observed,

> In its end lay the negation of its beginning: it created crimes against humanity and then punished them inhumanely. Twelve defendants were sentenced to death by hanging, after which—by some grisly irony appealing to the Allied high command—the bodies were cremated in the ovens at Dachau. The ashes were consigned to an unidentified fast-flowing river so no grave would ever serve as a place of neo-Nazi pilgrimage.[18]

The trials were also notable for the small number of defendants who were charged with war crimes. Thousands of offenders were never charged by the tribunal. Further, if the Nuremberg Trials were to serve as a deterrent to prevent future atrocities, they failed. Numerous instances of state-sponsored atrocities have occurred since Nuremberg, some of which are noted in Chapter 10 on genocide. Most of these horrendous acts have elicited only a tepid response from the international community.

Despite these limitations, the Nuremberg proceedings were much more than show trials. The defendants faced clearly articulated charges of crimes against humanity, and the proceedings followed a detailed series of legal procedures. Most important, the Nuremberg Trials laid the groundwork for later efforts at defining war crimes, for conducting war crime tribunals, for the principle that individuals could be held accountable for the acts of nations, and that "I was just following orders" was not an acceptable defense for all wartime atrocities. It has also been argued that the Nuremberg Trials inspired the development of the United Nations and the rise of nongovernment organizations (NGOs) that pursue human rights.[19]

THE UNIVERSAL DECLARATION OF HUMAN RIGHTS

Although Allied war atrocities were substantial, those of the Nazis were particularly horrific and caused nations to more formally recognize fundamental human rights and to move toward establishing a framework for punishing nations that flagrantly violated those rights. The United Nations, which had been formed in 1945, was a logical organization to direct this international effort. The Charter for the UN placed considerable emphasis on human rights, and the UN quickly established a Commission on Human Rights. The Commission on Human Rights included 18 member nations and was chaired by Eleanor Roosevelt, wife of President Franklin D. Roosevelt, with a Canadian, John Humphrey, serving as secretariat. One of the first items on the Commission's agenda was the creation of the Universal Declaration of Human Rights (see the appendix). The direction of the Commission may have been influenced by a speech given by President Roosevelt, in which he spoke of four fundamental freedoms—freedom of speech and worship and freedom from want and fear—ideas that had been outlined in the writings of science fiction author H. G. Wells.[20]

Although the practical work of constructing the Universal Declaration of Human Rights was in the hands of an American and a Canadian, there was a serious effort to include the perspectives of many cultures and from countries representing a broad range of economic development.[21] Altogether the Commission received input from 250 delegates representing 56 countries—in addition to seeking the advice of recognized authorities, including H. G. Wells. Giving a backhanded testimonial to its multicultural appeal, Robertson noted,

> That over the following half-century the Declaration would be flouted without regard to geography, by governments of every creed and color and often by or with the connivance of the U.S. and its European allies, amply demonstrates that its

guarantees are not "Western" in any meaningful sense. "Liberal" the Declaration is not, in any consistent way . . . [22]

Its broad appeal is even more surprising given the wide range of issues it includes among basic human rights. Aside from the obvious prohibitions against such things as slavery and torture, the Universal Declaration of Human Rights also includes the right to marry, work, join labor unions, have rest and leisure, free education, and the enjoyment of the arts.

The document was groundbreaking in another way. Influenced by what the Germans had done to their own people, the Universal Declaration of Human Rights also addressed the problems of human rights violations *within* nations. Interfering with a nation's sovereignty was justified by the assumption that serious human rights violations within a single nation threatened international peace and stability.[23] This created a precedent for subsequent international tribunals and interventions in what might previously have been considered purely internal matters.

The Universal Declaration of Human Rights was high on principles but made no effort to outline a mechanism for holding nations or individuals accountable for living up to those principles. Thus, the document was an important step toward global justice, but left the hard part for others who would follow.

Although the Universal Declaration of Human Rights has never had the force of law, as a model of what nations should aspire to it has been tremendously influential. As Robertson observed,

> What amazes today is the contemporaneity of the document, over half a century on. Roosevelt and her drafting committee produced an imperishable statement that has inspired more than 200 international treaties, conventions and declarations, and the bills of rights found in almost every national constitution adopted since the war.[24]

THE EUROPEAN COURT OF HUMAN RIGHTS

In 1950, a group of 12 European nations, known as the Council of Europe and eventually known as the Council of the European Union, held the European Convention on Human Rights. Signatory nations agreed to abide by the principles outlined in the Universal Declaration of Human Rights and, where necessary, to modify their legal codes to be consistent with the Universal Declaration.[25] More important, the European Convention on Human Rights created the European Court of Human Rights, which began hearing cases in 1959. The Convention also established rules and procedures for bringing alleged offenders to trial and for providing the accused with basic procedural rights drawn from the English common law tradition (see Chapter 4 for a discussion of that tradition). Most contentious of the procedural rights granted in the European Court has been the right of individuals and organizations to directly bring charges against a country before the court. This has meant that individuals could bring international charges against their own countries. The reluctance of nations to accept this provision delayed the active use of the court for nearly two decades.

Concerns about procedural issues were eventually worked out, and the frequency with which the court was used has increased. In 1983, about 500 cases were brought before the court. By 2000, more than 10,000 cases a year were brought before the court, and nearly 16,000 cases were pending.[26] After the Berlin wall came down in 1989, many nations that had been under the control of the Soviet Union sought to join the European Union and were willing to abide by the rules of the European Court of Human Rights.[27]

The European Court has been criticized for sometimes turning cases back to the country standing accused before it and for its requirement that whenever a nation is tried before it, the panel of judges deciding the case will have at least one of its judges drawn from the accused nation.[28] Despite these weaknesses, the European Court has been quite successful at persuading member nations to incorporate basic human rights protections into their laws. As Robertson observed,

> The European Court of Human Rights has become the model human rights court, proof positive that international law can work to enforce fundamental freedoms across a swathe of countries, as every one of its original member governments has made changes in its laws for the benefit of groups such as immigrants, transvestites, prisoners, and mental patients—reforms which would not have been sufficiently vote-winning in the absence of a decision from Strasbourg [France, where the court is housed].[29]

By the late 1990s, the court was used frequently, creating a 6-year backlog of cases. In 1998, the Council of Europe expanded the European Court, making its judges permanent and paying them respectable wages. At present, 41 member nations have willingly placed themselves under the jurisdiction of the European Court of Human Rights.[30] Ideally, the model presented by the European Court could be expanded to include nations from every continent to create a court with truly global jurisdiction. Although there has been some movement in this direction, the discussion that follows makes it clear that the process will be a long one.

TEMPORARY TRIBUNALS

Between 1945 and 1950, a flurry of international activity focused on human rights. The United Nations was formed, the Nuremberg Trials were held, the Universal Declaration of Human Rights was adopted, the Geneva Conventions issued rules of war, the Genocide Convention formalized the UN position on genocide, and there was a European Convention on Human Rights. Given all of these developments, it is surprising that international war crimes tribunals did not emerge for more than 40 years. The United Nations did not set in motion the process of establishing a permanent international criminal court to prosecute war crimes and the most egregious human rights violations until 1998.

The single biggest obstacle to setting up international courts with true enforcement power is that for such a court to be effective, participating nations must agree in advance to abide by its findings and thus to give up some of their sovereignty. A nation that agrees to be under the jurisdiction of such a court may easily find itself accused and tried by nations it does not trust.

International human rights activities between 1945 and 1950 described earlier fell far short of what was needed to hold people and nations fully accountable for war crimes and acts of genocide. These were, however, important steps toward the creation of a structure that would have the ability to examine specific cases and hand out punishments. The next significant steps toward a system of justice to deal with global atrocities did not occur until 43 years later, when the United Nations established a temporary war crimes tribunal in The Hague to hear cases of war crimes and genocide in Bosnia. Just one year later, the United Nations established another temporary tribunal to hear cases of war crimes in Rwanda. The Rwandan genocide was described in some detail in Chapter 10. A brief summary of the genocide in Bosnia will provide a context for understanding the reasons for creating the temporary tribunal.

Bosnia, now known as the Federation of Bosnia and Herzegovina, declared its independence from the former Yugoslavia in 1992. The region has a long history of violence, particularly among the Serbs (most of whom are Orthodox Christian), Croats (most of whom are Catholic), and Muslim populations. Intergroup violence in Yugoslavia was largely held in check under the strong rule of Marshal Tito, a Communist dictator. After his death, the economy of the country declined and ethnic tensions rose. From 1991 to 1995, a series of wars erupted when four of the six Yugoslavian provinces moved for independence. During these wars, atrocities were committed under the direction of political leaders—although because it was a time of war, the world did not distinguish legitimate warfare from "ethnic cleansing" or genocide for some time.[31] Though there were unconscionable acts committed by all sides in these battles, the Serbs, under the leadership of Slobodan Milošević, appeared to have engaged in the most systematic and ruthless acts, many of which were aimed at driving away the Muslim population, and killing those who did not leave.[32] In the town of Zvornik, for example, one UN official recalled the following scene:

> I could see trucks full of dead bodies. I could see militiamen taking more corpses of children, women and old people from their houses, and putting them on trucks. I saw at least four or five trucks full of corpses. When I arrived, the cleansing had been done . . . It was all finished. They were looting, cleaning up the city after the massacre.[33]

Scenes such as this were repeated throughout the country. In and around the city of Srebrenica, at least 7,000 Muslims were slaughtered and put in mass graves. There is a long list of atrocities committed by Christian Serbs seeking to create a new and ethnically pure state through ethnic cleansing. A UN commission investigating allegations of genocide concluded there was evidence of

> . . . murder, torture, arbitrary arrest and detention, extra-judicial executions, rape and sexual assault, confinement of civilians in ghetto areas, forcible removal, displacement and deportation of civilians, deliberate military attacks or threats of attacks on civilians and civilian areas, and wanton destruction of property.[34]

The Hague Tribunal for war crimes in Bosnia was the first international tribunal since the 1945 Nuremberg Trials. Unlike Nuremberg, The Hague Tribunal was truly international and not simply a situation in which the victors held the vanquished in judgment. The legal basis for creating The Hague Tribunal was not explicit but was inferred from the UN Charter, which gave the United Nations authority to act where there were threats to international peace and security. The tribunal was authorized to hear cases against individuals whose acts were committed after 1991 in what had formerly been Yugoslavia. It was given the authority to prosecute and punish serious violations of the laws of war outlined in the 1949 Geneva Convention and in the 1907 Hague Convention. The Hague Tribunal was also authorized to punish genocide and crimes against humanity.[35] In 1994, the UN Security Council created an extension of The Hague Tribunal to hear charges against those involved in the genocide in Rwanda. This tribunal was conducted in Arusha, Tanzania, and like the tribunal in The Hague, there were three trial chambers, each with an international panel of judges to hear the cases. To provide consistency across cases, the same body served as the Appeals Chamber for both The Hague and the Arusha Tribunals.

Someone accused of an international crime will be arrested by one of the countries that has agreed to cooperate with the international tribunals. The Hague and the Arusha Tribunals each have three courtrooms. In each courtroom, a panel of three judges hears each case, with a simple majority necessary for a conviction. Defendants are provided with the attorneys of their choice, and if they cannot afford an attorney, the fees will be paid for them. The accused is provided with many of the rights granted in common law courts. The only penalty that can be imposed by the tribunals is imprisonment and the return of improperly seized property to victims. Prison time is served in a country willing to take the offender, and the length of sentence is determined by the gravity of the offense.[36]

The Hague Tribunal was initially underfunded and understaffed. The first Serb was not arrested until two years after the tribunal was formed, although the whereabouts of Serbs accused of war crimes were well known. Over time, more resources came to the tribunal, and it became more aggressive in its pursuit of cases. By 2001, what began in 1993 as a small operation with one deputy prosecutor had expanded to a prosecutor's staff of 300 and a total staff of more than 1,000.[37] By April 2002, the tribunal's detention facility held 40 inmates, 8 were on provisional release, and another 30 remained at large.[38]

The Arusha Tribunals have processed even fewer cases arising from the Rwandan genocide than have been processed in The Hague Tribunals. Formed in 1994, the Arusha Tribunals did not hear their first case until 1996 and by early 2002 had only tried 9 of 50 suspects held in custody. There is no fixed pre-determined ending date for these tribunals, and it will likely be some years to come before they have finished their work. Considering that at least some of those on trial will be found not guilty, there are questions about the fairness of holding suspects in jails for years before their trials—a problem for which there is no obvious solution.[39]

Critics have argued that if the Nuremberg trials were used by victors to punish the vanquished, then the temporary tribunals for Bosnian and Rwandan war crimes were created as little more than symbolic gestures that allowed other nations to do nothing.[40] Inadequate funding may reflect the ambivalence that nations of the world feel toward these acts of genocide. The number of prosecutions is small considering the number of people who might be charged. Although resources have improved over time, these tribunals remain short on cash, short on personnel, and short on time. For example, in Rwanda, the government has taken to holding its own trials. An additional 120,000 have been arrested and are on trial in Rwanda by that nation's courts. Of these 6,000 have been tried.[41] At the current pace, it will take the Rwandan government 200 years to try the remaining suspects.[42]

What is the verdict on these temporary tribunals? Their weaknesses are many. They have received inadequate financial support from UN member nations. They have handled only a tiny fraction of the cases that fall within their jurisdiction. There is no evidence that the functioning of these courts has done much to prevent genocide. Many of the acts of genocide committed by the Serbs took place after The Hague Tribunal was called into being, as were the acts of genocide in Rwanda. Finally, it is not clear that the Tribunals have helped heal the emotional wounds of survivors. As Power noted,

> Despite the presence of high-powered defendants in UN custody, none of the early trials had the effect on survivors that the 1961 trial of Adolf Eichmann, the Nazi official in charge of Jewish deportations, for instance, had on Israelis. Citizens in Rwanda and Bosnia paid almost no attention to the court proceedings. Israelis recall the days when they huddled around their radios to hear for the first time the details of Nazi horrors, whereas Bosnians and Rwandans just shrug when the courts are mentioned. They are deemed irrelevant to their daily lives.[43]

Viewed in isolation, The Hague and Arusha Tribunals would appear to be of limited utility. Their value, however, can only be appreciated when they are viewed within a larger context. Both tribunals represent a small but important step in the evolution of a system of global justice. The tribunals have served an educative function, making it clear to the world that shared definitions of unacceptable behavior exist and holding up examples in which these shared rules have been violated. The tribunals have also clarified the boundaries of behavior that falls within the jurisdiction of international courts through their decisions in individual cases. For example, in February 2001, The Hague Tribunal ruled that sexual enslavement was a war crime, convicting three Serbs of "crimes against humanity for repeatedly raping and torturing Muslim women in 'rape camps.'"[44] Finally, aside from those facing trial, there have been no serious challenges to the authority of the tribunals, nor have there been questions about their fairness. The tribunals have been a success if viewed as steps in a longer journey rather than as the final destination. The next step in this journey is the development of a permanent international criminal court that has the authority to deal with cases wherever they might occur.

A Permanent International Criminal Court

In July 1998, 120 nations reached an agreement detailing the creation of a permanent international criminal court to hear cases of the most extreme human rights violations and to dispense punishments to those found guilty. The agreement, signed in Rome, Italy, was known as the Rome Statute[45] and was to go into effect one year after it had been ratified by at least 60 nations. On April 11, 2002, that threshold was passed, bringing the total number of ratifying countries to 65 and setting in motion the creation of the International Criminal Court (ICC). On March 11, 2003, opening ceremonies were held for the court.[46] In protest, the United States sent no representative to the ceremony.

The Rome Statute drew heavily on the experiences of Nuremberg and The Hague and from the examples of the many perpetrators of genocide and war crimes who had successfully evaded punishment.[47] The ICC is authorized to hear cases involving four types of crime: genocide, crimes against humanity, war crimes, and the crime of aggression. Each category of crime is defined in the Rome Statute, except for "crimes of aggression," which will be included when participating nations come to an agreement on the acts to be included within this category.[48]

The rules of the ICC generally follow those in common law adversarial systems.[49] Trials are open to the public, defendants are presumed innocent, and the burden of proof is on the prosecutor to show guilt beyond a reasonable doubt. Defendants have a right to remain silent, and if they cannot afford an attorney, one is provided for them. Those standing accused before the court have a right to review the evidence against them, to confront witnesses against them, and to call witnesses in their behalf. Convicted defendants have the right to appeal their convictions and their sentences, but contrary to most common law systems, the prosecution also has the right to appeal.

The ICC, consistent with an emerging world standard, cannot impose the death penalty on convicted offenders. Punishments are limited to life imprisonment for the most serious cases, as long as 30 years in prison for the majority of serious offenses, and 5 years in prison for lesser offenses. The court can also order defendants to return gains from their crimes, and there are provisions for reparations to victims.

Although the ICC has great promise, some are skeptical of its ability to have any meaningful authority. Robertson, for example, suggests that the final version of the Rome Statute included so many compromises that it will render the court largely ineffective.[50] He is particularly critical of the United States, which had opposed an international criminal court from the very beginning, indicating it could support such an institution only if there were absolute guarantees that no United States' citizen would ever be subject to the ICC. In 1998, 120 nations agreed to the Rome Statute creating a permanent International Criminal Court and 7 nations voted to oppose the court. In its vote against the ICC, the United States aligned itself with nations that have a questionable record for protecting human rights, including China, India, and Israel. Many modifications were made to weaken the authority of the court in the hopes of gaining the support of the United States, but that support did not materialize.

Here are a few of the many ways that Robertson believes the ICC was unnecessarily weakened.[51] First, cases can only be pursued if they are sent to the court through the UN Security Council, which is made up of the world's superpowers, or with the permission of the nation in which the state-sponsored atrocities occurred. Thus, major nations can block a prosecution, as can oppressors who remain in power. Second, the jurisdiction of the court and the rules that govern it cannot be modified until its review seven years after it has been put in place. Third, no one can be charged for actions that took place before their country ratifies the Rome Statute. Fourth, states have the ability to ratify the ICC but any time after that they may receive an exemption from the jurisdiction of the court for seven years. Thus, state officials planning to engage in war crimes or genocide may, before committing the acts, request a seven-year exemption from prosecution by the ICC. Fifth, under the ICC, individuals can be charged with international crimes, but nations, political groups, or corporations cannot. Finally, the court cannot proceed in cases prosecuted within a nation, unless it can be shown that the national prosecution was a show trial or was otherwise conducted in a way to avoid justice.

On March 11, 2003, ceremonies were held at The Hague officially opening the permanent international criminal court. Eighteen judges were sworn in before diplomats, politicans, and judges from more than 100 nations. The United States, a long-time opponent of the court, sent no representatives and has no judges sitting on the court.[52]

From the beginning, the ICC has been controversial.[53] The ICC holds the promise of a judicial body that will hold those who engage in genocide and war crimes criminally accountable. In its present configuration, the ICC is unlikely to fully meet this promise. However, the ICC has tremendous symbolic importance, and despite its limitations, it is a very small but important step toward the development of a more complete system of international justice. The same powerful nations that have shown little interest in stopping war crimes or genocide in developing countries have little interest in establishing a legal structure that would hold offenders accountable—at least for the moment.

TRUTH AND RECONCILIATION COMMISSIONS

Many times, courts do not have the resources to handle all the cases of human rights violations before them. In other cases, convictions are not possible because the perpetrators successfully destroy evidence or because the authorities now in power block efforts to gather evidence of past atrocities. Justice for gross human rights violations does not only mean legal prosecution and punishment. An alternative is the truth and reconciliation commission.[54] Between 1974 and 2000, there were at least 21 truth commissions,[55] usually following a transition from a brutal authoritarian regime to a more democratic system. The structure of these commissions has varied, as has the extent to which they were deemed a success. Sometimes they have been conducted in conjunction with prosecutions, whereas others have been conducted rather than prosecutions. They all have shared a belief that a full accounting of atrocities in the recent past is necessary to reach closure and move forward. As Rotberg observed,

> Truth commissions thus seek, whatever their mandate from a new government, to uncover the past in order to answer questions that remain unanswered: What happened to husbands, sons, wives, and lovers at the hands of the ousted regime? Who executed the orders? What was the grand design? Who benefitted? Getting the facts provides closure, at least in theory.[56]

Minow argues,

> The working hypothesis is that testimony of victims and perpetrators, offered publicly to a truth commission, affords opportunities for individuals and the nation as a whole to heal. . . . truth commissions presume that telling and hearing truth is healing.[57]

A common strategy is to allow offenders to publicly describe their crimes in full in exchange for amnesty. Sometimes this means amnesty for anyone who fully cooperates and sometimes it is amnesty for lesser offenses, but any serious offenses that are uncovered are forwarded for prosecution. Victims are also allowed to testify and may find it therapeutic to have their victimization publicly recognized. Thus, the focus is on healing and reconciliation rather than on vengeance and punishment. This is particularly appropriate where the victims and offenders are from the same country and of necessity must cooperate for the country to function smoothly. Not every instance of gross human rights violations is amenable to a truth commission, but in many circumstances, it is a viable alternative to a focus on punishment.

CONCLUSION

Is a global system of justice necessary or likely in the future? Quite probably. To explain why, we only need to look to the American experience in which the founding fathers left nearly all criminal matters to the states, with treason among the only crimes mentioned in the Constitution. Over time, the federal government has made an increasing number of behaviors federal crimes. As communication and transportation improved, what happened in one state had serious implications for what happened in another. Further, criminal enterprises came increasingly to cross state borders. The result was a geometric increase in the number of crimes that came to be defined as requiring federal intervention.[58] Parallel conditions can be seen in the world today as improved communications and transportation have dramatically increased the movement of goods, services, and people across borders.

As the world moves toward a global economy and nations are increasingly interdependent, it is becoming more difficult to view genocide and war crimes as purely internal matters. Nations that in the past have not been moved to stop such atrocities on purely moral grounds are increasingly finding intervention is necessary for their own economic and social stability. Thus, despite the reluctance of the United States and China, to name only two examples, to embrace an international system of justice, in the long run it will be in their interests to do so. The development of an international justice system has progressed at a glacial pace, but it has progressed. The key will be to devise a system that can address the most serious atrocities while allowing nations as much independence as possible.

Discussion Questions

1. What are the arguments for and against having rules of war and defining war crimes for those who violate the rules?
2. Why was the Universal Declaration of Human Rights important, even though it did not have the force of law?

3. What are the arguments for and the arguments against the U.S. position opposing an International Criminal Court?

Endnotes

1. Geoffrey Robertson, *Crimes Against Humanity: The Struggle for Global Justice* (New York: Free Press, 1999).
2. Ibid., p. 3.
3. Richard Norman, *Ethics, Killing and War* (New York: Cambridge University Press, 1995).
4. Robertson.
5. Richard Shelly Hartigan, *Lieber's Code and the Law of War* (Chicago: Precedent, 1983).
6. Robertson.
7. Norman.
8. Robertson. For an excellent discussion of what constitutes a war crime, also see Roy Gutman and David Rieff (eds.), *Crimes of War: What the Public Should Know* (New York: Norton, 1999).
9. Ibid., p. 176.
10. Ibid.
11. Ibid., pp. 210–211.
12. See The Avalon Project, *Nuremberg Trial Proceedings, Volume I: Rules of Procedure* (accessed online at www.yale.edu/lawweb/avalon/imt/proc/imtrules.htm on 26 March 2002).
13. Robertson, p. 214.
14. Martha Minow, *Between Vengeance and Forgiveness: Facing History After Genocide and Mass Violence* (Boston: Beacon, 1998).
15. Robertson.
16. Ibid.
17. Minow.
18. Robertson.
19. Minow.
20. Robertson, p. 23; Susan Waltz, "Universalizing Human Rights: The Role of Small States in the Construction of the Universal Declaration of Human Rights," *Human Rights Quarterly* 23 (2001), pp. 44–72.
21. Ibid.
22. Robertson, p. 32.
23. Ibid.
24. Ibid., p. 29.
25. Ibid.
26. European Court of Human Rights, *Information Note on the Court's Statistics* (accessed online at www.echr.coe.int/BilingualDocuments/infodoc.stats(2001).bil.htm on 10 April 2002).
27. Robertson.
28. Ibid.
29. Ibid., p. 58.
30. European Court of Human Rights.
31. See Steven L. Burg, "Genocide in Bosnia-Herzegovina?" in *Century of Genocide: Eyewitness Accounts and Critical Views*, Samuel Totten, William S. Parsons, and Israel W. Charny (eds.). (New York: Garland, 1997), pp. 424–433.

32. Ibid.
33. Gale A. Kirking, *Untangling Bosnia and Hercegovna: A Search for Understanding* (Madison, Wis.: Real World Press, 1999).
34. Cited in Samantha Power, *A Problem from Hell: America and the Age of Genocide* (New York: Basic Books, 2002), p. 483.
35. Robertson.
36. *Statute of the International Tribunal* (accessed online at www.un.org/icty/basic/statut/stat2000.htm on 18 April 2002).
37. Power.
38. International Tribunal, *Outstanding Public Indictments* (accessed online at www.un.org/icty/glance/indictlist-e.htm on 18 April 2002).
39. Power.
40. Robertson.
41. Arthur Asiimwe, *Arusha Tribunal to Move Some Genocide Cases* (accessed online at http://allafrica.com/stories/200202180774.html on 18 April 2002).
42. Danna Harman, "Rwanda Turns to Its Past for Justice," *Christian Science Monitor* (30 January 2002 edition, accessed online at www.csmonitor.com/2002/0130/p09s01-woaf.html on 30 January 2002).
43. Power, p. 496.
44. Lauren Comiteau, "'Sexual Enslavement' Established as a War Crime," *USA Today*, 23 February 2001, p. 10A.
45. Rome Statute of the International Court (accessed online at www.un.org/law/icc/statute/99_corr/cstatute.htm on 21 February 2002).
46. Stevenson Swanson, "1st Global War Crimes Court Poised to Open," *Chicago Tribune*, 11 March 2003, p. 3.
47. William A. Schabas, *An Introduction to the International Criminal Court* (New York: Cambridge University Press, 2001).
48. Rome Statute of the International Court.
49. Ibid.
50. Robertson.
51. Ibid.
52. Marlise Simons, "World Court for Crimes of War Opens in The Hague," *New York Times*, 12 March 2003 (accessed online at www.nytimes.com on 12 March 2003).
53. See Sarah B. Sewall and Carl Kaysen, *The United States and the International Criminal Court* (New York: Rowman & Littlefield, 2000); Alton Frye, *Toward an International Criminal Court: A Council Policy Initiative* (New York: Council on Foreign Relations Books, 1999).
54. See Minow; and Priscilla B. Hayner, *Unspeakable Truths: Confronting State Terror and Atrocity* (New York: Routledge, 2001); Robert I. Rotberg and Dennis Thompson (eds.), *Truth v. Justice: The Morality of Truth Commissions* (Princeton, N.J.: Princeton University Press, 2000).
55. Hayner.
56. Robert I. Rotberg, "Truth Commissions and the Provision of Truth, Justice, and Reconciliation," in Robert I. Rotberg and Dennis Thompson (eds.), *Truth v. Justice: The Morality of Truth Commissions* (Princeton, N.J.: Princeton University Press, 2000), p. 3.
57. Minow, p. 61.
58. See, for example, Daniel C. Richman, "The Changing Boundaries Between Federal and Local Law Enforcement," in *Criminal Justice 2000*, Volume 2, Charles M. Friel (ed.) (Washington, D.C.: U.S. Department of Justice, National Institute of Justice, 2000), pp. 81–111.

Postscript:
Justice as an Evolving Concept

Justice has been hard to define and even harder to implement. It would be a mistake, however, to view justice as something with a fixed definition whose achievement is objectively measurable. Rather than a destination, justice should be viewed as a journey and as a mirror reflecting the development of a particular people over time. As societies advance, injustices may continue, but sensitivity to injustice grows and the list of issues considered under the umbrella of justice expands.

In William Golding's book, *Lord of the Flies,* a group of children are stranded on an island with no adults to supervise them.[1] They form their own society, but that society quickly breaks into violent groups. The book illustrates the primitive instincts in humans and the brutality of humankind, but it also illustrates that humankind requires laws and structure to overcome those baser instincts. It might be argued that the pursuit of justice is a natural response to man's violent instincts. Golding wrote that book following the atrocities of the Nazis during the Holocaust, and although not everyone shares the author's dark view of human nature, it is a reminder that justice is a human construct raised in response to human injustices.

Evidence of concern about justice and institutions that support justice can be found in the earliest cultures. For early societies, and some modern ones, that emphasized religion as central to life, definitions of justice came from holy documents and prophets. Angry or merciful gods dispensed justice and gave humans guidance in dispensing their own justice. All humans would have their own judgment days when they died. Even secular leaders looked to priestly classes to justify their actions. When Moses and Pharaoh battled over the fate of an enslaved class, both called upon gods and religious arguments to justify their actions. Pilate and Herod bowed to the chief priests and scribes in the pretrial of Jesus. Subsequent monarchs in Europe laid claim to the Divine Right of Kings. Even in a highly secular society like the United States, presidents routinely use religious rhetoric to justify their positions. George W. Bush, for example, justified war by drawing on notions of justice and religion when he talked of an "axis of evil."

When some advanced civilizations subsumed religion into mythology, a long history of philosophical discussion on justice resulted. The importance of justice to Greek, Roman, and early Catholic thinkers attests both to its perennial attraction and to the difficulty of fully understanding the concept. Philosophers who have pondered the great human mysteries have found that one of them concerns what constitutes a just life, a just government, and a just society. That such discussion, begun thousands of years ago, continues today attests to the staying power and complexity of the concept.

As civilizations evolved and the nation state became more prominent, the legacy of religion lingered in the Divine Right of Kings. The citizenry accepted pronouncements about justice from these leaders as having come directly from God. Only after secular forces took over the state during the Renaissance did philosophers and politicans discuss justice in new ways. The state, needing the support of its citizens, focused on issues of the responsibility of government to its own citizens and to other countries. In doing so, ideas developed regarding political legitimacy, the nature of leadership, just wars, and law.

About this time, the most dramatic expression of political justice, criminal justice, was taken from religious and private hands and placed with the state. The development of criminal justice mirrored the development of society with harsh and unspeakably cruel punishments first couched in religious terms and institutions. When the state took over criminal justice, punishments became public spectacles, demonstrating for all the recently acquired power of the government. Criminal law reflected the nature of the state in which it emerged, leading to variations in criminal law in France and England in Europe, Muslim societies in the Middle East, and Asian culture in the Far East. Generally, courts emerged first, with police and prisons only developing later, or being connected to the military.

Political and economic revolutions of the eighteenth, nineteenth, and twentieth centuries ensured an ever-increasing development and expansion of democracy and capitalism. With some exceptions, feudalism and monarchies became less valid. These changes gave rise to questions of liberty and equality, as well as questions regarding the appropriate division of wealth. Political justice became increasingly important, there was a growing focus on economic justice, and still later this evolved into a concern with social justice.

As the state became more involved in justice, a variety of justice systems emerged. In Europe, the classic delineation was between common law and civil law. In the Middle East, the influence of Islam was pronounced. These justice systems reflected the particular values of the countries in which they emerged. For example, England was a highly stratified country in which upper classes were in firm control and judges were empowered to dispense law and justice. These elites answered only to the monarch. Even Parliament, which had a hard time getting started itself, was divided between Lords and Commons. Courts, with judges wearing aristocratic wigs and a stratified lawyer class of barristers, reflected the country's values. Even the police force, which did not emerge in

England until the early 1800s, was organized as a magisterial force. In contrast, France had experienced a spectacular revolution in which peasants took power from the aristocracy. Under such conditions, there was a strong interest in having a public check on those who made law, placing such power in the hands of elected legislators. Further, because Catholicism was stronger in France and the state was more bureaucratized, the transformation of canon law into civil law was relatively easy. The justice system and its practitioners were more centralized. These two systems, common law and civil law, spread and predominated throughout much of the Western world, largely through colonialism. However, particular ideologies, such as Islam and later Communism, overlaid their own worldview upon the law and on the meaning of justice.

The American justice system is interesting because it shows how a country's particular value system shapes the form a dominant justice system takes and because it reflects the tendency of many societies to draw selectively from different models of justice. The American system is built on the traditions of English common law. Founding members of the United States crafted a Constitution and Bill of Rights owing much to common law traditions and to earlier documents developed in England. The American Revolution was never as radical as the revolutions in France or Russia, and many of the English views of justice were adopted wholesale in America.

Although America was a democracy with common law roots, however, elements of civil law crept in. Over time, statutes became as important as judicial pronouncements in defining law and establishing punishments. Even today, through such things as mandatory minimum sentences, Congress continues to erode the power of judges, shifting that power to legislators. The influence of common law remains strong, however, particularly as seen through the importance placed on process. In most cases, for example, people convicted in court can only base an appeal of their convictions on mistakes made in the trial process, not on new evidence showing their innocence. In the United States criminal justice system, justice really means fairness in procedure, but this emphasis on procedure is not absolute. There is a continuous tension between thorough procedures (common law) and efficiency (civil law). During the past half century, a "Due Process Revolution" has occurred to make certain that the system does not place so much emphasis on efficiency that the rights of offenders are sacrificed. Despite these safeguards, numerous injustices have occurred.

The many injustices that exist throughout the world suggest that justice remains a work in progress. We have selected just a few to illustrate how persistent and pervasive some of these justice issues can be. The United States has a long history of radical dissent. Significant numbers of people have lost faith in the national government and have joined groups bent on revolution. A dramatic example was the bombing of the federal building in Oklahoma City in 1995, in which 167 people were killed. By the end of the nineteenth century, most countries had ended slavery, yet there are more slaves in the world today than at any other time. The particular form taken by slavery has changed and, in many ways, is far more brutal than the outlawed practices of the past. Similarly, genocide during the past 100 years has been more widespread than in any 100-year period in history. Despite the hollow promises of "Never Again," people continue to be slaughtered because of their religious beliefs, tribal affiliations, or skin color. Finally, the world has seen an unprecedented assault on the environment and that assault has led to war, disease, and untold brutality—bringing out the very worst in humankind.

How is it possible for society to advance while injustices seem to multiply? This question has arisen throughout the book in one form or another, but there is no obvious answer. One might just as well turn the question around: Is a world in which injustices are multiplying truly a world in which civilization is advancing?

Well, then, how is justice to be attained? Considerable religious, intellectual, and political energy has been expended but injustice remains. Perhaps this has to do with the nature of humans, a notoriously self-serving species. Perhaps humankind is as primitive and violent as is assumed in *The Lord of the Flies*. Perhaps ignorance or lethargy might explain the growth of injustice, or perhaps justice cannot be achieved.

The title of this book is suggestive. The pursuit of justice may be as important as attaining it. Several remarkable individuals and organizations seek to achieve a just world. Indeed, in another evolutionary step, several international organizations have been working to achieve global justice. Just as the United Nations works toward international cooperation in politics and the World Trade Organization tries to deal with multinational corporations, several organizations have been working to achieve global justice. Still, injustice persists, even in more advanced nations like the United States. Religious exhortations, academic discourses, political statements, individual activists, reformist groups, nonprofit organizations, and world courts all testify that justice has not been achieved but that the pursuit of justice continues to be a human obsession.

Perhaps there will never be true justice in the world. But even if justice remains elusive, it is such an important objective and the benefits of reaching it are so great that the pursuit of justice must continue. To say we should give up on justice because we have been unable to achieve it is like saying that because we have spent billions of dollars and millions of person-hours without successfully finding a cure for cancer, we should stop looking. Like the failed search for a cancer cure, we cannot define past failures to achieve justice as wasted efforts—those past failures may someday become the building blocks for a lasting answer. Ultimately, the old saying rings true—"No Justice No Peace."

Endnotes

1. William Golding, *Lord of the Flies* (New York: Perigee, 1959).

Appendix: *The United Nations' Universal Declaration of Human Rights*

Adopted by the General Assembly of the United Nations on December 10, 1948

PREAMBLE

Whereas recognition of the inherent dignity and of the equal and inalienable rights of all members of the human family is the foundation of freedom, justice and peace in the world,

Whereas disregard and contempt for human rights have resulted in barbarous acts which have outraged the conscience of mankind, and the advent of a world in which human beings shall enjoy freedom of speech and belief and freedom from fear and want has been proclaimed as the highest aspiration of the common people,

Whereas it is essential, if man is not to be compelled to have recourse, as a last resort, to rebellion against tyranny and oppression, that human rights should be protected by the rule of law,

Whereas it is essential to promote the development of friendly relations between nations,

Whereas the peoples of the United Nations have in the Charter reaffirmed their faith in fundamental human rights, in the dignity and worth of the human person and in the equal rights of men and women and have determined to promote social progress and better standards of life in larger freedom,

Whereas Member States have pledged themselves to achieve, in co-operation with the United Nations, the promotion of universal respect for and observance of human rights and fundamental freedoms,

Whereas a common understanding of these rights and freedoms is of the greatest importance for the full realization of this pledge,

Now, Therefore THE GENERAL ASSEMBLY proclaims THIS UNIVERSAL DECLARATION OF HUMAN RIGHTS as a common standard of achievement for all peoples and all nations, to the end that every individual and every organ of society, keeping this Declaration constantly in mind, shall strive by teaching and education to promote respect for these rights and freedoms and by progressive measures, national and international, to secure their universal and effective recognition and observance, both among the peoples of Member States themselves and among the peoples of territories under their jurisdiction.

Article 1.

All human beings are born free and equal in dignity and rights. They are endowed with reason and conscience and should act towards one another in a spirit of brotherhood.

Article 2.

Everyone is entitled to all the rights and freedoms set forth in this Declaration, without distinction of any kind, such as race, colour, sex, language, religion, political or other opinion, national or social origin, property, birth or other status.

Furthermore, no distinction shall be made on the basis of the political, jurisdictional or international status of the country or territory to which a person belongs, whether it be independent, trust, non-self-governing or under any other limitation of sovereignty.

Article 3.

Everyone has the right to life, liberty and security of person.

Article 4.

No one shall be held in slavery or servitude; slavery and the slave trade shall be prohibited in all their forms.

Article 5.

No one shall be subjected to torture or to cruel, inhuman or degrading treatment or punishment.

Article 6.

Everyone has the right to recognition everywhere as a person before the law.

Article 7.

All are equal before the law and are entitled without any discrimination to equal protection of the law. All are entitled to equal protection against any discrimination in violation of this Declaration and against any incitement to such discrimination.

Article 8.

Everyone has the right to an effective remedy by the competent national tribunals for acts violating the fundamental rights granted him by the constitution or by law.

Article 9.

No one shall be subjected to arbitrary arrest, detention or exile.

Article 10.

Everyone is entitled in full equality to a fair and public hearing by an independent and impartial tribunal, in the determination of his rights and obligations and of any criminal charge against him.

Article 11.

(1) Everyone charged with a penal offence has the right to be presumed innocent until proved guilty according to law in a public trial at which he has had all the guarantees necessary for his defence.

(2) No one shall be held guilty of any penal offence on account of any act or omission which did not constitute a penal offence, under national or international law, at the time when it was committed. Nor shall a heavier penalty be imposed than the one that was applicable at the time the penal offence was committed.

Article 12.

No one shall be subjected to arbitrary interference with his privacy, family, home or correspondence, nor to attacks upon his honour and reputation. Everyone has the right to the protection of the law against such interference or attacks.

Article 13.

(1) Everyone has the right to freedom of movement and residence within the borders of each state.

(2) Everyone has the right to leave any country, including his own, and to return to his country.

Article 14.

(1) Everyone has the right to seek and to enjoy in other countries asylum from persecution.

(2) This right may not be invoked in the case of prosecutions genuinely arising from non-political crimes or from acts contrary to the purposes and principles of the United Nations.

Article 15.

(1) Everyone has the right to a nationality.

(2) No one shall be arbitrarily deprived of his nationality nor denied the right to change his nationality.

Article 16.

(1) Men and women of full age, without any limitation due to race, nationality or religion, have the right to marry and to found a family. They are entitled to equal rights as to marriage, during marriage and at its dissolution.

(2) Marriage shall be entered into only with the free and full consent of the intending spouses.

(3) The family is the natural and fundamental group unit of society and is entitled to protection by society and the State.

Article 17.

(1) Everyone has the right to own property alone as well as in association with others.
(2) No one shall be arbitrarily deprived of his property.

Article 18.

Everyone has the right to freedom of thought, conscience and religion; this right includes freedom to change his religion or belief, and freedom, either alone or in community with others and in public or private, to manifest his religion or belief in teaching, practice, worship and observance.

Article 19.

Everyone has the right to freedom of opinion and expression; this right includes freedom to hold opinions without interference and to seek, receive and impart information and ideas through any media and regardless of frontiers.

Article 20.

(1) Everyone has the right to freedom of peaceful assembly and association.
(2) No one may be compelled to belong to an association.

Article 21.

(1) Everyone has the right to take part in the government of his country, directly or through freely chosen representatives.
(2) Everyone has the right of equal access to public service in his country.
(3) The will of the people shall be the basis of the authority of government; this will shall be expressed in periodic and genuine elections which shall be by universal and equal suffrage and shall be held by secret vote or by equivalent free voting procedures.

Article 22.

Everyone, as a member of society, has the right to social security and is entitled to realization, through national effort and international co-operation and in accordance with the organization and resources of each State, of the economic, social and cultural rights indispensable for his dignity and the free development of his personality.

Article 23.

(1) Everyone has the right to work, to free choice of employment, to just and favourable conditions of work and to protection against unemployment.
(2) Everyone, without any discrimination, has the right to equal pay for equal work.
(3) Everyone who works has the right to just and favourable remuneration ensuring for himself and his family an existence worthy of human dignity, and supplemented, if necessary, by other means of social protection.
(4) Everyone has the right to form and to join trade unions for the protection of his interests.

Article 24.

Everyone has the right to rest and leisure, including reasonable limitation of working hours and periodic holidays with pay.

Article 25.

(1) Everyone has the right to a standard of living adequate for the health and well-being of himself and of his family, including food, clothing, housing and medical care and necessary social services, and the right to security in the event of unemployment, sickness, disability, widowhood, old age or other lack of livelihood in circumstances beyond his control.
(2) Motherhood and childhood are entitled to special care and assistance. All children, whether born in or out of wedlock, shall enjoy the same social protection.

Article 26.

(1) Everyone has the right to education. Education shall be free, at least in the elementary and fundamental stages. Elementary education shall be compulsory. Technical and professional education shall be made generally available and higher education shall be equally accessible to all on the basis of merit.
(2) Education shall be directed to the full development of the human personality and to the strengthening of respect for human rights and fundamental freedoms. It shall promote understanding, tolerance and friendship among all nations, racial or religious groups, and shall further the activities of the United Nations for the maintenance of peace.
(3) Parents have a prior right to choose the kind of education that shall be given to their children.

Article 27.

(1) Everyone has the right freely to participate in the cultural life of the community, to enjoy the arts and to share in scientific advancement and its benefits.
(2) Everyone has the right to the protection of the moral and material interests resulting from any scientific, literary or artistic production of which he is the author.

Article 28.

Everyone is entitled to a social and international order in which the rights and freedoms set forth in this Declaration can be fully realized.

Article 29.

(1) Everyone has duties to the community in which alone the free and full development of his personality is possible.
(2) In the exercise of his rights and freedoms, everyone shall be subject only to such limitations as are determined by law solely for the purpose of securing due recognition and respect for the rights and freedoms of others and of meeting the just requirements of morality, public order and the general welfare in a democratic society.
(3) These rights and freedoms may in no case be exercised contrary to the purposes and principles of the United Nations.

Article 30.

Nothing in this Declaration may be interpreted as implying for any State, group or person any right to engage in any activity or to perform any act aimed at the destruction of any of the rights and freedoms set forth herein.

Source: http://www.un.org/Overview/rights.html

Index